Jesper Eckhardt Larsen (Ed.)

Knowledge, Politics and the History of [illegible]n

Studies on Education

Volume 2

LIT

Knowledge, Politics and the History of Education

edited by

Jesper Eckhardt Larsen

LIT

Bibliographic information published by the Deutsche Nationalbibliothek
The Deutsche Nationalbibliothek lists this publication in the Deutsche Nationalbibliografie; detailed bibliographic data are available in the Internet at http://dnb.d-nb.de.

ISBN 978-3-8258-1561-5

Verlagskontakt:
Fresnostr. 2 D-48159 Münster
Tel. +49 (0) 2 51-620 320 Fax +49 (0) 2 51-23 19 72
e-Mail: lit@lit-verlag.de http://www.lit-verlag.de

Distribution:

In Germany: LIT Verlag Fresnostr. 2, D-48159 Münster
Tel. +49 (0) 2 51-620 32 22, Fax +49 (0) 2 51-922 60 99, e-mail: vertrieb@lit-verlag.de

In Austria: Medienlogistik Pichler-ÖBZ, e-mail: mlo@medien-logistik.at

In Switzerland: B + M Buch- und Medienvertrieb, e-mail: order@buch-medien.ch

In the UK: Global Book Marketing, e-mail: mo@centralbooks.com

In North America: International Specialized Book Services, e-mail: orders@isbs.com

Contents

Foreword

This anthology is the result of a process that began with the international symposium "The Raison d'être of the History of Education" that was hosted by the *Danish University of Education*, and partly sponsored by this institution in spring 2008. *The Danish Society for the History of Education* took the initiative, and contacts were made to a number of scholars in mostly European countries but also from America. Since then quite a few contributors have been added to the list in a way that doesn't make this the exact proceedings of the symposium, but rather a very comprehensive and cohesive book on the topic of the politics of knowledge in the academic field of the history of education. A thank goes to all who on the way have agreed to contribute to this project. A thank also to *Aarhus Universitets Forskningsfond* for sponsoring this publication. A thank goes to the very thorough proofreading by Steven Cowan of the *Institute of Education,* London and for valuable comments from Gary McCulloch and Barry M. Franklin to the framing of the project. A thank for the competent layout by Ulrik Stylsvig Madsen that should be complimented. The members of the board in the *Danish Society for the History of Education* have all contributed valuably to this publication. However I must take the responsibility for any mistakes as the editor of this anthology.

On behalf of the *Danish Society for the History of Education*,
Jesper Eckhardt Larsen

Introduction

Introduction

The reasons for publishing a book on this theme are many. In many countries the historical and philosophical areas of research and education, the humanities as a whole, are under severe pressure to prove their renewed relevance in the knowledge economy. A new paradigm for research policy has functioned since at least the 1960s and 1970s, but increased in influence after 2000. In educational research the agenda in this policy research paradigm has been in the direction of "what works" or "evidence based research". By 1979 this had already been described as a performative turn in the legitimation of knowledge by Jean-Francois Lyotard.[1] A postmodern concept of capitalist or functionalist efficiency should govern the policy of knowledge in society. In this atmosphere the field of historical research in education is increasingly considered to be of negligible importance – or new demands on relevance are put forward in what can be considered a drift of epistemic criteria to use a concept introduced by the Swedish sociologist Aant Elzinga.[2] It is not enough for the researcher to do what he/she finds relevant – it is necessary to perform a political argumentation to prove this relevance in front of external bodies, whether these be national research councils, private foundations or regional and global research councils. To put it succinctly: excellence is not enough, peer review is not enough. Only the view from a political body is now crucial. The drift is therefore from internal to external epistemic and relevance criteria. In this situation opening an explicit discussion on the raison d'être of the history of education can be a first step in a productive dialogue between researchers and research politicians on the future politics of knowledge within this specific field.

---

[1] Jean-Francois Lyotard, *The Postmodern Condition: A Report on Knowledge* (Minneapolis: University of Minnesota Press, 1984 (1979)).

[2] Aant Elzinga, "Research, Bureaucracy and the Drift of Epistemic Criteria," in The University Research System. The Public Policies of the Home of Scientists, ed. Björn Wittrock and Aant Elzinga (Stockholm: Almqvist & Wiksell International, 1985).

Of course this claim deserves to be investigated in more detail within the field in question: the history of education. But an initial overview shows that educational scholars who where originally historical in outlook increasingly must find ways to re-school themselves as it where – into becoming students of policymaking or other fields of more immediate practical concern. In this collection of articles cases and overviews of the development of our field are presented from a number of European and American countries.

Secondly one should not forget the fruitfulness of comparisons in any field. If the situation in some countries shows a decline in the field, the situations in other comparable countries could produce both new arguments and other strategies to be followed. Thereby this work could provoke the political concept coined by the comparative educationalist Jürgen Schriewer and stand as a proactive "reference to abroad" - and counter a simplistic view of a general disaster. The array of scholars in this anthology who come from a range of different countries can more readily present a variety of perspectives on both declining and growing activities within the field of the history of education.

Lastly it can be observed that the situation described in the first paragraph of a new paradigm in the politics of knowledge strongly influences these individual scholars. It is as though a virtual microphone has over these years, been placed in front of every active and publicly paid scholar: What is your raison d'être? Why are you worth your salary? The demand for accountability in the aftermath of New Public Management is thereby turned into a potential delegitimation of almost any scholarly pursuit – maybe with the exception of technological research of various kinds. But especially in the tense atmosphere of external relevance pressures – unequally felt in differing countries, institutions and departments – these more personal motivations, albeit performed in a highly politicised environment, are driving research in ways that are sometimes highly inspiring for peers. The debates on relevance or reasons of existence are therefore also part of the self-understandings of researchers and the dynamics of individual research lives. An additional objective of this book is therefore to bring internal criteria of relevance to the fore, and combine them with external criteria of relevance to inspire and stimulate not only research but also research and education policy.

Possible approaches

To frame the empirical space for these investigations the concept of the history of education is viewed quite broadly. Local, national, regional and global histories of institutions, university history, histories of educational policy bodies, histories of curriculum and didactics, histories of educational ideas, and histories of socialization arenas of any kind are all seen as pieces of the jigsaw of history of education.

But how can this theme be addressed in diverse ways? The question of the raison d'être of a scholarly discipline is a meta-question dealing with the explicit or implicit uses and misuses of the field in question. It also deals with the objectives and cultural developments of the field. Therefore this pursuit is not educational history in itself. It is more likely to be a social, political or cultural analysis of the impact of research and scholarship on society. A few approaches might exemplify this endeavour:

A first approach to this theme would be arguing for and investigating specific and explicit formulations of the raison d'être and relevance to society of the history of education over time. Thereby the findings of considered explicit criteria of relevance could be analyzed to form their own historical development. Within this approach, the methods could examine analytical or rhetorical discourses in pinpointing the emergence of hegemonic views and creation of argumentations over time. Possibly this would be more loyal to the actors' self-understandings, more so than evidence of the actual impacts. Nevertheless this level of perceived criteria of scholarly works can be envisaged as a driving force in the actual choices of objects and approaches in writing histories of education.

A second way to approach the theme could be, as it were, going behind the backs of the actors. Through investigations of a number of cases differing uses of historical knowledge of education in educational, political or broadly cultural contexts, can show how history writing has influenced the everyday micro politics in institutions as well as macro politics in the public debates. This could be a way to show the raison d'être or deeper sub-current of relevance of the history of education in practice. The exercise will be to find clear examples of where history writing has informed the public debate or the minds of the actors in certain ways. An array of such examples shows the concrete uses and misuses of scholarship in the field. The theoretical assumptions of such case analyses could draw on both post-structural as well as neo-functionalist sociological interpretations of the impact of certain ideologies or system self understandings that frame certain values and reproduce premises of practical educational action that has been taken.

A third approach is to consider the historiography of the field and comment on differing implicit or explicit objectives that the tradition of works in the field has had. But only if historiography is connected with an investigation of the uses of these contributions in specific ways to political issues and to general cultural developments, it is seen as relevant to this anthology. This approach is for instance, seen in the investigation into how history of education in the 19th century served specific nation building agendas.

Each of these approaches has a place in the wider approach, complementing the other. The contributions to this volume are therefore diverse, but they share a common purpose of analyzing argumentations, discourses and public debates on the raison d'être, relevance and impacts of the history of education.

Perspectives

What are the possible wider perspectives of this analysis? What is already known? Although this outline in many respects overlaps with existing research – there are a few specific goals that can serve as the common ambition of the project – creating at the least some cohesion between our curiosities. What does this project do, that hasn't been done before?

By citing and listing works and their importance, existing historiographies within history of education have dealt mostly – if not exclusively, with internal debates on the objectives of educational history writing. As a somewhat new departure, this project tries through select cases to tell the story of the external impacts of this scholarly field on society as well as the reception of educational history writing in the public domain. How have actors in institutions and policy fora used and misused the history of education? And what have been the critical or affirmative roles of these intellectuals (the historians of education) in society? As this is a field involving both semantics and practice our concerns are with discourses and policy implementations. To anticipate the results of these studies a few general tendencies in the field raise specific questions concerning the social relevance of history of education.

A general development runs from historiography more or less explicitly serving nation building purposes and broad educational purposes in teacher education, to a fragmented and specialized pursuit without any obvious educational function. A suggestion of the way to reinvent the professional relevance of the history of education could be in adhering to the notion of historical consciousness – making professionals critical towards over simplistic views of – for instance "the black schools" of the past – or overly whiggish progressive narratives of optimistic reforms. The almost natural place of the history of education in teacher training was for a long time the one – and quite obvious – raison d'être of the history of education. That, and maybe also celebratory histories of individual institutions serving to strengthen and celebrate the unique identity of the institution in question. The last tendency is certainly clear in the field of university history, but also in school histories at the primary and secondary levels.

The development in the field has therefore in itself run counter to an obvious or straightforward external relevance. This is not only the case for the history of education, but for all humanistic and social science studies. An academic drift has gravitated towards more distanced, more specialized and more theorized approaches in all fields of social or humanistic research. There have been at least three major consequences of this development of the history of education. The first is that the field has splintered into a large number of different areas and specialisms, such as curriculum, teachers and teaching, girls and women, universities, the economy and the city, reflecting wider trends in historical writing over the past generation. This greater specialisation based on detailed research has tended to supplant works of synthesis with a broader scope which had a recurrent importance in the field for many years. Secondly there have been an increasing number of studies that seek to relate the history of education to issues and ideas drawn from across the social sciences and humanities, especially in sociology but also including other disciplines such as psychology, cultural studies, politics and philosophy. Thirdly, the inherently educational rationale of the history of education, once so strong, has been progressively undermined as it has been challenged and displaced by these other sources of ideas and argument. This latter trend has threatened the principal base of the history of education in university departments of education. It has also helped to permit the erosion of the historical memory of educational policies and institutions over the last thirty years. Some of these authors call it the systematic forgetfulness of policy makers.

So to pinpoint the present situation, internal tendencies characterised by an academic drift create a strong tension when faced with external tendencies of an epistemic drift. The activity of the scholars is more and more wissenschaftlich – but the funding demands are more and more performative. This can only result in a failing communication between the funding parties and the scholars. Some scholars – as indicated – therefore choose the strategy of finding hot topics in policy or practice to sex up the relevance factor – or X-factor as it were – of their research, thereby improving their career chances in a new environment. A few excellent scholars in large and prestigious institutions try to stick to basic research curiosity and fundamental questions. Many other strategies are chosen – but few scholars can remain indifferent.

Pro action – suggestions of possible paths to follow

Some of the proposed strategies are not specific to the history of education but are seen as general tendencies across the humanities and within branches of the social sciences. The dissemination argument used by research councils increasingly since the 1990s tries to argue that the act of communicating the results of this kind of research is equivalent to implementation for technical kinds of research. But this places a demand upon the scholars to reach out more openly – and maybe more normatively – than they usually do to regain the educational relevance once so dominant. Contributing to public debate is increasingly among the expectations directed at scholars. Besides research and teaching, public dissemination of knowledge and opinions is a part of the job description in today's academia. So the suggestion is for historians of education to counter the academic drift with quite normative and/or popular statements influencing the public debate in an informed but quite proactive sense.

Another strategy would be to regain educational relevance by not only producing short academic articles on hyphen-histories of this or that subfield – but again try to produce sweeping overviews of the history of education – maybe even international and comparative in outlook. This would inform the first dissemination activity producing hopefully provocative and eye-catching narratives to re-inform public debate. Never before has the market for well-told stories been larger – in quantitative book-selling terms – but the product needs to cater to the demands of the readership. Even if the research assessment exercises which indirectly guide the funding are the dominant influence over the drift of academic research programmes – the best strategy for the history of education within the new paradigm of the politics of knowledge seems to be to readdress the true market mechanisms and sell well-told narratives in the history of education. To put it shortly: regain the educational raison d'être in the 21st century. Scholars of history and the social world have always, and are still capable of producing premises of practice and politics. A new sense of having exactly this role in society is maybe a common trend in these observations. In the twenty-first century scholars again dare to say: this is best and this is worst – publicly.

Contributions

This anthology is divided into three sections that all address the common theme. The first section includes articles that present current challenges to the discipline of the history of education.

Gary McCulloch in his article looks to the varying constituent audiences and the changing rationales of the history of education, which he finds as being threefold: history, education and social science. His overall suggestion is that good scholarship in this discipline with historical examples of Emile Durkheim and Brian Simon actually speaks to all three constituencies at once. The tensions between the pure aspirations of historians just to depict the past on its own terms and the more applied interests of the educationalists can and have been bridged in a bicultural approach by many historians of education, standing as it were, with a leg in both camps at once. McCulloch pledges for the members of the discipline to find a common cause, to better able them to define and defend the history of education in both academic and in public discourse.

Marc Depaepe stands in opposition to McCulloch to the effect that he defends the pure aspirations of historical scholarship against any kind of purposeful use of the history of education. Examples are shown from the moralizing use of heroes of the educational past to the "dilettantish" aspiration concerning the relevance of the history of education to the solution of practical problems. Depeape has seen it as his duty to warn against a purely utilitarian treatment of the educational heritage of the past. The qualities of irrelevance are on the other hand described as a way forward. The history of education should deconstruct, demythologize and tarnish the great, heroic and often exaggerated stories of the past, not to ridicule our predecessors, their education, or their ideals but to demonstrate that they too, were human beings, living in a concrete, socio-historical context that can hardly be abstracted from. The relevance should, according to Depeape, only be of an intrinsic nature, one that is critical and inevitably uncomfortable.

Jukka Rantalas article tell us the story of a discipline in crisis. The discipline of the history of education is shown as threatened by extinction in the Finnish educational sciences. He uses the term of a new demand on pragmaticism in the educational field that disregards historical scholarship. Rantala defends a view of the history of education as a way of heightening the sensitivity to historical awareness in persons working with education. The danger in the straightforward deterministic view of history, which arises from limited historical knowledge, is the narrowing down of future hopes and options for decision. The article empirically show how historical chairs in educational settings are being cut, or never opened. The nonexistence of tenures in history of education thereby forms a self-feeding problem, ultimately leading younger scholars away from the field. The most important action to be taken is therefore to ensure that young educationalists have a chance to concentrate on the history of their own field, and become part of the scientific community specialized as historians of education.

Pierre Caspard and Rebecca Rogers introduce their article with a quote on the uselessness of the history of education: "teachers taught youth to the best of their ability, in line with parental demands... This sums up this history." To prove that there might be more to educational history writing the two authors go on to show that the curiosity towards the educational past has been widespread both in the public and among teachers, academics and policymakers. This sums up to continuity between familial, administrative and scholarly historical interest in education and learning. However, while both historicism and Marxism celebrated a historical viewpoint, history in the contemporary situation is no longer called upon to furnish managers with models, counter-models, examples and counter-examples of ideas, practices and educational institutions. The current critical situation for the research unit Service d'histoire de l'éducation (SHE) goes to show a new hostile environment to historical research in education in France. The suggestions to counter this tendency are threefold: to secure broadness of scholarly scope, to address teacher education needs and to engage actively in public debate.

The second section shows in various ways both examples of uses and abuses of the history of education and goes on to suggest ways of applying the discipline in various contexts. Thereby these articles both suggest ways to proceed and warn against abuses and pitfalls to be avoided.

Barry M. Franklin and Patricio R. Ortiz take their departure in the observation that several applied fields of knowledge have their own history writing. Other non-historical professional fields like law, economics and science have well-established historical scholarship. Referring to John Rury who have analysed the role of history in these professional fields, Franklin and Ortiz goes on to argue for historical scholarship to introduce new conceptual frameworks and methodologies and thereby challenge longstanding, virtually taken for granted assumptions in their related fields. Specifically the authors argue for the uses of ethnohistory in policy research, not only to recognize the historical roots of many of the issues that the practitioners and politicians mistakenly assume are new and novel, but also to trace in detail the implementations of various policies on the ground level. This article shows numerous examples of such bottom-up historical work that has informed us about the consequences of policy reforms.

Esbjörn Larsson in his article on the use and abuse of history of education in Sweden introduces a framework inspired by Friedrich Nietzsches famous analysis of the use and abuse of history for life from 1872. He finds examples of all the three types of the uses of history: a monumental, an antiquarian and a critical. The monumental use that shall inspire the present to great deeds Larsson finds has certain affinities to a Whig interpretation of history, as the past is subsumed under the present. But Nietzsche did not as Butterfield view this as a negative feature of good historical work, as it is important that the great deeds of the past may inspire visionaries of today. Larsson is however critical towards examples of this from the Swedish scene both analysing historical movies and historiography. The antiquarian tendency is shown in the character of Rudolf Hall who had a desire to preserve almost everything from even small schools archives. Finally Larsson suggests the critical history writing as the true way to proceed, to question and sometimes overthrow established narratives. He finds inspiration in the critical approach as history too often is used either to glorify our present accomplishments or gets caught up in empirical data.

Harry Haue writes about the use of history in didactics and curriculum planning under the title "History of Education Matters - If the Past is Present." He refers to the German sociologist Niklas Luhmann for a communicative interpretation of the different school subjects as systems of self-referential communication. This makes the historical genesis of school subjects central to the understanding of the way present school subjects are presently delimited and developed. He takes an example in the Danish discussions on the school subject of history for the upper secondary schools, the gymnasiums, with the specific formula "almendannelse" (general education) as the guiding principle. Haue sees a large affinity between the enlightenment, multicultural state of imperial Denmark of the 18th century to the new present day globalization agenda and states that the new rules of curriculum from 2005 corresponds to the cosmopolitan ideas of the enlightenment. The area of curriculum is actually stressed by many of the authors in this anthology to be a success story of the positive impact of historical scholarship on the present discussions. The past is present – in didactics and curriculum thinking.

Else Hansen also addresses both uses and abuses of educational history, with Danish university history as her case. She initially claims an obvious but important observation, which is that the question is not if a historical account will exist, but rather if the historical account should build on popular conceptions of recollection and experience or sound evidence based scholarship. Not that a popular conception can be totally avoided, but rather that it be more informed through empirical work as to depict more fully the unsolved conflicts, or forgotten tensions in complex institutions like universities. The history of universities contains numerous examples of being used and influenced by events contemporary to the historical analysis. Just one example was the surprising alliance between right wing politicians and critical activist students, both groups agreeing on the need for change in the leadership structure of the universities in 1968. All parties quickly forgot this alliance – and the activists got the credit or blame in popular accounts. Neither right wing politicians nor leftist activists now like to hear the, perhaps, true story.

Marcelo Caruso chooses to depict the complex connections between politics and educational historiography through four selected short biographies of educational scholars in the field of the history of education. He warns not to conceive of this relation as in any way linear, leading from a specific historiography to certain political viewpoints in the present situation. But to a large degree historians of education have actually been paramount in shaping educational policies in Latin America. He even claims the opposite connection too: that a kind of politicization of scholarly work may lead to a more professional and differentiated standard of scholarship. The cases also bare witness to a regionally specific close connection between an engagement in scholarly work and political activities on the side, or more often, a scholarly career that ultimately leads to positions in the scene of educational politics. This is the case in all the mentioned four biographies that goes to show a new more explicit level of entanglement between politics and the historians of education in Latin America.

The third section addresses examples of educational historiography from different countries and on that basis go on to discuss the raison d'être of the history of education more broadly. The examples all show a vigorous and lively discipline that may contradict the diagnosis of a crisis in the field. The viewpoint of the editor is however that the crisis is there, not IN the field but in the relation between the field and the politicians of knowledge. However, it is refreshing to counter the pressures from outside with a positive statement of the health of the discipline. All is well; send more money!

Carola Groppe traces in her article the history of education in Germany in both its historic development, in some of its results and in a suggested raison d'être. In its historic development it is specific for the German case that chairs of history of education were established within educational science. There are hence still numerous chairs in the history of education in larger German universities. However since 1990 the increasing importance of PISA, of school education and didactics, has turned the history of education into one of the endangered sub-disciplines of educational sciences in Germany. The development of the field has been from a humanistic pedagogy that argued for the autonomy of pedagogy on the basis of historical developments with Herman Nohl and Wilhelm Flitner as examples into a more autonomous discipline inspired by the social sciences and freer from normative efforts. This, according to Groppe, may be positively interpreted as a process of emancipation and constitution of an independent field of research. But at the same time the history of education is deeply rooted in educational science and must deal with and convey its function and relevance within the latter. Its raison d'être should not only be orientation, but also the critical highlighting and distancing of oneself from current institutional structures and conventional thought forms.

Alfred Oftedal Telhaug introduces his article with a critique of the all to gloomy editorial introduction. Both in vigour and impact the discipline is faring well in Norway. Telhaug describes a long journey from descriptive to theory-oriented research within Norwegian historical-educational research. Through three stages of the Norwegian modern history the history of education has played an important part. The historians of education in the liberal state of the late nineteenth century Norway felt it as their most impelling duty to identify the real Norway in times of nation building in the young independent state. Until the 1930 school history had a dominant position compared to educational psychology. Through the social democratic state the social sciences gained importance as steering sciences. However, Telhaug points out that the discipline of the history of education still constituted a significant part of the total research effort in education during this period. In the final, post-national phase, more and more reference is made to studies undertaken by the EU, WTO, World Bank and OECD, so that the Norwegian sense of self-satisfaction in educational matters perhaps could be described as dented.

Telhaug cites Kaare Skagen for the counter statement that educators with an interest in history should now be put to work to see schools as cultural products. In spite of these new developments prospects are however, states Telhaug, perhaps brighter than they appear in the view of the editor.

Christian Larsen and Jesper Eckhardt Larsen look to the political implications of educational historiography in Denmark. Different viewpoints in the historiography tend to support and deliver premises for certain political positions. These different viewpoints are to some extent chronologically presented, but the point that is made clear is that all of the viewpoints are represented in the present literature. Five positions in the historiography are listed: a conservative neo-humanist position, a Grundtvigian liberal position, a cultural radical position, an emancipatory revisionist position and finally a post-revisionist position. As the educational scholar Jürgen Schriewer states it, both references to history and references to abroad are used politically to position oneself in any debate. These references are mostly either Nordic or continental in the Danish historiography. A single raison d'être is not pointed to, but an acknowledgement of the role as clarifying and delivering premises for educational practice is a suggested way out of an overly purist conception of the history of education.

Section 1

The present challenges to the history of education

The Changing Rationales of the History of Education: History, education and social science

Gary McCulloch

The history of education may be treated as having a broad, overarching set of rationales, reaching across its constituent audiences of education, history, and the social sciences. Conversely, it may be addressed as having a narrower rationale, speaking particularly to only one or two of these potential audiences. Some of the foremost historians of education in the twentieth century, including Emile Durkheim in France and Brian Simon in Britain, articulated a broad and encompassing vision for the field as a whole in relation to their own educational, social and political contexts. Yet a range of tensions and debates have tended to encourage fragmentation in the field, and the development of distinctive and rival rationales. These have often come into conflict with each other, sometimes with creative effect and at other times to the detriment of the field as a whole. This paper will appraise these changing and competing rationales, with an emphasis on educational, historical and social science perspectives. It will then examine some of the consequences of these changes for the field of history of education, and the threats and challenges that they carry, before going on to discuss current needs and suggested priorities in the light of these developments.[1]

To understand the nature of these trends, and to assess the prospects for addressing them effectively, we must of course consider them historically – to look, as Sol Cohen once put it, at the history of the history of education. In his major essay on this subject, published in the *Harvard Educational Review* in 1976, Cohen made the important point that such an approach should not simply be about filling in a missing chapter in the history of education as a field of study, or discussing the uses of history in schools of education, but should aim to "restore the broken links between our generation and our predecessors, to fill

---

[1] For a fuller and more detailed discussion, see also McCulloch, Gary, *The Struggle for the History of Education* (London: Routledge, 2011).

in certain gaps in our memory".[2] Indeed, this is far from being simply an intellectual exercise. The shifting patterns of our academic labours affect status, resources, identities, careers and lives. More profoundly still, they reflect developments in the historical and social memories of institutions, systems and societies as they change over time. We can certainly identify broadly international trends and contours over the past half century, although again it is important to recognise that the key issues have played themselves out in particular ways in different national and cultural contexts. There are therefore significant differences to take into account between different countries, systems and experiences.

Over a century ago, Emile Durkheim, the French sociologist and professor of pedagogy at the Sorbonne in Paris, expressed an expansive vision for the history of education in his lectures on the formation and development of secondary education in France. His rationale for the study of the history of education embraced education, history and the social sciences. Durkheim argued eloquently that it is only by carefully studying the past that we can come to anticipate the future and to understand the present, so that the history of education provides the soundest basis for the study of educational theory. History could also help us to understand the organization of education and to illuminate the educational ideals which the organization was designed to achieve, while in broader terms it helped us to understand humanity itself and the aspirations of individuals and groups. The present was itself merely "an extrapolation of the past, from which it cannot be severed without losing the greater part of its significance".[3] Thus, he insisted,

> ...only history can penetrate under the surface of the present educational system; only history can analyse it; only history can show us of what elements it is formed, on what conditions each of them depends, how they are interrelated; only history, in a word, can bring us to the long chain of causes and effects of which it is the result.

It was for these reasons, according to Durkheim, that we should carry out historical research into the manner in which educational configurations have progressively come to cluster together, to combine and to form organic relationships.

---

[2]Cohen, Sol "The history of the history of American education, 1900-1976 the uses of the past" in *Harvard Educational Review* 46 (1976), pp. 298-330.

[3] Durkheim, Emile, The Evolution of Educational Thought: Lectures on the Formation and Development of Secondary Education in France (London: Routledge & Kegan Paul, 1977), p. 15.

At the same time, Durkheim linked these concerns systematically with his broader sociological interests. He argued that historical and social studies were "close relatives" that were "destined eventually to merge with one another",[4] and that education was bound up with both. For example, he defined education as the methodological socialization of the new generation, through which society renewed itself under the supervision of the State.[5] Moreover, an understanding of psychology was also necessary in order to comprehend the diversity of human intelligence and character.[6] This led another leading sociologist, Talcott Parsons, later to stress Durkheim's contribution not only to sociology but also to psychology, and that it was his work in education that was fundamental in "leading him to the insights which made this articulation of psychology and sociology possible".[7]

For his part, Brian Simon, the leading historian of education produced in Britain since the Second World War, insisted that the study of the history of education should be designed to illuminate the nature of education as a social function, of primary importance in every society. According to Simon, "It should be one of the main tasks of historical study to trace the development of education in this sense, to try to assess the function it has fulfilled at different stages of social development and so to reach a deeper understanding of the function it fulfils today."[8] Simon's work emphasized the differences of social class interests: "Modern education systems, it seems to me, are an area where the interests and objectives of different social classes, strata and even groups meet and very often clash".[9] This approach to the history of education had clear implications for an understanding of contemporary policies and problems. It should, he insisted, "bring educational developments into perspective, and in so doing open the teacher's eyes to the real nature of his work".[10] It should enable the student to understand that educational ideas and institutions contained historical components, some of which might no longer be relevant or viable, and should be open to reconsider-

---

[4] Durkheim, Evolution of Educational Thought, p. 331.
[5] Durkheim, Emile "Education: its nature and role" in Durkheim, Education and Sociology, chapter 1.
[6] Durkheim, Emile "The nature and method of pedagogy" in Durkheim, Education and Sociology, chapter 2.
[7] Parsons, Talcott "Foreword" in Durkheim, Education and Sociology, pp. 9-10.
[8] Simon, Brian "The history of education" in The Study of Education ed. J.W. Tibble (London: Routledge and Kegan Paul, 1966), p. 91.
[9] Simon, Brian "Can education change society?" in Brian Simon, Does Education Matter? (London: Lawrence and Wishart, 1985), p. 27.
[10] Simon, "The history of education", p. 92.

ation; and he concluded famously, "There is, perhaps, no more liberating influence than the knowledge that things have not always been as they are and need not remain so."[11]

Both Durkheim and Simon, in their different ways, emphasized the importance of cultivating the history of education within a broad framework involving education, history, and the social sciences. Yet despite such distinguished and influential contributions, there has been a strong tendency for the study of the history of education to fragment into these component parts. This was evident first in a long dominant approach that stressed its importance for education above all and neglected its historical and social scientific dimensions. Following the eclipse of this model in the 1960s, an alternative historical justification largely replaced the educational approach. Third, a further rationale emerged that insisted on the central importance of the social sciences. Fourth, the underlying tensions between these competing approaches were encouraged by developments within the organised national systems of education, which influenced the character of educational research, teacher education and education policy.

For many years, as is well known, the dominant rationale of the history of education was to support the further development of the national systems of schooling that had arisen around the world in the nineteenth and early twentieth centuries. Its main tendencies were to celebrate the spread and growth of education, to proselytize on behalf of the teaching profession, and to underpin further advances in the form of gradual, progressive reform, presenting these as symptoms and stimulants of gradual social and economic improvement. While this general approach tended to favour a catalogue of "Acts and facts", it gave rise to many uncritical exercises in nostalgia and myth making, written mainly by educationists for the benefit of teacher trainees.[12] The historical value of such work was somewhat limited, and it placed little store by social science methods and perspectives, but it fostered a convenient and usable version of the educational past that teachers, educators and policy makers could use to support their own endeavours. In other words, it tended to be highly instrumentalist in nature, fashioning a usable past in the interests of contemporary institutions and policies.

---

[11] Ibid.

[12] McCulloch, Gary and Richardson, William, Historical Research in Educational Settings (Buckingham: Open University Press, 2000), pp. 34-37.

By the 1960s, this traditional "educational" model was being decisively undermined, partly because it was so unhistorical but also because increasingly its optimistic narrative did not ring true alongside the deep-seated dilemmas of western schooling. In the United States, scholars such as Bernard Bailyn and Lawrence Cremin led the way in questioning the general thrust of writing in the history of education,[13] and their critique was echoed and developed further in other western countries over the following decades. In their attacks on the established tenets of educational historiography, the revisionists of the 1960s did not necessarily intend to undermine the idea that history could contribute to an understanding of current educational issues. Bailyn for example argued strongly that the history of education should be able to provide what he called "historical leverage on the problems of American education".[14] Nevertheless, the discrediting of the received accounts of educational history damaged the convenient assumptions about the present that they had helped to generate. It became more difficult to claim that teachers were on a steady upward climb to respectable, professional status, or that educational policies were building in a rational, incremental way on the foundations successfully laid in the past. A once powerful rationale for the field that had emphasized its specifically educational purpose, at the expense of its base in history and the social sciences, was soon in precipitate decline.

In its place, there rose an alternative, rival rationale that emphasised the historical claims of the field. According to this general formulation, the history of education should be viewed as an aspect of social history, in such a way that it would be concerned principally with discovering the historical connections between education and other aspects of society. In Britain, this key objective was expressed most forcefully perhaps by the leading social historian Asa Briggs, writing in the first issue of the journal *History of Education*, when he argued that the study of the history of education was best considered as part of the wider study of the history of society: "social history broadly interpreted with the politics, the economics, and, it is necessary to add, the religion put in".[15] One implication of this approach, at least for some, was that the history of education should concentrate on its mission to illuminate

[13] Bailyn, Bernard, *Education in the Forming of American Society* (Chapel Hill: University of North Carolina Press, 1960); Cremin, Lawrence, *The Wonderful World of Ellwood Patterson Cubberley* (New York: Teachers College, Columbia University, 1965).
[14] Bailyn, Education in the Forming of American Society, p. 4.
[15] Briggs, Asa "The study of the history of education" in History of Education 1 (1972), p. 5.

the past for its own sake, rather than become contaminated with concerns about the present.

This potential tension between the "historical" and the "educational" has been underlined by some scholars to the extent that it is often viewed as the basis of a key divide within the field. William Richardson in Britain, for example, has suggested that there developed a conflict between historians and educationists, with the former concerned with the pure and disinterested pursuit of historical knowledge, and the latter preoccupied with the applied and committed engagement with the improvement of education.[16] It is certainly possible to be too rigid in presenting this as a fundamental dichotomy. After all, there were many historians of education who regarded themselves as both historians and educationists. If there were two different audiences to their work, they tried to engage with both. In the case of the History of Education Society in Britain, established in 1967, most of the original members were teachers of the subject in colleges and departments of education. Yet individuals involved in the Society such as Brian Simon, W.H.G. Armytage and Kenneth Charlton were well able to engage with historians and educationists alike, and there were, and are, many others who could be described as bicultural in their approach.[17]

Nevertheless, to the extent that history and education represented competing rationales, the rise of the historical standpoint was a major challenge to a rationale that depended principally on the value of the field to education. Briggs was surely right to maintain that historians of education should at all times be aware of what he described as the "broad trends of historical scholarship".[18] Yet those employed in university education departments should also remember and cater for the varied requirements of their own constituency. Their role may continue to produce tensions as it has in the past, but it is not inherently contradictory. For example it is possible to say, as did David Layton in his excellent book *Science for the People*, published in 1973, that the historical endeavour is useful in order "to step back occasionally from the ferment of present day problems", and yet at the same time to try to address "the striking similarities between many of the issues which engaged science educators in the mid-nineteenth century and those which occupy

---

[16] Richardson, William "Historians and educationists: the history of education as a field of study in postwar England" in *History of Education* 28 (1999), pp. 1-30 and 109-41.
[17] See McCulloch, Gary " Forty years on: the presidential address to the History of Education Society" in History of Education 36 (2007), pp. 1-16.
[18] Briggs "The study of the history of education", p. 160.

their latter-day counterparts".[19] In this sense there is perhaps something to be said for the comments of Jurgen Herbst in a much-quoted essay:

> Historians in schools of education...should continue to participate in the work and debates of academic historians and pursue their teaching and writing for the joy of discovering the past and extending our human sympathies for heroes and victims alike. But at the same time they must keep in mind the professional concerns of their students, concerns that pertain to practical, utilitarian considerations as much, if not more, as to philosophical issues of the liberal arts. They cannot forget that they must respond to the questions of present and future classroom teachers, educational administrators, and specialists in public as well as private settings, and that their published scholarship must reflect these concerns as well.[20]

Such issues are a sharp reminder of Cohen's point about the effect of such debates on the position of individual scholars in the field, and even the health and viability of the field itself.

The third basic challenge to a broad-based rationale has emanated from the social sciences. There have long been significant contributions to the history of education by a wide range of social scientists. In Britain, for example, sociologists such as A.H. Halsey and Olive Banks have produced important historical work,[21] and more broadly the insights of social theorists such as Pierre Bourdieu have stimulated many new approaches.[22] Yet there have often been tensions that have developed as a result. Sociologists and historians have tended to have an uneasy intellectual relationship, the former being concerned with developing theory and articulating methodological concerns in a way that historians have often found strange and difficult. The cultural historian Peter Burke has characterized the mutual relationship of historians and sociologists as a "dialogue of the deaf" in which "each group tends to perceive the other in terms of a rather crude stereotype". According to Burke, indeed,

---

[19] Layton, David, *Science for the People: The Origins of the School Science Curriculum in England* (London: George Allen and Unwin, 1973), p. 167.

[20] Herbst, Jurgen "The history of education: state of the art at the turn of the century in Europe and North America" in Paedagogica Historica 35 (1999), pp. 737-47.

[21] See e.g. McCulloch, Gary "Parity and prestige in English secondary education revisited" in British Journal of Sociology of Education 29 (2008), pp. 381-89.

[22] McCulloch and Richardson, Historical Research in Educational Settings, chapter 4.

> Even today, some historians still regard sociologists as people who state the obvious in a barbarous and abstract jargon, lack any sense of place and time, squeeze individuals without mercy into rigid categories, and, to cap it all, describe these activities as "scientific". Sociologists, for their part, have traditionally viewed historians as amateurish, myopic fact collectors without system, method or theory, the imprecision of their "data base" matched only by their incapacity to analyse it.[23]

These tensions have been mirrored in and around the history of education.[24] There has also been an emergent tension over the past two decades between broadly social scientific and interdisciplinary rationales, and other established justifications for the history of education.

The social sciences often seek explanations for general social configurations in which education is only one aspect, whereas an educational rationale would be seeking to highlight the implications for education above all else. One interesting example of this is an edited collection on "Governing children, families and education: restructuring the welfare state", published in 2003. This presents itself as an investigation of "welfare state reforms and new discourses that are constituting and reconstituting the family, the child, and his/her care and education". Its key rationale is that it "draws on an interdisciplinary group of social scientists whose focus is on the *theoretical* assumptions and *empirical* implications of welfare policies on children, their care, education, and schooling in (and across) numerous national contexts and state traditions".[25] The major focus as it explains is on "how new governing patterns are restructuring the ways we understand childhood, families, schooling, and care in a time of increasing complexity, uncertainty, and rising cultural and economic globalization of ideas, patterns of regulation, and what we might call a social administration of 'freedom".[26] This serves to connect education and schooling to broader social and cultural debates in a constructive manner, but at the same time tends to limit and displace a focus on education itself.

---

[23] Burke, Peter, *History and Social Theory*, 2nd edition (London: Polity, 2005), pp. 22-23.
[24] See e.g. Herbst, "The history of education".
[25] Bloch, M., Holmlund, K., Moqvist, I., Popkewitz, T. (eds) Governing Children, Families and Education: Restructuring the Welfare State (New York: Palgrave Macmillan, 2003), p. vii. Emphasis in original.
[26] Ibid., p. viii.

While as already noted, there have been tensions between history and social sciences, when these rationales have been combined they have also been turned against an educational approach. There is a notable instance of this in a recent critique by a senior historian of education in Europe, Marc Depaepe, in relation to an edited collection, "History of education for the twenty-first century". Depaepe complained that this work "echoes in my opinion still far too much the functionalist demand to make history, via 'lessons', useful for contemporary policy", which in turn in his view would risk history of education "degenerating into an ahistorical supply firm of hidden political agendas – educational and otherwise". To this historical criticism he added a social scientific note that this particular work lacked reference to "the theoretical and methodological positioning of the subject in the context of postmodernism".[27] More generally, Depaepe has insisted that the history of education should "avoid the pitfalls of ahistorical utilitarianism as well as of the legitimizing and/ or mythologizing belief in a particular pedagogical system, in which the history of this specialist field is so rich", to the extent that he concludes that "there are hardly any lessons to be learned for education from the history of education".[28] Against this kind of view, there have continued to be spirited defences of the idea that the history of education is relevant and indeed important for a fuller understanding of education, from David Tyack, Larry Cuban and William J.Reese in the United States for example.[29] The potential tensions raised by these differing rationales here become fairly explicit.

Fourthly, we should acknowledge that education as a field has largely turned away from historical approaches in some countries including Britain, and this has made it stony ground for the cultivation of a broadly based rationale for the history of education. Education has been a contested subject over the years, for example between a disciplinary-based approach to educational studies and a quasi-scientific

---

[27] Depaepe, Marc "What kind of history of education may we expect for the twenty-first century? Some comments on four recent readers in the field" in *Paedagogica Historica* 39 (2003), pp. 195-96; Crook, David and Aldrich, Richard (eds) *History of Education for the Twenty-First Century* (London: Institute of Education, 2000).

[28] Depaepe, Marc "How should the history of education be written? Some reflections about the nature of the discipline from the perspective of the reception of our work" in Studies in Philosophy and Education 23 (2004), p. 336.

[29] See for example Tyack, David and Cuban, Larry, Tinkering towards Utopia: A century of Public School Reform (London: Harvard University Press, 1995); and Reese, William J., History, Education and the Schools (New York: Palgrave Macmillan, 2007).

and relatively autonomous educational research.[30] In the United States, Ellen Lagemann has demonstrated how educational research developed historically as a "contested terrain", but one that has been dominated principally by the idea of an empirical and professional science, based mainly on behaviourist psychology and quantitative measurement.[31] This research environment has not been especially conducive to supporting the educational base for the history of education, and has sometimes, certainly in Britain, been openly hostile to history of education as a contributory discipline. Although Brian Simon was one of the earliest presidents of the British Educational Research Association, in more recent times BERA seems to have taken little interest in history as a discipline or its contribution to an understanding of education. Relatively few historically-based papers are presented at its annual conferences, unlike the European Educational Research Association which has a significant historical dimension. BERA's journal, the *British Educational Research Journal*, describes itself as "interdisciplinary" but has tended to include few historical articles.

In terms of education policy, too, the past generation of education reform since the 1970s and 1980s has tended to be but little informed by historical perspectives and insights, in sharp contrast to the reforms of the mid twentieth century, generally taking a managerial or technical fix approach to reform that disregards the cultural and historical context. "Evidence-based policy", which has often been invoked in Britain in recent years, rarely seems to involve the use of historical evidence. As Charles Webster noted over thirty years ago,

> It is only by reference to history that we will understand both the root causes of the present crisis of confidence, and the sources for our inegalitarian and heavily bureaucratized educational system, and it is only by this means that we will be able to retrace the steps by which progress has been made at the cost of insensitivity to the cultural aspirations of the classes which the system was intended to serve.

---

[30] McCulloch, Gary "'Disciplines contributing to education'? Educational studies and the disciplines" in *British Journal of Educational Studies* 50 (2002), pp. 100-119.
[31] Lagemann, Ellen (2000) An Elusive Science: The Troubling History of Education Research (London: University of Chicago Press, 2000).

Yet as Webster also predicted, "These are lessons which the bureaucrat and the politician are very unlikely to wish to learn."[32] Examples of new initiatives reinventing the wheel, and failing to learn from the experience of previous initiatives developed even a short time ago, within the last thirty years, have become rather a regular event. In Britain, also, government policy has undermined the position of historical approaches in the curriculum of teacher education over the past twenty years, so that the history of education now barely exists in teacher education, weakening still further the educational base of the history of education.

It is the combination of these four developments – the rise and fall of the traditional "educational" model of educational history, the rise of distinctive historical and social science based rationales for the history of education, and the effects of an uncongenial environment within education itself – that has progressively undermined more inclusive types of justification. This trend, in Britain at least, has threatened the principal base of the history of education in university departments of education. It has also helped to permit the erosion of the historical memory of educational policies and institutions over the last thirty years.

The increased importance of historical and social science rationales over the past generation has also tended to encourage the history of education as a whole to splinter into a large number of different areas and specialisms with sub-fields such as curriculum, teachers and teaching, girls and women, universities, the economy, and the city, reflecting wider trends in historical writing over the past generation. These different subfields have tended to develop their own rationales. For example curriculum history, which enjoyed a relatively brief vogue in the 1980s, developed a strongly educational rationale in Britain at least under the influence of Ivor Goodson, who emphasized its potential worth as a way of addressing the restructuring of state schooling and the emergence of the National Curriculum in contemporary education policies. According to Goodson, curriculum history was "less interested in history for its own sake, much more with history for the sake of curriculum – to aid understanding of fundamental curriculum issues", and he argued that this objective should stand as the "litmus test" for those undertaking such history.[33]

---

[32] Webster, Charles, "Changing perspectives in the history of education" in Oxford Review of Education 2 (1976), p. 211.

[33] Goodson, Ivor, The Making of Curriculum: Collected Essays (London: Falmer, 1988), p. 53.

At the same time, some scholars who are particularly interested in social science-based approaches, developments in theory and methodology would suggest that such sub-fields are based on receptivity to developments in theory and methodology. There have been some very exciting advances in these respects, for example in oral and visual approaches to history, but scholars who are committed to these novel approaches sometimes complain of their differential impact and the cultural resistances of the field as a whole. In the early 1990s, for example, June Purvis could argue in relation to the history of women's education that British history of education was "remarkably slow" to respond to the challenges posed by feminist history: "While feminist researchers document and chart the history of women's education, their findings remain ghettoized and isolated from what is seen as the 'main body' of work".[34] According to Grosvenor and Lawn, similarly,"scholars with an interest in historical explanation move into or remain in disconnected sub-fields of study which encourage innovation; this has the consequent effect of allowing the main field of study to remain secure in its approaches while impairing its development".[35]

There has thus been a process of compartmentalization or balkanization, fragmenting the field at the same time that tensions have developed between the potential rationales involved. Reacting against this tendency in the discipline of history as a whole, the British historian David Cannadine has noted a tendency for specialisms to proliferate, often taking up "extreme and entrenched adversarial positions".[36] The sub-fields of the history of education have in some cases taken on the character of pockets or enclaves of activity, embodying often some very interesting and important advances in different areas but developed in relative isolation, albeit with shifting alliances with different individuals and groups. This image of the field is more complex than the essentially bipolar characterization of a Cold War proposed by William Richardson, but hardly less hazardous or insecure as a world order.

[34] Purvis, June "The historiography of British education: a feminist critique" in *Rethinking Radical Education ed.* A. Rattansi and D. Reeder (London: Lawrence and Wishart, 1992), p. 264.

[35] *Grosvenor, Ian and Lawn, Martin "Ways of seeing in education and schooling: emerging historiographies" in History of Education 30 (2001), p. 105.*

[36] *Cannadine, David "Perspectives: One hundred years of history in Britain" in D. Cannadine, Making History Now and Then: Discoveries, Controversies and Explanations (London: Palgrave Macmillan, 2008), p. 33.*

"Post-revisionism" has become popular as a description of the state of the field as a whole, following the pioneering work of the revisionists of the 1960s and 1970s, but it does not suggest a general rationale as such but rather complexity and diversity. In the United States, Reese and Rury portray post-revisionism as eclectic, broad and diverse in its range, although they also suggest that it represents "a new maturity in the field, a willingness to embrace the complexity of education as a social and political process of change, entailing struggle but also growth and the hope of progress".[37]

The greater specialisation based on detailed research has again produced work of great distinction and sophistication in recent years, but has tended to supplant works of synthesis with a broader scope which had been familiar in the field for many years. In Britain, for example, Simon's four volume history is still the standard work, and it is now fifty years since the publication of the first of its four volumes.[38] It does not seem a coincidence that no general history of education in Britain in the nineteenth and twentieth centuries has been produced in the last thirty years, during which time new work has always been restricted by focus on a particular sector or period.

These considerations give rise to a number of strategic issues in developing the *raison d'etre* of the history of education over the coming generation. First, we should consider how best to find common cause, or a set of common causes, for the field as a whole despite its recent compartmentalization into a range of specialisms. This is important for strategic as well as epistemological reasons, as we seek ways of defining and defending the position of history of education in the academy and in public discourse. But finding ways of sharing and highlighting our common concerns as historians of education is a key task ideologically no less than pragmatically, in binding together individuals and groups whose work has sometimes come to appear disparate and even incoherent. Second, it is necessary to seek further ways of enriching the history of education by engaging with the social sciences and humanities,

---

[37] Reese, William J. and Rury, John "Introduction" in *Rethinking the History of American Education* ed. W. Reese and J. Rury (New York: Palgrave Macmillan, 2008), p. 7.

[38] Simon, Brian, Studies in the History of Education, 1780-1870 (London: Lawrence and Wishart, 1960). This was later renamed The Two Nations and the Educational Structure, 1780-1870, and was joined by Education and the Labour Movement, 1870-1920 (London: Lawrence and Wishart, 1965), The Politics of Educational Reform, 1920-1940 (London: Lawrence and Wishart, 1974), and Education and the Social Order, 1940-1990 (London: Lawrence and Wishart, 1991).

while maintaining its integrity as a form of history. The rise of these approaches over the past generation has reinvigorated research in the field in a number of directions over the past half-century, and it is very important that they be encouraged to develop further.

We should also attempt to regain and renew vigorous educational rationales for the history of education without losing the advances that have been made through greater awareness of historical and social scientific developments. History as a means to anticipate the future and understand the present, and to reconsider educational ideas and institutions that may no longer be relevant or viable, remains a key theme that has tended to be neglected over the past generation as a *raison d'etre* for the history of education. In the spirit of Durkheim and Simon, it is urgent that historians of education consider new ways of promoting connections between historical insights and interpretations on the one hand, and the needs of education on the other. Yet this should be realized not as a return to the pious platitudes that were once so prominent, or the "ahistorical utilitarianism" deplored by Depaepe, but building on the insights of Durkheim and Simon, as part of a broad and interdisciplinary vision for the history of education as a whole.

Qualities of Irrelevance: History of Education in the Training of Teachers

Marc Depaepe

Almost a decade ago, Jurgen Herbst, one of the former presidents of the *International Standing Conference for the History of Education (ISCHE)*, wanted to portray the State of the Art of the History of Education at the end of the Twentieth Century in North America as well as in Europe. In his final considerations he said that historians of education have to "consider *anew* [italics added] their presence as academics in programmes of professional education"[1]. "Anew" implies, in this context, that there once existed a truly relevant history of education that was, indeed, integrated into teacher training programmes. But what kind of history of education was that? And does it still have the potential to attract educationalists today? These questions[2] seem to me, as a historian of education, a good starting point to open an international conference on enhancing the quality of education for teachers in the Twenty First Century[3].

As Marie-Madeleine Compère[4] and I myself[5] among others, have

---

[1] J. Herbst, The History of Education: State of the Art at the Turn of the Century in Europe and North America, Paedagogica Historica, XXXV (1999) 737-747 (here 747).

[2] See first of all my reply, M. Depaepe, A professionally relevant history of education for teachers: does it exist? Reply to Herbst's the State of the Art Article, Paedagogica Historica, XXXVII (2001) 631-640, of which this article is a further elaboration. See furthermore my review article M. Depaepe, What Kind of History of Education May We Expect for the Twenty-first Century? Some Comments on Four Recent Readers in the Field. Essay Review in Memory of Maurits De Vroede (1922-2002) and Brian Simon (1915-2002): D. Crook & R. Aldrich (ed.), History of Education for the Twenty-First Century; R. Aldrich (ed.), A Century of Education; P. Götte & W. Gippert (Hg.) Historische Pädagogik am Beginn des 21. Jahrhunderts & T.S. Popkewitz, B.M. Franklin & M.A. Pereyra (ed.), Cultural History and Education, Paedagogica Historica, XXXIX (2003) 187-199, and, finally, my Spanish reader: M. Depaepe, Vieja y nueva historias de la educación. Ensayos criticos (Barcelona, Octaedro, 2006).

[3] This text was presented as a key-note at the ATEE (Association for Teacher Education in Europe) Spring University 2008, held at the University of Letvia in Riga on May 2nd, 2008. The general theme of this congerence was: Teacher of the 21st Century: Quality Education for Quality Teaching.

[4] M.M. Compère, L'Histoire de l'éducation en Europe. Essai comparatif sur la façon dont elle s'écrit (Paris/Berne, INRP/Lang, 1995)

[5] M. Depaepe, Entre pédagogie et histoire. Questions et remarques sur l'évolution des objectifs de l'enseignement de l'histoire de l'éducation, Histoire de l'Education, n° 77 (janvier 1998) 3-18.

tried to explain, from the last quarter of the nineteenth century the success of the history of education in teacher training – in the United States as well as in Europe – depended on the theoretical relevance of the educational thought of the "great masters" (like Montaigne, Comenius, Fénélon, Rousseau, Pestalozzi, and Fröbel), and, probably, even more on the prospect of inculcating a "pedagogically correct" attitude into future teachers. Gabriel Compayré (1843-1913), the standard bearer of the French "history of pedagogy", stated in 1884 that the various pedagogical systems of the great thinkers elevated the level of moral exhortation. We cannot imagine that Herbst simply wants to restore the moralizing of that old-fashioned history of education. Along with other leading scholars in the field who participated last year in a conference about "New Directions in the History of Education" sponsored by the Spencer Foundation[6], he believes that the "golden era" of American educational history is not to be situated in the 19th century but in the age of cultural revisionism of the 1960s and 1970s during which the research agenda in the United States was strongly determined by the "methodologically organized historiography"[7] of Bailyn, Cremin and others. Indeed, we may well assume[8] that a "paradigm shift" took place under the inspiration of cultural revisionism: the history of ideas was replaced by the postulate of the social history of education.

A closer look at this evolution, however, reveals a number of differentiations that can serve as an antidote to a monolithic and ahistorical conceptualization of the "history of the history of education", as Sol Cohen put it.[9] Heinz-Elmar Tenorth and other German researchers observed already in the mid-1970s[10] that the "new paradigm" of the "social" history of education could boast only a relative consensus and that was with regard to the methodological problem in a narrower

[6] R. Donato & M. Lazerson, New Directions in American Educational History: Problems and Prospects, Educational Researcher, XXIX, 8 (November 2000) 4-15.

[7] Herbst, The History, 738 paraphrases H.E. Tenorth in that respect.

[8] Among others: M.M. Compère, L'Histoire, 18 ff.; A. Nóvoa, L'histoire et l'histoire de l'éducation, in: A. Nóvoa, Histoire & Comparaison (Essais sur l'Education) (Lisbonne, Educa, 1998) 31 ff.

[9] S. Cohen, The History of the History of American Education: The Uses of the Past, in: S. Cohen, Challenging Orthodoxies: Toward a New Cultural History of Education (New York, Lang, 1999) 3-34.

[10] See, e.g., IZEBF: Informationen zur Erziehungs- und Bildungshistorischen Forschung, Heft 3: Herbsttagung 1975: Aufgaben und methodologische Probleme historischer Forschung im Erziehungs- und Bildungswesen (1975); W. Böhm & J. Schriewer (Hrsg.), Geschichte der Pädagogik und systematische Erziehungswissenschaft. Festschrift zum 65. Geburtstag von Albert Reble (Stuttgart, Klett-Cota, 1975); V. Lenhart (Hrsg.), Historische Pädagogik. Methodologische Probleme der Erziehungsgeschichte (Wiesbaden, Akademische Verlaggesellschaft, 1977).

sense: the general acceptance of social historical tools and research techniques, including quantitative methods. But this did not eliminate the fundamental diversity with regard to the methodological problem in a broader sense, namely the relationship between theory and history, not only in the field of education but also in that of the social sciences in general. As I have indicated elsewhere,[11] there was a fairly high degree of dissension in the theoretical positioning of the discipline in West Germany. For the historian of education, of course, it made a big difference whether the role of his research was limited, as the godfather of empirical research, Wolfgang Brezinka, argued, to that of a pre-scientific "reservoir of hypotheses", or whether it was at the heart of educational theory formation, as in the historical socialization research of Ulrich Herrmann or as in the ideological-critical and neo-Marxist approaches in both West and East Germany.[12]

These differences in theoretical conceptions also had practical consequences in the international organization of the scientific community of historians of education. It may be true that, under the impetus of chairholders like Brian Simon, Maurice De Vroede, and Jurgen Herbst himself, the "new" social history of education was inspirational in the founding and development of the International Standing Conference in the History of Education,[13] but this certainly did not hinder the flourishing of old-fashioned and, in my view, even dilettantish aspirations within the same organization concerning the "relevance" of the history of education to the solution of practical problems[14]. One of the editors of a book, presenting itself as the outcome of the meetings of the International Standing Working Group for the History of Education as a Field of Research and as a Teaching Subject within ISCHE, simply echoed the assumptions of the old-fashioned 19th century "historical pedagogy":

---

[11] M. Depaepe, On the Relationship of Theory and History in Pedagogy. An Introduction to the West German Discussion on the Significance of the History of Education (Leuven University Press, 1983).

[12] See also, in this respect, B. Rang, Pädagogische Geschichtsschreibung in der DDR. Entwicklung und Entwicklungsbedingungen der pädagogischen Historiographie 1945-1965 (Frankfurt/Main, Campus Forschung, 1982); M. Heinemann (Hrsg.), Historische Pädagogik in Europa und den USA. 2 vol. (Stuttgart, Klett-Cota, 1979-1985).

[13] J. Herbst, The International Standing Conference for the History of Education after the first decade, Paedagogica Historica, XXVI (1990) 85-89; M. Depaepe, International Standing Conference for the History of Education (ISCHE), in: P. Caspard (dir./ed.), Guide international de la recherche en histoire de l'éducation/ International Guide for Research in the History of Education (Bern/Paris, Lang/INRP) 227-232. See also M. Depaepe, It's a long way to... an international social history of education. In search of Brian Simon's legacy in today's educational historiography, History of Education, XXXIII, 5 (2004) 531-544.

[14] See, e.g., K. Salimova & E.V. Johanningmeier (eds.), Why should we teach history of education? (Moscow, The Library of International Academy of Self-Improvement, 1993).

> "Through such examples [as Comenius, Pestalozzi, Dewey, Makarenko, and Sukhomlinsky], taken from the heritage of the past, we may form the future teachers' mode of thinking, their pedagogical outlook, their attitude towards their future position [...] Positive contribution of this or that epoch fulfils a *prognostic* function of history of education because it shows vitality of some or other conceptions, practical decisions and possibilities of using them and taking into consideration the requirements of a new epoch [...]. History of education is the science about the regularities (laws) of theoretical and practical development [...] So, the history of education will make further contribution to the solution of new tasks, set by our time and dictated by the demands of modernization and educational reforms oriented to the twenty-first century"[15].

Without wanting to be exposed to the charge of methodological imperialism, I saw it as my duty in 1992 when president of ISCHE, to warn against a purely utilitarian treatment of the educational heritage of the past[16]. In my judgement, the explicit striving for ideological, theoretical, or practical advantage will inevitably lead to mystification and even the prostitution of history to hagiographic, pedagogical hero worship and a partisan and presentistic reading of history - an opinion of which I became more and more convinced after the invitation, in October 1994, to participate in a "Sino-Swiss Pestalozzi Project" as well as after a mission, in September 1995, to evaluate the existing research and teaching in the history of education at the universities of the province of Gauteng (the former Transvaal) in South Africa. In both cases my critical comments[17] encountered simplistic reasoning about "lessons" of the past, for a large

---

[15] K. Salimova, Educational Wisdom of the Past: A message for the future, in: Salimova & Johanningmeier, Why should we, 104-106.

[16] M. Depaepe, History of Education anno 1992: 'A tale told by an idiot, full of sound and fury, signifying nothing?', History of Education, XXII (1993) 1-10.

[17] M. Depaepe & H. Van Crombrugge, Using or Abusing the Educational Past? - Some methodological reflections on the place of Johann Heinrich Pestalozzi in the educational historiography, in: H. Gehrig (ed.), Pestalozzi in China. International Academic Symposium on the Occasion of the Publication of Johann Heinrich Pestalozzi's Selected Works in Chinese. Beijing, 10-14 October 1994 (Zürich, Pestalozzianum, 1995) 51-62; M. Depaepe, My way to the new 'cultural' history of education: from 'historical pedagogy' to the history of 'educational mentalities', in: J.H. Coetzee & T.G. Smith (eds.), International conference on education and change. A selection of papers of a conference held in September 1995 at Unisa, Pretoria (Pretoria, University of South Africa, 1996) 1-11.

part hiding specific pedagogical and political interests in educational reform.[18]

The nationally orchestrated attempts to popularize Pestalozzi's thought in China coincided with large scale literacy campaigns, in which the integration of manual labour and formal education was central[19]. What makes Pestalozzi attractive in China is not so much his "profound historical significance" but his "great immediate significance" which is reflected in conclusions like: "People of the contemporary era can absorb the quintessence [of Pestalozzi's educational thoughts] so as to direct and promote educational reform today"; "At present the kernal [of activity teaching] ... is still the basic ideas of Pestalozzi"; "With life-long devotion to education and indomitable willpower, Pestalozzi will always be a shining example for educators all over the world"; "Pestalozzi's thought on [labour and technical] education still has far reaching significance for guiding educational practices nowadays"; "If one has Pestalozzi's universal love and readiness to save the world, he will be filled with 'saint's zeal' and become ever succesful", and so on[20]. Ironically enough, analogous attempts to make good use of the heritage of the educational past can be found in some conservative (White) circles in South-Africa, where "historical pedagogy" is still used to legitimate traditional values (even unofficially under the flag of ISCHE!). On the basis of the so-called *paedagogica perennis* - a phenomenological construct about the essences of education derived from history - one can hear the plea for a "cultural based" (that is: unicultural) education for the diverse ethnic and religious groups in the country:

> "Education through the ages was always culturally interrelated. Culture, religion, vernacular and historicity were always inherently part of authentic education. Remember this when re-evaluating the integration of schools in South Africa [....] Cramming children from all these divergent cultural groups into the same classrooms negates

---

[18] See, e.g., J.H. Jordaan, How a course in the history of education serves as a changing factor in the education and lives of first year students, in: Coetzee & Smith (eds.), International Conference, 259-263.

[19] See the report of Zhang Ziyong about the conference in Paedagogica Historica, XXXI (1995) 310-312.

[20] Quotations from: Ren Zhong Yen, Pestalozzi and Modern Education, in: Gehrig, Pestalozzi, 111.Yuan Rui, Pestalozzi and Modern Activity Teaching, id., 116.Zhou Huiying, Johann Heinrich Pestalozzi on Labour Education - His Theory and Practice, id., 121. Sun Jianguo, Integration of Education and Productive Labour - Through Offering Courses of Labour Techniques as the Main Channel, id., 125; Teng Dachun, Carry Forward Pestalozzi's Dedication to Education - in Commemoration of his 250th Birthday, id., 83.

> the *paedagogica perennis*. Whose language, history, religion, norms and values and cultural heritage are going to be taught? These essences of education must never be neglected if children are to be educated authentically towards proper adulthood. We owe our children this. In multicultural schools many children are going to be deprived of their vernacular, cultural heritage and religion. Overemphasis on knowledge, skills and vocational preparation is inadequate. Cultural based schools are pedagogical [sic] verified"[21]....

Although the political and ideological power implications of such reasoning by historical researchers (not in the least the historians of education themselves) still have to be brought to the surface by studying the concrete, social and cultural-historical context to which they relate, they nevertheless instinctively make me think back to how the Catholics fleshed out the subject of "the history of education" in pre-conciliar Flanders. After the First World War, the priest-educationalists De Hovre and Decoene made an attempt to underpin education from a Catholic point of view through the publication of the *Vlaamsch Opvoedkundig Tijdschrift.*[22] What they were ultimately aiming for was a "conservative revolution", "a rebirth through rebaptisation in the eternal rejuvenating source of Catholic educational philosophy". For De Hovre, the Catholic philosophy of life was the "cornerstone" of all modern life theories, "the prototype, the Platonic idea, the essence of all real pedagogical thinking, the '*paedagogia perennis*', the foundation of real educational tradition, the mother tongue of educational wisdom, the herald of educational truth," from where all "idols" or "false sources" of modern educational theory would be judged. This combative position meant that historiography could not be neutral, nor educational theory. "All the theory from the modern understanding of historical data, has shown", again according to De Hovre, "that personal sympathy constitutes a primary condition for understanding a man, a work, or event". Thereby indicating that the past

---

[21] J.H. Jordaan, Schooling in Changing African Societies: Before and after Independence, 1950-1996, in: C. Majorek & E.V. Johanningmeier (eds.), Educational Reform in National Perspectives: Past, Present and Future (Cracow, Polish Akademy of Sciences Publishing House in Cracow, 2000) 137-148 (Quotation: 146).

[22] See M. Depaepe, Normatief-pedagogisch denken in Vlaanderen. Continuïteit en discontinuïteit in de katholieke pedagogiek sedert 1918, Pedagogische Verhandelingen, X (1987) 270-291; Idem, De spanning van verborgen agenda's. Ontwikkelingen inzake het onderwijs in de historische pedagogiek, Comenius, XVII (1997) 200-215, where the reader can find all references to the original works of De Hovre and Decoene.

had to be seen through Catholic eyes, in which the extent of admiration for the great educational heroes depended on the building blocks that they supplied to Catholic educational practice. Hence innovators (in this case "reform educationalists who wanted to start with the child") such as Ellen Key, were labelled by Decoene and De Hovre as "big children" who have surfaced in the century of the child "in order to put their great childishness in the place of age-old values".

That these assumptions in Catholic Flanders have continued to resound for a long time requires little debate. Much more remarkable is perhaps their theoretical scientific analogy with the Marxist-Leninist principles of educational history and educational theory in the former Eastern block, and more particularly in the DDR, where a lot of consideration was given to the theoretical-methodological foundation in this respect[23] (of course as a counter to the Western "imperial", read "capitalist", educational theory in Germany). There too, the (dialectical) unity of the "logical" (theoretical) and "historical" formed the core of (historical) educational theory. Within the bounds of the Marxist-Leninist epistemology, the past appeared as the inevitable and necessary developmental process towards the socialist society. The history of human society was regarded as a succession of class conflicts. The different episodes of the class struggle were demarcated by a revolution, which in itself constituted the climax of the conflict. Once the class society had been transformed into a socialist (communist is meant) society as a result of the great revolution, the ordered nature of their blind determinism was disposed of. In this socialist form of society, people got to know the forces that determine society. As a result they became masters of history and they could apply this knowledge to the realisation of the socialist message of salvation. This principle applied *mutatis mutandis* to Marxist-Leninist educational theory. Without a systematic exploration of the past, the progressive construction and planning of the future was impossible. Just like the past, present and future, theory and practice in Marxism-Leninism were inseparable ("dialectically") from one another.

A number of functional consequences arose from these theoretical-methodological fundamentals for education in the history of education that were not only conceived as the centre of educational theory, but also as an essential component of general cultural history. First of

---

[23] See M. Depaepe, De marxistisch-leninistische opvatting over historische pedagogiek in de D.D.R. (ca. 1965-1980), Pedagogische Studiën, LIX (1982) 507-518, in which you can find a list of East German discussion articles of the time.

all, the "pedagogic heritage" of the past had to be laid bare, as familiarity with the "progressive" legacy of former educationalists was very useful for historical, shall we say socialist awareness in general, and that of teachers in particular. Moreover, the association with the "socialist" heritage could be placed in the struggle against "imperialist", and/or even "fascist" influences from abroad (in this case related to West Germany). Thirdly it was hoped that a problem-oriented reading of the past would provide help in resolving contemporary problems, and finally it also seemed to be an aid in making forecasts for future policy.

Such "strange uses of the past"[24] – which were not just reserved for East Germany, but were also perceptible throughout the sphere of influence of the Soviet Union,[25] with Latvia being no exception,[26] bring me back to the issue of cultural revisionism in the United States. But the associated question of the functional value of the history of education is better viewed in the light of the long-term history of the subject. While the "history of education" from the end of the Nineteenth Century seemed to be a permanent feature on the curriculum of teacher training in the United States as well, mistrust grew after the First World War, because this part of the training did not seem to keep its pragmatic promises.[27] In the 1920s and '30s this led to an extensive debate on the functional value of the history of education, which lost confidence as a subject in teacher training. A survey in 1917 showed that only 12.7% of the teachers surveyed were convinced that the subject had been of any use to them.[28] The answer of academics involved in the history of education primarily related to the content. They referred to the role, in this case the benefits, of public education in relation to the structure of American society. The school was the engine of democracy (read meri tocracy), as Ellwood P. Cubberley called it.[29] He set the tone with the

[24] See R. Lowe, History as Propaganda: The strange uses of the history of education, in: P. Gordon & R. Szreter (eds.), History of Education: The making of a discipline (London, Cass, 1989).

[25] Which makes the ideas of K. Salimova– even after the "Peristroika" – understandable. See K. Salimova, Educational Wisdom.

[26] See I. Kestere, The use of textbooks in the history of education. The experience of the Univeristy of Soviet Latvia from the 1940s until the 1980s. Paper presented at 11th Conference of the Internationale Gesellschaft für Historische und Systematische Schulbuchforschung. Ypern, 5-6/10/2007.

[27] J. H. Stoutemeyer, The Teaching of History of Education in Normal Schools, School and Society, XVII,177 (1918) 571-573.

[28] L.A. Cremin, The Recent Development of the History of Education as a Field of Study in the United States, History of Education Journal, VII (1955) 1-5.

[29] E.P. Cubberley, The History of Education: Educational practice and progress considered as a phase of development and spread of western civilization (London, Constable, s.d. [1920]); E.P. Cubberley, Public Education in the United States (Cambridge, MA, Riverside Press, 1919).

construction of a linear-progressive account of progress of the history of education.[30] This narrative, which was not devoid of triumphalism, joined in with the general ("Whig") interpretation of the target-oriented progress in (Western) civilisation, from which nothing but good was expected (in the sense of "more and more" and "better and better").

However the "functional fallacy", as Frederic Lilge characterised the American expectations of the history of education in 1947,[31] was far from finished. To begin with, the "success story" according to the Cubberley style, further accentuated the professional discourse and ethos of the educationalists. In addition, the demand for a problem-oriented approach in social sciences from a social-reconstructivist point of view increasingly resounded in the 1930s. Only in this way could a "new" society come into being, capable of managing contemporary problems. As a result, the history of education risked being reduced to a part of a "social foundations" course focused on current affairs. It was only after the Second World War that the way was cleared for a wider sociocultural perspective, in which educational history was no longer seen as the development of "formal pedagogy but rather as the entire process by which culture transmits itself across the generations."[32] In favour of this "paradigm shift" was the so-called revisionism of the 1960s, which on a scientific-organisational level was accentuated by the foundation of the *History of Education Society* in 1960 and the publication of *History of Education Quarterly* as of 1961. Incidentally, this (re?)development of the educational past by historians resulted in Edgar B. Wesley changing his thirty six year old lament "Lo, the poor history of education"[33] to the jubilant: "Hail, the flourishing history of education"[34]!

In practice the revisionism, of which Bernard Bailyn and Larry Cremin were the protagonists, meant a wider view of upbringing and education. In essence, as professional historians, the revisionists have attacked the narrow-minded thesis of educationalists like Cubberley about the "victory" of public education in American democracy. They charged it with being burdened with methodological sins like

---

[30] L.A. Cremin, The Wonderful World of Ellwood Patterson Cubberley (New York, Columbia University, 1965).

[31] F. Lilge, The Functionalist Fallacy and the History of Education, School and Society, LXV, 1648 (1947) 241-243.

[32] B. Baylin, Education in the Forming of American Society: Needs and opportunities for study (Chapel Hill, University of North Carolina Press, 1960) 14.

[33] E.B. Wesley, Lo, the Poor History of Education, School and Society, XXXVI (1933) 619-621.

[34] E.B. Wesley, Lo, the Poor History of Education, History of Education Quarterly, IX (1969) 342.

presentism and evangelism. "The past was simply the present writ small", it ran.[35] "But the supreme irony of the golden era was" – as Donato and Lazerson has put it in their review of last year's debate on the new directions in American history of education – "that radical revisionists gained attention by doing what previous generations of educational historians had done: They claimed an immediate connection to the present,"[36] Indeed, the radical revisionists, with among others Michael Katz as the pioneer, turned the old Cubberley thesis on its head. Far from having acted as an engine of democratisation, the school lay at the basis of racism, class inequality and unequal opportunities in the United States. As a kind of therapeutic assessment with an idealised past, educational history had to indicate the possibilities and priorities of future educational developments, within the critical and also generally neo-marxist, perspective held by the radical revisionists. Hence post-revisionists such as Ravitch blamed the radicals for opening the door again for propaganda and the politicization of history with their "leftist" interpretation. However, they may not forget that their own research has been coloured by their assumptions about the present, even if they pleaded for a history of education in "its own right and in its own terms"[37] – an observation that other researchers, in addition to Ravitch, also made[38]. Today revisionism may be dead, as Herbst already noted in the 1980s,[39] but that does not automatically imply that the search for lessons from the history of education is over. On the contrary Ravitch and others do not stop "learning from the Past."[40] But their stories are much more sophisticated and therefore, perhaps more veiled and dangerous than the utilitarist examples discussed above.[41]

During the 1980s, another "new" history of education emerged in the United States and elsewhere, the so-called new "cultural" his tory of education, which was perhaps not so "new", since the "old" new

---

[35] See S. Cohen, The History, 22, originally from B. Bailyn, Education, 9.
[36] Donato & Lazerson, New Directions, 6.
[37] D. Ravitch, The Revisionists Revised: A Critique of the Radical Attack on the Schools (New York, Basic Books, 1978).
[38] See, e.g., D.R. Warren, A Past for the Present: History, education and public policy, Educational Theory, XXVIII (1978) 264-265.
[39] J. Herbst, Beyond the Debate over Revisionism: Three Educational Pasts Writ Large, History of Education Quarterly, XX (1980) 131-145.
[40] D. Ravitch & M.A. Vinovskis (eds.), Learning from the Past. What History Teaches Us about School Reform (Baltimore, The John Hopkins University Press, 1995).
[41] See in that respect also the critique of R. Aldrich towards our understanding of the "British" situation: R. Aldrich, Lessons from History of Education. The selected works of Richard Aldrich (London/New York, Routledge, 2005).

history of education in Germany - to use the term of Jarausch[42] - considered the social as well as the cultural dimensions of education from the outset as aspectual expressions of a rich intellectual life. Moreover, this same qualification of the often inflated "paradigm shifts" applies, in my view, to the American development. Indeed, historians like R. Freeman Butts may have believed, as Cubberley did, in the benefactions of American public education. Also, by the 1940s and '50s they showed, at least embryonically, the way for a thoroughly socio-cultural analysis of education. Butts for example tried to find a balance between giving history a meaning for the present and upholding the integrity of the past.[43] However that may be, this "new" cultural history of education – to which, among others, Sol Cohen contributed[44], although his concept of "linguistic turn" recently came under fire from a methodological point of view[45] – clearly gives evidence for presentism being more a condition of historical research than an abstract methodological sin. Writing and rewriting history ultimately belong to the present. In this respect postmodernism does not really force us to do anything new, "but it does oblige us to do it well and to be seen to doing it well", to quote Roy Lowe.[46] And whether we label these activities "postmodern" or "high modern", as historical explanations, they always will need a kind of "hermeneutics", which, as Gadamer understood it, "is based on the historicity and linguisticity of experience, seeks the identification of meaning and the sense of memory which the narrator as mediator elaborates as a text, restoring and re-establishing the gaps in the story, even critically, so as to give the analysis the coherence it requires regarding the totality of the discourse and the context."[47]According to Foucault, we are as human beings "condemned" to write and rewrite history from the present. This does not imply legitimizing the systematic distortion of the past in function of an ideologically fixed position. It does mean

[42] K. Jarausch, The Old 'New History of Education': a German reconsideration, History of Education Quarterly, XXVi (1986) 225-241.
[43]S. Cohen, The History, 19.
[44] E.g. S. Cohen, Representatins of History in the Linguistic Turn, in: Cohen, Challenging Orthodoxies, 65-85.
[45] K. Brehony, From the particular to the general, the continuous to the discontinuous: progressive education revisted, History of Education, XXX (2001) 413-432; See also the critical book review of Sol Cohen's Challenging Orthodoxies by H.E. Tenorth, Linguistic Turn und Konstruktionsmetaphern, Zeitschrift für Pädagogische Historiographie, VII (2001) 134-137.
[46] R. Lowe, Postmodernity and Historians of Education: A View from Britain, Paedagogica Historica, XXXII (1996) 307-323 (Quotation: 323).
[47] A. Escolano, Postmodernity or High Modernity? Emerging Approaches in the New History of Education, Paedagogica Historica, XXXII (1996) 325-341 (Quotation 340).

that we, as professional historians, have to investigate how we ourselves rationalize and camouflage our own research strategies, research questions, and interpretative themes just as much as we have to unmask the hidden agendas and rhetoric of the educational discourse of previous generations.[48]

To the degree to which we succeed in this "endless task", the history of education will acquire a post-modern added value: it deconstructs, demythologizes, and tarnishes the "great", "heroic" and often exaggerated stories of the past, not to ridicule our predecessors, their education, or their ideals but to demonstrate that they, too, were "human beings", living in a concrete, socio-historical context that can hardly be abstracted from. It qualifies the great emancipatory meta-narratives about education and shows that, at least from the 19th century onwards, education increasingly revealed a dynamic of its own that seems of itself, not to have guaranteed the greater emancipation of the individual. The increase of educational opportunities did not necessarily provide increased opportunities for empowerment and autonomy but could also led to subjection and dependence.[49] Herbst is absolutely right in picking up Tenorth's demand[50] to investigate this paradox within the "new" cultural history of education from the inside and not with conceptualizations and frameworks from the outside, i.e. the mainstream history or sociology. And he is also right in describing with Tenorth these "import theories" as a most critical factor in the absence of knowledge about the history of everyday pedagogical practices in the classroom to the point that there is almost no place for "education" in the history of education,[51] which indeed can help to explain the absence of historical awareness among teachers and educators. Recently, however, in line with the current outstanding Spanish research on school culture,[52] some studies are

---

[48] M. Depaepe, Demythologizing the Educational Past: An Endless Task in History of Education, Historical Studies in Education/Revue d'histoire de l'éducation, IX (1997) 208-223.

[49] M. Depaepe, Educationalisation: A key concept in understanding the basic processes in the history of Western education, History of Education Review, XXVII,2 (1998) 1-15.

[50] H.E. Tenorth, Lob des Handwerks, Kritik der Theorie - Zur Lage der pädagogischen Historiographie in Deutschland, Paedagogica Historica, XXXII (1996) 343-361.

[51] M. Depaepe & F. Simon, Is there any Place for the History of 'Education' in the 'History of Education'? A Plea for the History of Everyday Educational Reality in- and outside Schools, Paedagogica Historica, XXXI (1995) 9-16.

[52] A. Esscolano Benito, Las culturas escolares del siglo XX. Encuentros y desencuentros, Revista de Educación, núm. Extrordinario (2000), 201-218.

dealing with the silences of classroom practices,[53] but it is very much the question whether they will provide answers teachers and educators are willing to hear.

Historical demystification about, for example, the practical impact of educational research or about the influence of educational innovation, always seems to annoy and frustrate the believers. For this reason, in contrast with Herbst[54] (who relies for this particular idea on Geraldine Clifford), I really do not believe that much in "learning from the past" or in the "lessons" that history will teach about school reform.[55] Nor would I hold with the privatizing of the educational past by the individual or collective memory in order to put into action the lessons drawn from former experiences.[56] Certainly, policy makers - as well as teacher trainers[57] - will continue to use "historical perspectives", but they do so primarily to advance their own agendas.[58] Let us not be naive about this, as the latest book of the right wing historian of education - or should I say conservative politician - Diane Ravitch about the historical damages of progressive education (with its "hedonistic, individualistic, anarchistic spirit of the sixties") proves.[59] The relevance of the history of education for the educators of the 21st century can in my view only be the relevance of an intrinsic nature, i.e., one that is critical and inevitably uncomfortable,[60] even for the "time-tested truths" of the educational goals of "self-restraint", "self-discipline, and humility" that Ravitch wants to learn from the history of education.[61] But such a history of education is, all in all, far from a being a superfluous luxury for teachers. For what can the professional competence of practical educators consist of other

---

[53] I. Grosvenor, M. Lawn & K. Rousmaniere (eds.), Silences & Images. The Social History of the Classroom (New York, Lang, 1999); M. Depaepe et al., Order in Progress. Everyday Educational Practice in Primary Schools - Belgium, 1880-1970 (Leuven, Leuven University Press, 2000).

[54] J. Herbst, The History, 747.

[55] See also M. Depaepe, Some statements about the nature of the history of education, in: Salimova & Johanningmeier (eds.), Why should we, 31-36.

[56] G. McCulloch, Publicizing the educational past, in: D. Crook & R. Aldrich (ed.), History of Education for the Twenty-First Century (London, Institute of Education University of London, 2000) 1-16.

[57] See, e.g. my critical review of J. Wolfe, Learning from the Past. Historical Voices in Early Childhood Education (Mayerthorpe, Piney Branch Press, 2000): M. Depaepe, Ein Beispiel klassischer Hagiographie, Zeitschrift für pädagogische Historiographie, VII (2001) 57-58.

[58] Donato & Lazerson, New Directions, 9.

[59] D. Ravitch, Left Back. A Century of Failed School Reforms (New York, Simon & Schuster, 2000).

[60] Depaepe, Demythologizing.

[61] D. Ravitch, Left Back, 407 & 453.

than in critical reflection on their activities past and present, especially now that the ideological coverage of normative philosophy has fallen away? As Tom Popkewitz has pointed out, "concepts of educational research, like our commonsense ideas of teaching, cannot be treated as if they were natural but must be interrogated as historical monuments in social relations."[62]

The representation that is taking root in our current European society is largely one of economic cost-effectiveness and utility. The education sector is not escaping from the current washing away of this neoliberal ideology. Educational institutions are considered to be playing "the market" and "capturing" a specific "segment" or "niche" with their offering. "Clientism" has not just been plucked out of the air. Quality controls are generally done from the point of view of the satisfaction of the "user", rather than from a critical reflection of what is to be achieved with education. Education is said to be a "business" that delivers knowledge and skills (neatly operationalised in final attainment levels and development objectives) for the purpose of securing a place on the job market. Far from us risking a cultural-critical debate on the sense and nonsense of the "performative requirements" that are currently being placed on schools, it nevertheless has to be said that the dominance of such a representation strongly threatens to lead attention away from the cultural history of education. Investing in research into history (also the history of education) is now difficult to reconcile with the priorities of *management* and *efficiency* thinking. Rather than willingly going along with the desiderata of market thinking (such as the demand for "profit" and the "cost-benefit analysis" of education), history enunciates an inconvenient discourse. The historical approach cultivates, as it were, the utility of the non-utilitarian. It sets itself up as a dam against the terror of the immediate practical benefit. From the critical distance of the cultural-historical view, research and education in history (also educational history) aims to go beyond the short-sightedness of modern times, by placing its genesis into a lengthy story that will probably not be devoid of paradoxes.[63] Thus the desire for rationality, where the prevailing drive for utility is obviously no more than an

---

[62] T.S. Popkewitz, The Denial of Change in Educational Change: Systems of Ideas in the Construction of National Policy and Evaluation, Educational Researcher, XXIX,1 (January-February 2000) 17-29 (Quotation 27).

[63] See M. Depaepe, F. Simon & A. Van Gorp (red.), Paradoxen van pedagogisering. Handboek pedagogische historiografie (Leuven/Voorburg, 2006^2).

expression, is more than likely linked to the process of modernisation, a modernisation of which the school itself laid the foundations in the distant past. To believe that by ignoring history it will be possible to escape the social processes that it generates itself, is of course a bitter illusion, even for curriculum builders, educational innovators, and policy bureaucrats and technocrats, who in the meantime have turned their backs on history. To paraphrase Nietzsche,[64] the task is and remains one of constantly reconciling oneself with the historicity of existence, one of the inconveniences that will never pass away in this earthly world.

[64] See M. Depaepe, Gesplitst en gespleten.De kloof tussen wetenschappelijke en praktische kennis in opvoeding en onderwijs (Leuven/Leusden, 2002) which takes F. Nietzsche's, Vom Nutzen und Nachteil der Historie für das Leben (1874) as starting point.

History of education threatened by extinction in Finnish educational sciences

Jukka Rantala

This article examines the position of the history of education in the Finnish scientific community, especially in educational sciences. The only professorship in history of education was recently abolished. Bachelor and Master level teaching has also been drastically reduced, and supervision of doctoral studies has floundered. History of education has become a mere "by-product" for university teachers of education.[1] In their research and teaching, they have had to blend into their own scientific community as broad-based educationalists and groups focused on history of education have not formed. Besides educational sciences, history of education is also studied in historical sciences, but history departments do not have specific tenures or teaching in that field. So far, collaboration between educational sciences and historical sciences has been minimal. This can be seen as a result of universal downgrading of pedagogic research, which stems from the pragmatic orientation of educational sciences and the unevenness of research quality. The Finnish scientific community shows no signs of improvement in the position of history of education in degree requirements or tenure structure. The future of the field therefore depends on the success of cross-disciplinary collaboration and networking.

---

[1] Sources: Degree requirements for bachelor's and master's degrees at the home pages of the faculties of education and behavioural sciences of the universities of Helsinki, Joensuu, Jyväskylä, Lapland, Oulu, Tampere and Turku and the Åbo Akademi. Accessed in March 2006. Journals and yearbooks used as data: Historiallinen Aikakauskirja 1995–2004 (Finnish-language journal of historical sciences),Historisk Tidskrift för Finland 1995–2004 (Swedish-language journal of historical sciences), Kasvatus 1995–2004 (journal of education), Koulu ja menneisyys 1935–2004 (yearbook of the Finnish-language society for the history of education), Skolhistoriskt Arkiv 1952–2003 (yearbook of the Swedish-language society for the history of education)

The weak position of history of education in degree requirements

The meaning of history of education can be seen as the heightening of the sensitivity to historical awareness in persons working within education, which means making connections between explanations of the past and expectations for the future. Past decisions have not been without alternatives; this is revealed when the past is studied from different viewpoints. The danger in the straightforward, deterministic view of history, which arises from limited historical knowledge, is the narrowing down of future hopes and options for decision. That is why knowledge of the history of one's own field of study is important to educationalists.

For a long time, history of education was considered an important part of training in educational sciences. In the 1970's, however, the perceived value of historical self-understanding began to diminish as the demands for pragmaticism in the field began to increase. Studies in history of education diminished when it had to engage in competition with other fields of education that was argued to be of more importance from a present-day point of view. Arguing the case for a historical viewpoint to students and senior teaching administrators became more challenging and studies in history of education were gradually dropped from degree requirements.

Preserving the vitality of various fields of educational science – history of education, philosophy, sociology etc. – is largely based on their presence in bachelor and master level studies. Even concise courses can encourage students to become more deeply acquainted with the thematics of these fields. It is even more essential, however, that university teachers who are responsible for these study modules take responsibility for developing these fields. If one field of education is marginalized in degree requirements, the experts in this field have to redirect their professional contributions elsewhere. This leads to the withering or even complete eradication of fields that have been downsized in this manner. This is now happening to history of education in Finland where the proportion engaged in this field in degree requirements has decreased sharply. The field began to be marginalized in the 1960's and 1970's, when demands for the autonomy of educational sciences led to the trimming of elements from other disciplines.[2] Introduction to history was

[2] See S. Anttonen, "Kasvatustieteen suunta kamppailujen kohteena – autonomiaan vai vallan alle" in S. Anttonen & V. Huotari (eds.) Työn alla kasvatustiede (Tampere: Tampereen yliopiston kasvatustieteiden laitos, 1996), 49–65 pp. 54–56

often left to a single examination text, especially in teacher training institutions that had only recently been integrated into the scientific community. In the following decades, history of education has been integrated into hybrid study modules that often involve philosophy of education and sociology along with history. Based on the degree requirement descriptions and course literature, these study modules emphasize the viewpoints of philosophy and sociology, leaving history as a mere curiosity. In some universities, it is possible to finish a master's degree in education without studying history of education at all, as shown in the tables below.

Table 1. The proportion of history of education in study points in the degree requirements of education or adult education between 2004–2007[3] (one study point equals approximately 27 hours of work for the student. The length of a master's degree is 300 study points).

University	Compulsory methodology studies	Optional methodology studies	Other compulsory studies	Other optional studies
University of Helsinki		2		5 + 2,5
University of Turku	2		3	
University of Tampere			2,5 + 2	
University of Jyväskylä			4	3
University of Joensuu		4	2,5	
University of Oulu				2,5
University of Lapland			1,5	
Åbo Akademi			5	

[3] History of education is often combined in the same study module with other fields of education, especially philosophy of education and sociology. In such cases, the study points awarded for the module have been divided by the number of fields involved. This data comes from the degree requirements given on the home pages of the faculties of education of different universities.

Table 2. The proportion of history of education in study points in the degree requirements of teacher training programmes between 2004–2007.

University/ Teacher training institute	Compulsory methodology studies	Optional methodology studies	Other compulsory studies	Other optional studies
University of Helsinki	1		2	
University of Turku	1			
Rauma teacher training institute			1,5	
Hämeenlinna teacher training institute			2,5	
University of Jyväskylä				3
University of Joensuu		4	2,5	
Savonlinna teacher training institute			2,5	
University of Oulu				
Kajaani teacher training institute				
University of Lapland			1,5	
Åbo Akademi	1			

Studies in history of education are also part of the master's programmes in special education, home economics, craft science and early childhood education, as well as home economics, craft and kindergarten teacher training programmes. The status of history of education in these fields of study follows the general trend shown in the tables.

The tables above show the weakness of the role of history of education in degree requirements. Students do get a general outline of education in the past, but exploring historical methods of study is left to their own initiative. Therefore it is crucially important that a student preparing a thesis on a historical topic chooses history as a minor subject. A deeper introduction to the nature and methods of historical research is still largely left to teachers conducting seminars relating to education theses. They can be divided into experts and novices according to how deeply they understand the tradition of historical research and how much historical research they have undertaken themselves. The Finnish scientific community of education currently includes four docent-level university teachers[4] whose research has involved studies in history of education. In addition, a few professors and about half a dozen other educationalists with a PhD degree have done research in this field at some

[4] In Finland docent (Adjunct Professor) is an academic title and it is rank between Lecturer and full Professor.

point in their career. The nonexistence of tenures in history of education forms an undeniable and self-feeding problem: scholars of history of education find themselves having to become involved in other fields of education, and the study of history wanes. In their research and teaching, experts in history of education must concentrate on tasks outlined in their own tenure descriptions; history becomes an area that is studied only if there is time left over from other tasks. The situation is particularly depressing for young historians of education who have only just started applying for university positions: with purely historical research, they are in danger of being overshadowed by other educationalists. Because of this, concentrating on studies in history of education is not beneficial to those seeking a university career.

When the proportion of history of education in degree requirements is diminished, even experts in the field have to do most of their teaching in other fields of education. Grasping the research tradition of a less familiar field is often laborious, and historians of education have to direct their resources outside their original field of expertise. History of education becomes a mere by-product for them.

Teaching in this field is also often given to novices who have done limited research of their own in this area, and whose knowledge of the historical research tradition may be inadequate. This pattern is part of the nature of hybrid studies. Responsibility for studies involving the philosophical, historical and social aspects of education is often given to philosophically or sociologically oriented university teachers with history of education being perceived the weakest link.

The problem for novice teachers instructing bachelor and master students is the question of how to differentiate between fully scientific historical research and methodologically less rigorous historical surveys. The problem stems from the dual nature of history of education involving both effective historical research and pure historicism. Even in the publications of the Finnish Society for the History of Education, historical research and amateur histories appear side by side. The criteria of historical research defined by the scientific community itself have changed over time – the so-called "grand narratives" that were common in early 20th century, for example, are now viewed quite critically.[5] A teacher unfamiliar with the paradigmatic changes in science may have difficulty in separating quality research from amateur research. A novice thesis

[5] cf. Ahonen, S. "Kouluhistorian vaihtuvat paradigmat" in "Kasvatuksen monimuotoinen sarka. Koulu ja menneisyys XXXVII" (Helsinki: Suomen Kouluhistoriallinen Seura, 1999), p.32–51.

instructor may allow students to write chronicle-like theses of little intellectual or academic value. The dangers of plagiarism are also apparent due to inadequate knowledge of research methods and source materials. It does not take too many scientific blunders to ruin the credibility of the entire field.

Narrowness in the instruction of postgraduate studies

The almost nonexistent status of history of education in bachelor and master level degrees in education is reflected in a number of problematic ways in relation to the situation of teachers in this field. In the instruction of postgraduate studies the situation is even more difficult due to the heterogeneity of the postgraduate students and the small number of qualified teachers.

There are many postgraduate students of history of education, and the number of doctoral dissertations in this field has been growing for a long time (see table 3). In the past decade, an average of three educationalists per year have defended doctoral dissertations on history of education. Of this group, one out of three has been over 60 years of age; many of them are people with long careers in the schooling system. Doctoral students who finished their basic degree decades ago need intensified instruction, as they often lack the routines of scientific work. Instructional capacity has been limited and resources for intensified instruction for doctoral students have not been found.

Table 3. Doctoral dissertations in education 1904–2004[6]

	Dissertations in history of education	Other dissertations in educational science	Total
1904–1909	3 (75 %)	1 (25 %)	4 (100 %)
1910–1919	3 (43 %)	4 (57 %)	7 (100 %)
1920–1929	1 (50 %)	1 (50 %)	2 (100 %)
1930–1939	5 (38 %)	8 (62 %)	13 (100 %)
1940–1949	5 (38 %)	8 (62 %)	13 (100 %)

[6] The statistics on doctoral dissertations are based on an article by Joel Kivirauma: "Faktorianalyysin kautta teemahaastatteluun – Suomalaisen kasvatustieteen paradigmamurrokset 1900-luvulla väitöskirjojen valossa" in J. Kivirauma & R. Rinne (eds.) "Suomalaisen kasvatustieteen historia – lyhyt oppimäärä" (Turku: Kasvatustieteiden laitos, 1997), p. 5–60, and a list of dissertations compiled in the spring of 2005 by Leena Lehtimäki (http://www.helsinki.fi/vokke/Tyoryhmat/Liite3b%20tohtorin%20vaitoskirjat_140405.pdf), accessed November 28, 2005. Based on material collection and processing. The list consists of dissertations that can be classified as historical research. Sometimes the distinctions were difficult to make, so the list should only be considered suggestive.

1950–1959	5 (33 %)	10 (67 %)	15 (100 %)
1960–1969	6 (32 %)	13 (68 %)	19 (100 %)
1970–1979	5 (8 %)	54 (92 %)	59 (100 %)
1980–1989	9 (9 %)	92 (91 %)	101 (100 %)
1990–1999	26 (8 %)	280 (92 %)	306 (100 %)
2000–2004	17 (5 %)	332 (95 %)	349 (100 %)
Total	85 (10 %)	803 (90 %)	888 (100 %)

For a quarter of a century, thesis instruction and official expert assignments related to postgraduate research were the responsibility of the only professor of history of education in Finland, whose tenure was abolished after his retirement in 2004. While holding this chair in history of education, he participated in the instruction and examination processes of over 70 licentiate and doctoral theses.[7] He was involved in practically every doctoral dissertation in history of education. Docents of history of education working within the scientific community of education were rarely used as official instructors for doctoral theses. Neither did the instructors come from the spheres of historical sciences, ethnology or church history. Besides the aforementioned professor, thesis instruction was handled by experts from other areas of education, few of whom had distinguished themselves as historical researchers.

After the turn of the millennium, more than one third of the pre-examiners and opponents involved in evaluating doctoral dissertations in history of education have been retired docents or professors, and the proportion of emeriti seems to be increasing (see Table 4). Many of the defendants are seniors, and the same applies to the researchers in Finnish Societies for the History of Education. The board of the Finnish Society for the History of Education, for example, consists mostly of retirees. The Society's yearbook is similarly a publishing channel for over 60-year olds; in the past decade, only one writer in four has been under the age of 50.[8]

The age of the persons participating in the examination process is not a problem as such. On the contrary, utilizing the expertise of senior researchers would be particularly beneficial in a field with few docent-level researchers. The problem is that young researchers tend to orient

[7] Kuikka, M. T. "Kasvatuksen historian tutkimus – ollako vai eikö olla" in "Koulu kansakuntaa rakentamassa" (Helsinki: Suomen Kouluhistoriallisen Seura, 2005), p.7–24, see p.15
[8] Rantala, J. "Kasvatuksen historian asema uhattuna" in Kasvatus 37 (2006:5), p. 442–452

towards other fields of education if they cannot secure responsible posts in their own field. Young historians of education should be brought into the thesis instruction and examination process. This would, however, require better familiarity with specialized educational historians from those who hold academic chairs in education. A broader use of experts in history of education, including representatives from other disciplines, would also help prevent the danger of narrowing viewpoints, a risk involved in relying on only a handful of experts. Some of the researchers who prepared their theses in history of education have ended up in cross-disciplinary projects, such as history of technology or women's studies. The networking of researchers with different backgrounds is a good thing. It is alarming, however, that due to the lack of a community whose specialism is in history of education, young researchers have to look for cross-disciplinary projects to find a research community.

Table 4. Experts (pre-examiners and opponents) in doctoral dissertations in education 2000–2004

Number of dissertations	Educationalists	Historians	Other disciplines	Experts total	Emeriti
2000 (2)	7	0	0	7	0
2001 (5)	12	3	2	17	4
2002 (5)	14	3	0	17	4
2003 (4)	10	3	1	14	7
2004 (1)	3	0	0	3	3
17	46 (79 %)	9 (16 %)	3 (5 %)	58 (100 %)	18 (31%)

The weak status of educational sciences prevents cross-scientific collaboration

When the Academy of Finland evaluated the state of educational sciences two decades ago, one flaw discovered by the advisory board was that opponents for doctoral dissertations rarely came from outside the discipline itself.[9] History of education has had a fair number of opponents and pre-examiners from other disciplines, but instructional collaboration has been scarce. Yet instructional collaboration would be particularly important given the inadequacy of historical methodology training of postgraduate students in the scientific community of education.

The relationship between educationalists who dabble in historical research and historians has been complex. Educationalists have stayed

[9] Anon. Kasvatustieteellinen tutkimus Suomessa (Helsinki: Suomen Akatemia 1990), p.111

away from the publishing channels of historical sciences – over the past few decades, only a few educationalists have written for the leading Finnish publications in the field of history, Historiallinen Aikakauskirja and Historisk Tidskrift för Finland. Educationalists have rarely been seen at the historians' conferences. The absence of doctoral students of education at the open forum of the doctoral schools of history is of particular concern.[10] Educationalists have been shy with historians because of their own – often inadequate – training in history. When educationalists have been unable to bring anything methodologically or theoretically new into historical science, they have felt their position as that of some sorts of apprentices in the scientific community of historians.

Another obstacle for the collaboration between educationalists and historians has been the implicit assumption of a scientific hierarchy, which has been heavily discussed especially in the Anglo-American world (cf. Herbst 1999; Richardson 1999a and 1999b; Aldrich 2003; Rinne 1998, 3). Although the representatives of different sciences have not publicly discussed the inequality between sciences in Finland, the state of affairs here is hardly different from the rest of the world. Historians are occasionally used as opponents in educational dissertations. Educationalists, on the other hand, very rarely perform such tasks in historical science. Among historians, accepting an educationalist as an opponent was – especially in the past – sometimes seen as a sign of the dissertation's poor quality. The mutually exclusive attitude of educationalists and historians can also be seen in doctoral schools, which have remained polarized. Publishing traditions have also become separated: if educationalists do not publish in historical forums – as has been pointed out – neither do historians write for educationalist publications.[11] No wonder joint research projects have also been few and far between.

Collaboration between historians and educationalists was common during the early 20th century. Before World War II, historians were involved in the Finnish Society for the History of Education. As late as the 1980's, professional historians published in the field of history of education but since then, professor-level historians have abandoned the field. Historians have done research in history of education in the early stages of their academic careers, but have then moved on to other subjects after establishing themselves in their own specialist academic community.

---

[10] Hietala, M. "Minne menet historiantutkimus? Pohdintoja suuntautumisesta ja metodeista" in Historiallinen Aikakauskirja 101 (2003: 1), p.105–125, see p.106f

[11] Rantala, J. 2006a. Kasvatustiede on vaarassa menettää historiallisen näkökulmansa. Historiallinen Aikakauskirja 104 (2006: 2), 176–180, see p.179

The lack of respect from many historians for educational studies is based on the inconsistent quality of educationalist research and the essentially pragmatic nature of the discipline something that is not entirely a Finnish phenomenon. The study of history of education within the field of educational studies is barely noticed in the wider academic community of historical studies.[12]

In 1990, the advisory board of the Academy of Finland criticized the descriptive nature of research in history of education. In addition to broader research projects, the advisory board called for researchers in the field to deepen their collaboration with the field of cultural history, history of ideas, and history of mentalities. At the same time, there was also broader discussion about broadening the viewpoints of history of education from the study of institutional education to the study of the family, childhood, and the history from below.[13] In the 1990's, history of education began to show signs of new forms of collaboration and influences from so-called new histories. This influence was probably not a response to the advisory board's criticism, but an outcome of the more general paradigmatic discussion in historical science. Within historical studies, new approaches had been laying a claim to recognition for some while. Instead of taking an institutional starting point, the history of education also began to study phenomena from a bottom-up perspective, from the participants' point of view. The macro-level gave way to the micro-level, commonly shared experience and the perspectives of previously hidden minorities took the place of once dominant figures who had featured prominently in historical accounts. History of mentalities, everyday history, psychohistory and women's studies raised new types of questions and introduced new source materials into the research of history of education.

The emergence of new histories in Finland took place in the 1980's and 1990's, as evidenced by the Historia nyt (History Now) anthology, published in 1990, where historians of the younger generation evaluated the state of their discipline. At the time, representatives of

---

[12] Tommila, P. Suomen historiankirjoitus. Tutkimuksen historia (Helsinki: WSOY, 1989), Tommila, P. 2000. "Historia" in P. Tommila (ed.) "Suomen tieteen historia 2. Humanistiset ja yhteiskuntatieteet" (Helsinki: WSOY, 2000), p. 64–139

[13] Herbst, J. "The history of education: state of the art at the turn of the century in Europe and North America" in Paedagogica Historica 35 (1999: 3), p.737–747, see p.739, Schnell, R. L. "Sources for Constructing a New History of Education" in R. F. Lawson, V. D. Rust & S. M. Shafer (eds.) "Education and Social Concern" (Michigan: Prakken Publications, 1987) p.35–47, Szabolcs, E. "Recent Research in the History of Education in Hungary" in Koulu ja menneisyys XXXI. (Helsinki: Suomen Kouluhistoriallinen Seura, 1993), p. 137–145

psychohistory, micro-history, women's history and other new histories still work to establish the legitimacy of their approaches and studies. New histories did not become mainstream even though they won some support especially among younger researchers.[14]

The turning point for history of education studies came later through the Kasvatushistoria nyt (History of Education Now) anthology (2003), which introduced new approaches to history of education.[15] The editors wanted to strengthen the position of new subjects and methods of study that were establishing themselves within historical studies including the sub-field of history of education. New histories seem to have rooted themselves particularly as approaches to women's studies. However, this new type of research approach has not sparked the kind of discussion among Finnish historians of education as it did among general historians or Anglo-American historians of education.[16] Perhaps the discussion and the arguments used need not be repeated. A more obvious explanation is probably the splintering of the field of history of education and its weak academic position – there are no schools of thought to defend.

Presently there is no single dominant paradigm in history of education; different paradigms are visible simultaneously. For the future of history of education, it would be important for participants in the field to clearly separate critical historical research from studies with little scientific significance. This would help fledgling students and novice teachers to direct their efforts at questions relevant for study. At the same time, this would help to re-balance the weak reputation of research in history of education. Researchers of history of education have not drawn the line between scientific studies and amateur surveys clearly enough, having little public discussion about their methodological starting points or conclusions. Avoiding distinctions between amateur and professional researchers is probably a result of the lack of an appropriate discussion forum. The lack of debate could also be the result of an identity crisis amongst educationalists with researchers not being able to settle into

[14] Ahtiainen, P. et al. (eds.) Historia nyt. Näkemyksiä suomalaisesta historiantutkimuksesta. (Helsinki: WSOY, 1990), Ahtiainen, P. & Tervonen, J. "Menneisyyden tutkijat ja metodien vartijat. Matka suomalaiseen historiankirjoitukseen" (Helsinki: Suomen Historiallinen Seura, 1996), p. 173, Katajisto, K. "Historiantutkimus ja uusintaminen" Ennen ja nyt 2/2003.
[15] Nieminen, M. "'Uusien historioiden' avaamia näkökulmia kasvatushistoriaan" in J. Rantala (ed.) Koulu ja kansalaisyhteiskunta historiallisessa perspektiivissä. (Helsinki: Historiallis-yhteiskuntatiedollisen kasvatuksen tutkimus- ja kehittämiskeskus, 2003) p.14–30
[16] Lowe, R. "Do we still need history of education: is it central or peripheral?" in History of Education 31 (6), (2002) p. 491–504, see p.494

the educational community, while others rarely move outside of it. In short, the identity of historians of education is fickle, and researchers do not know where and with whom they should be having discussions.

The pragmatic nature of educational sciences is another reason historians have tended to be sceptical about them. In Finland as well as other countries, historians have tried to stay outside government control,[17] while educationalists have eagerly responded to society's expectations of them. The number of professorships in education in Finland has increased in two decades from 85 to 131. The number of tenures for historians has not increased during the same time.[18] Although the reason behind the growing number of tenures in education is the similar or even stronger growth in the number of students,[19] an uninformed observer might consider educationalists to be "lap dogs of power", who have benefited from their pragmatic attitude.

Publications as embodiments of the substance of history of education

An indication of the twofold nature of research in history of education is the observation made by the advisory board of the Academy of Finland that most of the monographs and edited volumes in the field are published outside the scientific community.[20] The monographs are divided into academic studies and historical surveys written by amateurs. Two studies were published at the turn of the 1970's and 1980's that examined the status of history of education within the field of educational sciences.[21] Since then, no holistic presentation of publications in history of education has been made. However, the yearbooks of Finnish societies for the history of education offer a view into the contextual and methodological trends. They have been the main publishing channel for

---

[17] McCulloch, G."'Disciplines contributing to education'? Educational studies and the disciplines" in British Journal of Educational Studies 50 (2002: 1), p.100–119, see p.112, McCulloch, G. & Richardson, W. "Historical research in educational settings" (Buckingham & Philadelphia: Open University Press, 2000), p.40

[18] Hietala, M. "Minne menet historiantutkimus? Pohdintoja suuntautumisesta ja metodeista" in Historiallinen Aikakauskirja 101 (2003: 1), p.105–125, see p.111

[19] Rinne, R. "Muotokuvassa kasvatustieteen professori" in J. Kivirauma & R. Rinne (eds.) "Suomalaisen kasvatustieteen historia – lyhyt oppimäärä" (Turun yliopiston kasvatustieteiden laitoksen tutkimuksia A:182, 1997), p. 61–124, see p.93f

[20] Anon. 1990. Kasvatustieteellinen tutkimus Suomessa (Helsinki: Suomen Akatemia 1990) see pp.176, 179, 182 and185

[21] Remes, P. "Suomalaista kasvatustutkimusta vuosilta 1966–75" (Jyväskylä: Kasvatustieteiden tutkimuslaitos, 1979), Kyöstiö, O. K. Viimeaikaista kasvatustutkimuksestamme III. Kasvatushistorialliset tutkimukset. Jyväskylän yliopiston kasvatustieteiden tutkimuslaitoksen selosteita ja tiedotteita 198 (1982)

articles on history of education, as relatively few texts from the field have been published in Finnish yearbooks of educational sciences and history.

The yearbook of the Finnish Society for the History of Education, Koulu ja menneisyys (The School and the Past) has been published since 1935. As of 2004, the series includes 42 volumes consisting of a total of 289 articles.

Table 5. Articles in the Koulu ja menneisyys yearbook (1935–2004) divided by content (N 289)

	1	2	3	4	5	6	7	8	9	10	Total
1935–1944	5 14 %	3 8 %	15 41 %	7 19 %	1 3 %	3 8 %	2 5 %	0 0 %	0 0 %	1 3 %	37 101 %
1945–1954	0 0 %	1 11 %	3 33 %	2 22 %	1 11 %	0 0 %	1 11 %	0 0 %	0 0 %	1 11 %	9 99 %
1955–1964	5 15 %	5 15 %	5 15 %	7 21 %	2 6 %	0 0 %	4 12 %	0 0 %	0 0 %	6 18 %	34 102 %
1965–1974	4 27 %	1 7 %	3 20 %	2 13 %	2 13 %	0 0 %	2 13 %	0 0 %	1 7 %	0 0 %	15 100 %
1975–1984	2 20 %	1 10 %	1 10 %	0 0 %	0 0 %	1 10 %	1 10 %	1 10 %	2 20 %	1 10 %	10 100 %
1985–1994	5 6 %	16 21 %	9 12 %	0 0 %	10 13 %	1 1 %	8 10 %	6 8 %	2 3 %	20 26 %	77 100 %
1995–2004	22 21 %	29 27 %	7 7 %	2 2 %	3 3 %	0 0 %	10 9 %	12 11 %	0 0 %	22 21 %	107 101 %
Total	43 15 %	56 19 %	43 15 %	20 7 %	19 7 %	5 2 %	28 10 %	19 7 %	5 2 %	51 18 %	289 102 %

1 Biographies
2 Structure of education
3 Local history
4 Histories of individual schools
5 Teaching of subjects
6 Recollections
7 Nature, practice and sources of history of education
8 Teacher training
9 Syllabi
10 Other (includes articles on teachers' salaries and organizational activity, school inspections, school legislation, course books and history of educational sciences)

The proportion of articles about methods, philosophy of history, the history of historiography and teaching academic history of education is significantly low – only about ten percent. History of education has been less self-reflective than other specialism within historical studies, where over one fifth of the articles in the leading national publication,

Historiallinen Aikakauskirja, deal with the aforementioned topics.[22]

The Koulu ja menneisyys yearbook initially published many articles about local history and individual schools. In the 1980's, their number began to decrease sharply, while discussion about different types of schools and the school system became more prominent. Topics related to teacher training also gained more focus, which demonstrates the researchers' response to the demands of pragmatism in educational sciences.

The articles reflect the discussion about institutional education characteristic of each different period. The topics of the articles in the yearbook show that researchers of history of education have participated in the public discussion of their own time. This kind of development is less evident in the yearbook of the Swedish-language society for the history of education. In the Skolhistoriskt arkiv, surveys of individual schools are more numerous. It is also interesting to note how little the writers of the Swedish-language yearbook deal with teacher training or syllabi, topics Finnish-speaking school historians seek to illuminate from a historical perspective to join in current pedagogical discourse.

Table 6. Articles in the Skolhistoriskt arkiv yearbook (1952–2003) divided by content (N 151)[23]

	1	2	3	4	5	6	7	8	9	10	Total
1952–1961	7 25 %	0 0 %	8 29 %	6 21 %	1 4 %	2 7 %	3 11 %	1 4 %	0 0 %	0 0 %	28 101 %
1962–1971	4 18 %	1 5 %	0 0 %	11 50 %	0 0 %	1 5 %	3 14 %	1 5 %	0 0 %	1 5 %	22 102 %
1972–1981	0 0 %	1 3 %	3 10 %	15 52 %	0 0 %	0 0 %	2 7 %	1 3 %	0 0 %	7 24 %	29 99 %
1982–1991	3 10 %	5 16 %	3 10 %	5 16 %	2 6 %	2 6 %	2 6 %	2 6 %	0 0 %	7 23 %	31 99 %
1992–2001	20 47 %	3 7 %	0 0 %	5 12 %	0 0 %	6 14 %	7 16 %	1 2 %	0 0 %	1 2 %	43 100 %
2002–2005	4 13 %	4 13 %	4 13 %	2 (7 %)	1 3 %	0 0 %	5 17 %	2 7 %	2 7 %	6 20 %	30 100 %
Total	38 (21 %)	14 (8 %)	18 (10 %)	44 (24 %)	4 (2 %)	11 (6 %)	22 (12 %)	8 (4 %)	2 (1 %)	22 (12 %)	183 (100 %)

[22] Ahtiainen, P. & Tervonen, J. "Historiatiede oman aikansa tulkkina. Katsaus suomalaisen historiankirjoituksen vaiheisiin viimeisen sadan vuoden ajalta" in P. Ahtiainen et al. (eds.) Historia nyt. Näkemyksiä suomalaisesta historiantutkimuksesta. (Helsinki: WSOY, 1990), p. 11–38, see p.32f

[23] The yearbooks from 1999 and 2005 are missing from this survey. The total number of published yearbooks is 28. A total of 151 articles have been published in the 26 yearbooks included in the survey. The yearbook of 1955 has been included in spite of its monographic nature. Dissertations published as parts of the series have been excluded.

1 Biographies
2 Structure of education
3 Local history
4 Histories of individual schools
5 Teaching of subjects
6 Recollections
7 Nature, practice and sources of history of education
8 Teacher training
9 Syllabi
10 Other (includes articles on teachers' salaries and organizational activity, school inspections, school legislation, course books and history of educational sciences)

In the leading Finnish journal of education, Kasvatus, texts dealing with history of education have been published occasionally. Within the last ten years, a few articles from the field of history of education have been published annually. Articles on history of education have represented about seven percent of the contents of the journal. Although history of education has not been prominently represented in Kasvatus, the number of published texts can be considered large in relation to the number of academic positions in history of education within the scientific community. The number is also large compared to historical yearbooks. In the Finnish-language Historiallinen Aikakauskirja, history of education is the focus of only a handful of articles within the same ten-year period. In the Swedish-language Historisk Tidskrift för Finland, on the other hand, the field is represented by eleven articles.

The invisibility of researchers with a background in history of education in the discussion of historical sciences, and the absence of traditional historians from educationalist discourse is undesirable, since it upholds the twofold nature of history of education, where historians and educationalists have drifted apart from each other.

Multi-disciplinary collaboration as the salvation of history of education

The status of history of education within educational sciences has hit rock bottom. As has been pointed out above, the status of history of education within educational sciences in degree requirements is weak and tenures are nonexistent. This implies that history of education is no longer considered an essential part of educational science. Relaying a historical viewpoint is seen as unnecessary, especially for future teachers.[24] Even if the academic educational community of education

[24] Elliott, B. J. "Researching the History of Education" in Research Intelligence 3 (1977: 2), p.16–19, see p.16, Richardson, W. "Historians and educationists: the history of education as a field of study in post-war England. Part II: 1972–96" in History of Education 28 (1999:2), p.109–141, see p.116. See Table 2.

suddenly woke up to revive this waning field, rescuing it without outside help will be difficult. Raising a new generation of historians of education will require the help of ethnologists, church historians, and above all, historians.

Genuine collaboration can only be based on mutual respect. Scientific scowling probably stems mostly from poor knowledge of other disciplines. To reach a status equal to historians, historians of education should shake the burden of the past from their shoulders. At the same time, the high-quality historical research being done within educational sciences should be brought to the forefront. The answer here is networking.

In 2005, educationalists formed a network that seeks to increase collaboration between researchers working in different scientific communities and at different universities. At the moment, the network includes over one hundred educationalists, historians, ethnologists and church historians. The network has been quite active, as shown by active participation in the national conference of history of education, organized for seven consecutive years, the launch of open Internet-based methodology training and the founding of a new peer-reviewed publication. The most important product of the network is cross-disciplinary collaboration, which enables young researchers to integrate into the research community of their own field. Until now, doctoral students of education have been forced to prepare their historical dissertations virtually by themselves, so the change has been quite remarkable.

Historical sciences seem to have taken possession of history of education in the Anglo-American world.[25] Fresh signs of similar development can also be seen in Finland. Unlike in educational sciences, where the theoretical-methodological development of history of education is left on the margins of academic discussion due to lack of interest in the field, in historical sciences it has offered researchers a subject of study based on cross-disciplinary collaboration. In historical sciences, the study of history of education has been active lately, especially among young female researchers. The Finnish Historical Society has chosen education as the subject of its large project; between 2009–2011, the society has published a three-volume series of books on the subject, written by over twenty researchers. Although representatives of

---

[5] Richardson, W. "Historians and educationists: the history of education as a field of study in post-war England. Part II: 1972–96" in History of Education 28 (1999:2), p.109–14, Herbst, J. "The history of education: state of the art at the turn of the century in Europe and North America" in Paedagogica Historica 35 (1999: 3), p.737–747, see p.738 and p.743f

historical sciences have started studying questions related to education more actively, this should not be seen as a threat to the research done within educational sciences. The rise of the study of the educational phenomenon in another field could give a boost to educational sciences as well. An example of this is the historians' book project, which also encourages educationalists to collaborate. The increased interest in history of education from historians is also welcome, because it sensitizes university teachers of history to the subject. Hopefully this will be reflected in education students doing minor subject studies at history departments.

Without the pull from historical sciences, the study of history of education within educational sciences will struggle to rise from the low position it currently occupies. The most important thing, however, is to ensure that young educationalists have a chance to concentrate on the history of their own field, and become part of the scientific community specifically as historians of education. Getting the dedicated academic chair back will be difficult, but it would be desirable to create some new tenures in history of education that researchers could aim at. If young educationalists give up history of education, over time the field of educational sciences will lose its historical viewpoint.

The history of education in France: a laboriously useless science?

Pierre Caspard & Rebecca Rogers

"There exist a number of laboriously useless sciences; among these one finds the history of education and learning, which emerged in the early nineteenth century". This radical and peremptory declaration comes, not from a new public manager, but from a very old one: Théodore Barrau, the director of the official journal of the French Ministry of Public Instruction, the *Manuel général de l'instruction primaire*. His critical remarks about what he considered a new field were written in 1857.[1]

He marshaled a variety of arguments in defence of his judgment. He claimed the new field was naïvely idealistic because it presented even the most minor pedagogues as "historical figures who had influenced their countries and inspired progress in their century" thanks to their ideas. His second criticism concerned the ways the history of education sought to establish itself as a separate field in relation to general history: "If one seeks knowledge of the history of education, one should carefully read political and social history; this suffices". In the past, "teachers taught youth to the best of their ability, in line with parental demands. This sums up this history [...]. Those who teach children are not sufficiently gifted to do anything more than transmit what the laws and morals of their century require of them". Barrau concluded: one should study the morals of the period, not the educational past, in order to raise the country's youth; the history of education was a pure waste of time, particularly for the young schoolteacher or the young professor at the beginning of his career.

Do these considerations shed any light on the questions of "relevance" that concern the history of education today? At the very least, they reveal the way French educational administrators questioned from the outset the usefulness of this field. For officials, such as Barrau, the history of education was both academically misguided and politically

[1] Text published initially in the Manuel général de l'instruction primaire, 3e série, n° 1, 1857, p. 4 et 5, and quoted in Histoire de l'éducation 30 (mai 1986), pp. 67-71.

useless, but his remarks inadvertently shed light on what gives meaning to our research: the individual and collective social practices that lead parents to educate their children, the State or individuals to open schools, and students to learn.

The article that follows begins by exploring this historical interest in education before briefly describing the characteristics of French historiography under the influence of "academic drift". It then questions the social usefulness of the history of education in France today, through an examination of the research unit best-known in the field: the Service d'histoire de l'éducation (SHE). The recent difficulties of this unit provide grist for our final comments on the role and mission of the field in today's knowledge economy.

Curiosity and demand for knowledge

Western culture, at least since the Renaissance, has trumpeted the idea of the necessary progress of instruction for both public and private reasons. For historians, evaluating the characteristics of this progress represents an important goal in understanding the educational past. This implies the comparison of the present with earlier periods, for example, within educational institutions. At the end of the sixteenth century Jesuit colleges were required to note year by year in their Annals the most significant events as well as information about student numbers, programmes and other details that revealed progress in the education they offered. These documents allowed the Jesuits to evaluate their schools and adjust their policies, and in the process constitute precious sources for historians interested in tracking the relationship between the supply and demand of schooling. Townships, which were important actors in the development of schooling, also accumulated documents that allowed local elites to establish comparisons with earlier periods and to argue for the pertinence of their decisions given a past record. Over the course of the seventeenth and eighteenth centuries municipal archives swelled with the accumulation of data concerning expenses, student numbers, and school programmes that constitute a mine of information for historians. Moreover, the study of these sources over time offers insights into how local officials in the past used or misused this material to determine and defend educational policies.

The concern to evaluate the changing "level" of students quickly emerged in Western culture. Within families themselves parents have long compared their children's education to that which they had received. This sort of spontaneous intergenerational comparison, which may or may not leave historical traces, bears testimony to individual interest in changing educational practices. For some this sparked an interest in earlier generations. For example, a worker in the region of Le Mans, under Napoleon I, explored the archives of his parish and discovered his ancestors were able to sign their marriage records...since the end of the sixteenth century.[2] This worker's curiosity antedated that of a high-ranking educational officer, the rector Louis Maggiolo, who launched a vast literacy survey in the 1880s, comparing couples' ability to sign marriage registers since the sixteenth century. Although he never really commented on the results, Maggiolo positioned his study with respect to nineteenth-century political debates about the role of the Church and the Revolution in promoting education. In the 1970s, the historians François Furet and Jacques Ozouf once more analyzed this survey with a far more sophisticated scientific method. They began their study noting the ways the history of literacy in France has long mobilized passions and served to spark political debate about the school. Their introduction states: "The French are probably more invested socially and psychologically in school education and literacy than any other people in the world. Why, how, at what cost and with what results; these are the questions we would like to ask if not to answer."[3] Their study highlights how, in 1977, the history of education, through the pursuit of academic knowledge, sought nonetheless to answer questions about the links between past literacy practices and public policy.

Comparative curiosity also exists about schooling results, beyond such cultural practices as reading and writing, which could be acquired both within and outside the school. Here we are thinking of the curiosity that has stimulated inquiries into how different generations of students perform the same school exercise. In the 1820s the authorities of a small village in the Jura decided to compare writing exercises of contemporary pupils with those of preceding decades that were preserved in the school archives.[4] Again, in 1867, the State demonstrated this same curiosity when the Minister of Public Instruction, Victor Duruy, compared the Latin discourse of a student in the rhetoric class of a Parisian *collège*

[2] Fillon, Anne, Louis Simon, villageois de l'ancienne France (Rennes: Ouest-France, 1996).
[3] Furet, François and Ozouf, Jacques, Lire et écrire. L'alphabétisation des Français de Calvin à Jules Ferry, 2 vol. (Paris: Editions de Minuit, 1977), pp. 9-12, quotation p.12. The book was translated into English as: Reading and Writing: literacy in France from Calvin to Jules Ferry (Cambridge: Cambridge University Press, 1982).
[4] These examples are taken from Caspard, Pierre, "L'éducation, son histoire et l'Etat. L'exemple français" in Annali di Storia dell' educazione e delle istituzioni scolastiche 5 (1998), pp. 101-123.

in 1736 with discourses on the same subject given to students at the lycée Louis-le-Grand. And once again, in the 1980s, scholars adopted this same method when they gave students in 1986 the identical dictation exam given in the 1870s in order to compare spelling performances. The State repeated this same experiment in 1994 through the comparison of student results in French composition, mathematics, and spelling. Thirteen-year-old students were given the same exercises as their peers in the 1920s. This ambitious study sprang from the intellectual curiosity of a high-ranking and cultivated civil servant, Claude Thélot, who initiated it within the Ministry he was responsible for. The study sought to defend the ministry's educational policy by showing that the academic "level" of students' had not declined as much as public opinion generally thought or, when necessary, explaining declining results through other reasons than the Ministry's "laxism."[5]

This series of examples exemplifies the continuity between familial, administrative and scholarly historical interest in education and learning. These examples may also usefully serve to remind us that this shared curiosity about education and the school in the past relies on comparisons of social practices, which are both ancient and widely shared. Recognition of this phenomenon may be a way to anchor the discipline in a historical continuity and, thus, ensure its survival.

Thoughts on historical research in education

Over the past forty years, the evolution of historical research, in the history of education as elsewhere, has resulted in a dizzying proliferation of themes, objects, and approaches, a phenomenon François Dosse described as a history "in crumbs" as early as 1987.[6] In the history of education, the rise of cultural and social methods produced studies that diverged notably from the predominant traditions in the field. The waning of political and institutional approaches, as well as those centered on the history of ideas and pedagogical theories can retrospectively be seen as carrying a political cost. Educational administrators were intrinsically most interested in the former, and were often historians themselves,

---

[5] Chervel, André and Manesse, Danielle, La Dictée. Les Français et l'orthographe, 1873-1987 (Paris : INRP and Calmann-Lévy, 1989). Ministère de l'Éducation nationale, « Connaissances en français et en calcul des élèves des années 1920 et d'aujourd'hui. Comparaison à partir des épreuve du certificat d'études primaires », Les dossiers d'éducation et formation, 62 (février 1996).

[6] Dosse, François, L'histoire en miettes : des "Annales" à la "nouvelle histoire" (Paris: La Découverte, 1987). The English-language translation does not attempt to translate the French title; it was rendered as: New History in France: the Triumph of the Annales.

while the history of pedagogy had significantly contributed to the moral, ideological, and professional training of schoolteachers in the normal schools of the Third Republic (1870-1940). Moreover, this early pedagogical history was often the product of educational administrators, such as the Rector and Inspector General Gabriel Compayré, who wrote the main textbook used in the teacher-training field.[7]

The recent diversification of approaches, described elsewhere as *academic drift*, has implications, however, for the "relevance" of the field, as a glance at historical studies of the baccalaureat reveals. Over the past two hundred years, this exam has held a particularly emblematic place in the French educational system crowning as it does secondary studies and opening the doors to higher education. And yet, until the 1970s, only one serious study of the exam existed: a dissertation in history, published in 1937 by Jean-Baptiste Piobetta, who was at the time the director of the Central Services for Exams of the University of Paris.[8] In the nineteenth century other civil servants had produced interesting but more perfunctory studies: Antoine-Augustin Cournot (1801-1877), the Rector of an Academy and an Inspector General of Public Instruction[9] or Octave Gréard (1828-1904), also an Inspector General and Director of Primary Education for the Ministry of Public Instruction.[10] Little serious scholarship was available on the exam, beyond the works just cited that were the product of university teachers who had become educational civil servants. Their positioning made them particularly sensitive to the themes and problems that would interest educational administrators. It bears mentioning that in the 1930s when J.B Piobetta published his dissertation, scholars and educational administrators had formed the "French commission of the Carnegie survey on exams and *concours* in France" to study the docimological and sociological aspects of the *baccalauréat*[11]. Public and academic interest in the exam coincided at the time.

The contrast with the situation today is particularly striking. Over the past two or three decades, historical research on the *baccalauréat*

[7] Compayré, Gabriel, Histoire critique des doctrines de l'éducation en France (1879), and many others.
[8] Piobetta, Jean-Baptiste, Le Baccalauréat (Paris: Baillière, 1937).
[9] Cournot, Antoine-Augustin, Des institutions d'instruction publique en France (Paris, 1864).
[10] Gréard, Octave, Éducation et instruction. Enseignement supérieur (Paris, 1889).
[11] La correction des épreuves écrite dans les examens. Enquête expérimentale sur le baccalauréat (Paris: A la maison du Livre, 1936) and Enquêtes sur le baccalauréat. Recherches statistiques sur les origines scolaires et sociales des candidats au baccalauréat dans l'académie de Paris (Paris: Hachette, 1935).

has proliferated but along very different lines, as the international conference organized in Lille in 2008 for the bicentennial of the exam demonstrated.[12] The published acts of the conference testify to the huge changes that have occurred. The twenty-odd articles examine such aspects as familial strategies with respect to the *baccalauréat*, the content and objectives of the different examination subjects, the modes of preparing candidates for the exam, its opening to a variety of new students (girls, students in technical tracks or the students in colonized countries), or the image of the exam in literature or the press. The subjects reflect the ways micro-history, the history of representations and cultural practices, gender and post-colonial studies have enriched the history of education over the past few decades. While the institutional history of the exam is not absent, it is not central in the volume. As it stands, the collection clearly represents current scholarly interests and practices. Does it at the same time hold interest for the administrators and managers of the educational system, given the context within which they operate? The answer is not obvious.

The contemporary context

Politicians and academics share the same *Zeitgeist* but their responses to the problems of the present bear the imprint of their radically different positioning. In what follows we will highlight the relationship between the contemporary spirit of the times and the external impact of the history of education within the public domain. We particularly focus on the factors that mitigate against the social usefulness of the history of education.

In this respect, it seems to us, that one of the most important characteristics of our time is the decline of historicism, which had gradually triumphed in the West over the course of the nineteenth century, in conjunction with the construction of the Nation-State and the development of an ideology of progress. This ideology, in both its liberal and Marxist forms, used history to understand, guide, and justify reforms of the educational system. History offered the proof of what had been accomplished and highlighted what remained to be done. Indeed some of the great reforming educational Ministers were themselves historians (F. Guizot, V. Duruy); in the 1880s Ferdinand Buisson, as Director of Primary education, published the immensely influential *Dictionnaire de*

---

[12] Marchand, Philippe (Ed.), Le Baccalauréat, 1808-2008. Certification française ou pratique européenne ? (Lille: Revue du Nord, Lyon, INRP, 2010), 446 p.

pédagogie et d'instruction primaire, which was full of articles on the history of education and where even the contemporary entries began with historical reminders. It is scarcely necessary to highlight the extent to which this ideology of progress has declined, particularly within France where scepticism has led to the invention of the neologism "déclinisme". History is no longer called upon to furnish managers with models, counter-models, examples and counter-examples of ideas, practices and educational institutions.

In publishing circles, a growing number of books in the history of education are now directed toward a general public, where nostalgia reigns supreme, particularly when the subject is elementary schooling. Here a mythologized past serves to highlight the contrast with an incomprehensible or unacceptable present day.[13] The journal *Histoire de l'éducation* periodically reviews these books, while insisting on what distinguishes the imagery and stereotypes such books convey with the most recent results of historical research in the field.[14] Still, one cannot help but acknowledge that for the most part, the history of education and learning deals with events and ideas that remain terribly abstract, except perhaps in the area of childhood education. The means and results of the transmission of knowledge and competencies, the cultural and social goals attached to knowledge do not easily translate into "sexy" historical narratives, as in other fields of research, unless one accepts gross simplifications or decides to heroize the different actors, thus falling prey to the failings that Th. Barrau highlighted back in 1857.

At the same time, contemporary schools are confronted by a series of problems that the history of education is ill equipped to illuminate. Take, for example, the question of youth or even children's violence both within and outside the school. A recent issue of *Histoire de l'éducation* addressed the theme "School and violence", highlighting the radical discontinuities that characterize school violence from the Antiquity to the present if one disregards the obvious anthropological insights concerning youthful turbulence which do not require detailed historical research to bring to light. Jacques Verger concluded that the comparison of contemporary violence with "the wilder side of [institutional] life" in

---

[12] Caspard, Pierre, "L'historiographie de l'éducation dans un contexte mémoriel. Réflexion sur quelques évolutions problématiques" in Histoire de l'éducation 121 (janvier 2009), pp. 67-82.
[14] It is extremely rare to find historically relevant commentary associated with images or photography. Two exceptions come to mind : Alexandre-Bidon, Danièle et al., Le Patrimoine de l'éducation nationale (Paris: Flohic, 1999), or Luc, Jean-Noël and Nicolas, Gilbert, Le temps de l'école. De la maternelle au lycée, 1880-1960 (Paris: Chêne-Hachette, 2006).

the past was a difficult if not impossible task.[15] Similarly, contemporary questions related to student drop-out rates are not usefully illuminated through the historical study of school absenteeism. The latter can largely be explained through the familial economy that depended on children's labor, whereas the current problems of "décrochage" stem from the ways school has lost any meaning for certain youth, particularly those raised in families that have recently migrated from some of the world's countries with the lowest schooling rates.[16] Within the media, drop-out rates and school violence are the object of frequent debate, notably around highly spectacular *faits-divers*; in these debates historians of education are seldom resorted to for advice.

Is the history of education in a position today to act as a *magister vitae* for managers? The French education system, more than others, has reached a degree of bureaucratization that significantly diminishes the capacity for initiative or autonomy of its actors at all levels. This is true at the ministerial level, as well as at the level of local and intermediary actors, such as the Rectors of academies, who were created to relay the central authority's decisions at the level of the regions. Recent historical studies have shown, however, the degree to which rectors have lost their range of manoeuvre, in comparison to the early Third Republic.[17] Today, the "lessons of history" have little impact on managerial decisions in education, but are rather the result of negotiations between different pressure or interest groups, or a calculated response to expectations concerning media and political benefits. The arguments used to justify these decisions rely on statistical "facts", established by national or international experts who, to our knowledge, do not include historians.

The contemporary tendency to use international criteria for the evaluation of educational systems has had a particularly negative impact on the ability of historians of French education to intervene in public debate. A single example illustrates this point. The French school system has developed over the past two centuries around highly distinct school disciplines, taught by specialized teachers, organized within disciplinary associations that were dedicated to the defense of their field within school programmes, examinations and *concours* that were established

---

[15] Verger, Jacques, "Ecole et violence. Faits, perception, discours", spécial issue "Ecole et violence", Histoire de l'éducation, 118 (2008), pp. 5-10.

[16] This information is generally omitted in statistics and indicators about French schools.

[17] Condette, Jean-François, Les recteurs d'académie en France de 1808 à 1940, 3 vol. (Lyon: INRP, 2006-2009).

nationally. In the past few years, French managerial approaches have focused on the question of competencies, as they sought to improve French ranking within such programmes as PISA or PIRLS. As a result, the considerable existing knowledge of the history of school disciplines, an area the French have explored for years, appears irrelevant except to the extent that it illuminates teachers "conservative" defence of a French school culture. This disciplinary history is not seen as useful in efforts to improve students' school performance nor is it seen as a means of reflecting on ways to help students from families of foreign cultures. Increasingly, a form of "progressive" pedagogy, in name if not content, positions the equality of school results for all students as its primary objective. This new objective in school history, which is both politically correct and popular in the media, has led at times to the expression of contempt for the educational past and its history. The example of the Service d'histoire de l'éducation illustrates this evolution in pedagogical circles.

The example of the Service d'histoire de l'éducation

The difficult positioning of the history of education can be illustrated through the case of a typically French research unit, the Service d'histoire de l'éducation (SHE). It was created in 1970 as a branch of the Ministry of Education, not of the Ministry for Higher Education and Research. Its first three directors were higher civil servants: two Rectors of an Academy and then an Inspector general of the administration. The SHE's mission was to "take all suitable measures to promote the history of education". This involved creating research instruments that would facilitate the work of historians in the field, and attract others to it, notably through the development of themes that were considered to be under-studied, such as the history of the administration of education. At the time several other ministries created similar historical units.

In 1977, the SHE was transferred to the Institut national de recherche pédagogique (INRP), while remaining under the tutelage of the ministry of Education. Created in 1976 from an existing Institute dedicated to pedagogical research, the INRP has a two-fold mission, acting as an "expert" for public leaders but also producing knowledge about education and pedagogy. The SHE's integration involved reconciling the criteria of academic excellence with the unit's original mission by combining the production of first-rate research with the creation of resources for the historical community: bibliographies, the constitution of oral archives, research guides for sources, data bases (on schoolbooks, on educational institutions...). The unit's academic quality has been recognized over the years through its association with the Centre national de la recherche scientifique (CNRS), through the ranking of the journal it produces, *Histoire de l'éducation* (ranked "A" by the E.S.F), and through a recent project to collaborate with the prestigious École normale supérieure (ENS) in Paris. In 2010, the SHE, with its fifteen scholars and research technicians, dominated the history of education, mobilizing as it does a large network of scholars associated with the unit's collective surveys. It constitutes the most important and only French research laboratory specialized in the history of education, although, of course, individual scholars in the history of education are active in French universities or in the CNRS.

Despite this situation of recognized intellectual excellence, the Ministry that oversees the INRP, has increasingly demonstrated its disinterest in historical research. Its own political decisions with respect to education have been made more and more frequently under the pressure of both politics and the media, little informed by knowledge of past pedagogical or educational measures. At the beginning of 2010, the prospects for the SHE appeared to be its integration within a specifically academic research environment, thus constituting a significant break with its initial responsibility with respect to the Ministry of Education. The director of the INRP, a professor in biology, with little interest in humanities and social science in general and the history of education in particular, announced a very different project in early July 2010 when he unilaterally declared to the governing board of the INRP that he intended to eliminate the SHE. The immediate protestations this generated, both in France and the international community, convinced the Ministry of Education that the SHE should proceed with its plans to become a research team within a larger structure that included the CNRS, the ENS and the university of Paris I-Panthéon Sorbonne. In September 2010 both the Ministry of Education and the Ministry of Higher Education and Research solemnly proclaimed their interest in the work produced by the SHE, as well as their concern to preserve this work within the above-mentioned joint research structure, which should emerge in 2011. This about-face, rather typical of French managerial practices, reflects nonetheless more broadly some of the problems confronting the history of education in its on-going tension between striving to meet criteria of academic excellence and its ability to illuminate political decisions or intervene in public debate.

Three perspectives for the future

The two authors of this text combine an experience in research, teaching and the management of an historical unit–the SHE. It is from this positioning that we would like to propose three principles and objectives for the history of education within the knowledge economy:

a) In scientific terms it is vital to avoid the ghettoization or marginalization of the history of education with respect to social, political, and cultural history, as well as the history of institutions or that of science and technology. On this issue, Théodore Barrau's criticisms in 1857 appear remarkably relevant, even if he underestimated the relative but increasing autonomy of educational institutions that justify the existence of studies that are specifically focused on them. For the history of education to maintain vitality in the academy it must consistently connect its research to broader themes, not only those that have long structured historical narratives such as democratization and the rise of the nation state. It needs to intersect as well with new areas of research including human rights and transnational history. But this is not enough ...

b) The history of education also has a role to play in the training of future teachers. The most recent reforms of teacher training in France have placed this training within universities offering an opportunity for historians of education to influence more broadly the knowledge future teachers have about the educational system and the history of individual disciplines. At the level of secondary teaching, competitive exams in history and geography, for example, require students to mobilize scientific and epistemological knowledge, but also to link this knowledge to a history of the discipline and its teaching, as well as to the didactic and civic dimensions of the field. This requirement offers an opportunity to spread knowledge about the rich scholarship concerning the history of history education. More broadly, however, all future teachers are expected to have knowledge about the French educational system and its history, so they understand how their actions contribute to a certain vision of society. Historians of education have a key role to play in showing future teachers how French schools have sought over time to integrate students into a community, the role of schools in the formation of national identity, as well as the place of the school in the Republican project. The history of disciplines and curricula offers important insights into the hierarchies of disciplines, the significance of the French language, as well the political uses of disciplines in specific historical contexts.[18] The history of education has a special role in communicating a critical awareness of how education has been used and misused in the past, encouraging future teachers to question the limits and blind spots in French Republican educational ideology.[19]

c) Finally, we would like to argue that the task of historians of education should be to nourish through their research all of the actors who participate in public debate, not just educational administrators and politicians; this includes adult trainers, teachers, students and parents.[20] Knowledge on education, produced through historical research should seek a distinctive place in the formation of a critical mind.

To achieve these objectives in the age of the internet and *digital humanities*, the history of education, like the other humanities and social sciences should strive to occupy a new frontier on the world wide web through the creation of digital platforms that offer reliable, coherent, systematic and even attractive information in the different areas it explores: school legislation, historical cartography, pedagogical media, teaching and apprenticeship practices, school iconography. These platforms would encourage multidisciplinary and multinational co-operation, along the lines that schoolbook scholars are currently developing.[21]

It is also worth remembering, that the history of education by nature, addresses issues that interest a wide range of people, well beyond the academic sphere, and that its rhetoric and language is (usually) easily understandable for the non-specialist. In France *Le Monde de l'éducation* offered a venue for scholars to "vulgarize", as the French say, the results of current scholarship. Antoine Prost, for example, used his notoriety as a historian of education in this weekly publication to show how the field had the capacity to engage in public debate in ways that

[18] For an example of such a treatment of the teaching of French, see André Chervel, Histoire de l'enseignement du français du XVIIe au XXe siècle (Paris: Retz, 2006).

[19] For a similar argument see Rogers, Rebecca: "Do we need commandments ?" response to Marc Depaepe's "The Ten Commandments of Good Practices in History of education Research", Zeitschrift für pädagogische Historiographie, 16 :1 (2010), pp.35-38.

[20] There are venues in France for historians of education to make their scholarship known in teaching circles. See Textes et documents pour la classe, "L'école en France, XVIIe-XXIe siècle", 48 (15 December 2009) with articles about, for example, the development of schooling since the 17th century, school iconography, girls' education, the different actors of the educational system (the Church, towns, and the State).

[21] Bandini, Gianfranco and Bianchini, Paolo (Eds), Fare storia in Rete. Fonti et modelli di scrittura digitale per la storia dell' educatione, la storia moderna e la storia contemporaneo (Florence : Carocci, 2007). Alain Choppin (member of the SHE) was one of the pioneers in the creation of this international network.

spoke to citizens as a whole.[22] The recent demise of this weekly publication suggests, of course, that this sort of public discourse on educational matters is no longer economically viable. The challenge for the future lies then in finding other ways to make our voices heard, and in maintaining our confidence that curiosity about the historical processes of learning exists widely among citizens throughout the world.

Since the writing of this article, the INRP has been absorbed into the Ecole Normale Supérieure de Lyon (ENSL). The SHE, as a result, has become a research unit within the ENSL.

[22] Prost, Antoine, Regards historiques sur l'éducation en France XIXe-XXe siècle (Paris: Belin, 2007). The book is composed of the articles he wrote for Le Monde de l'éducation between 2001 and 2007.

Section 2

Uses and abuses of the history of education

Educational History, Policy Research, and Ethnohistory

Barry M. Franklin & Patricio R. Ortiz

First appearance in the mid-nineteenth century American normal school, educational history was one of the earliest subjects to comprise the professional teacher education curriculum in the United States.[1] Yet despite its long lineage, the field has always had a difficult time of it. University historians have been as skeptical about its academic legitimacy and the scholarly competence of its practitioners as were their liberal arts faculty colleagues about virtually everything and anyone associated with the training of teachers and the study of education. At the same time, however, educational history was criticized by many faculty members in schools of education as lacking the relevant focus on the professional training of teachers and other immediate educational problems to merit a place within their midst.[2]

In recent years the status of educational history among professional historians has actually improved. In part this has been the result of the growing interest of faculty in university departments of history in the study of education. Equally, if not more important, is the fact that a new generation of educational historians have come of age since the 1960s who see the purpose of their field of study as broader than simply the professional preparation of teachers. Unlike their predecessors who taught the subject at the turn of the twentieth century, these scholars are more likely to have had formal training in history and to share the outlook of their counterparts in university history departments that the history of education is a liberal study.

The place of educational history among those who teach and do research in education is less clear. There are certainly indicators that the field is well regarded among educational scholars. At less than

---

[1] Ogren, Christine, The American State Normal School: "An Instrument of Great Good" (New York: Palgrave Macmillan, 2005), pp. 132-135.
[2] Cohen, Sol, "The History of the History of American Education, 1900-1976: The Uses of the Past," Harvard Educational Review 46 (1976), pp. 303-308.

600 members, the division of educational historians within the American Educational Research Association (Division F) is the smallest of its twelve standing divisions. Yet, educational historians have received five of the Association's annual outstanding book awards since the prize was established in 1983. The publication efforts of American educational historians point to the robustness of current research within the discipline, and the field's premier journal, *History of Education Quarterly*, enjoys a strong reputation for its standards in accepting articles and for the high quality of the articles that it ultimately publishes.

At the same time, however, the suspicion that many in the educational disciplines have about the field's lack of application to the problems of teacher education and educational practice remain. The dominant role that social efficiency thinking has played and continues to play within the educational disciplines since the 1920s has created a less than hospitable setting for any discipline that defines itself as a liberal study. An alternative disciplinary tradition, social foundations of education, which has from time to time challenged efficiency thinking in the name of social reform, has not provided a more welcoming terrain for educational historians. From its early appearance on the scene during the 1930s, this field has sought to direct the educational disciplines away from a traditional academic focus toward a commitment to at least social change if not outright social reconstruction. Rather than favoring educational history or any single social science discipline as the vehicle for studying schools as institutions, it promoted under the rubric of social foundations a new, integrated, and decidedly reform minded subject. Some social science disciplines, namely sociology, anthropology, political science, and philosophy have been able to find a place within this new discipline of social foundations while at the same time continuing their own distinct identities as lenses for exploring issues of schooling. This dual identity however, has been less comfortable for educational historians.[3]

Educational historians have certainly not been refused a place within the social foundations family. It is not unusual for educational historians to be members of both the History of Education Society (HES) and the principal organization of the educational foundations, the American Educational Studies Association (AESA). The two organizations in fact often hold their annual conferences jointly. Education historians are frequent contributors to the principal AESA journal, *Educational Studies*.

[3] Ibid, 311-313.

Notwithstanding all of this, however, there is something of an underlying tension that strikes us as present in the views of some educational historians when they talk about the social foundations of education. These historians are, we think, somewhat uncomfortable with the decidedly more practical orientation of those who identify themselves with the social foundations of education. They are not as willing as their counterparts in the foundations seem to be in according teacher education a central focus of their discipline. And while certainly not any less "left" in their political viewpoints than are the vast majority of social foundations practitioners, these educational historians seem less accepting of the role of their discipline as a vehicle of explicit social reform.

In a recent article in *History of Education Quarterly*, John Rury has raised the issue of the place of educational history within the broader field of education by comparing it with other similarly situated historical studies in science, law, and economics. What seems to provide these other historical studies with their place within their respective parent disciplines, he argues, has been the ability of scholars to connect their historical research to the concerns of these professional fields. His recommendation for addressing the problem is that educational history reorients itself as a field so that its research agenda is more in line with the immediate concerns of professional educators.[4] The purpose of this essay is to consider the prospect that a focus on policy on the part of educational historians might better connect the field with the concerns of the broader field of education and how that connection might be achieved. We will begin by looking at the comparison that Rury draws between the work of educational historians and those historians who work in other non-historical professional fields. We will then consider the record of current efforts on the part of educational historians to focus their work on the exploration of educational policy. Finally, we will look at how an approach to research modeled after the discipline of ethnohistory might serve to provide a needed connection between educational history and the research agenda of the broader field of education.

---

[4] Rury, John L., "The Curious Status of the History of Education: A Parallel Perspective," History of Education Quaqrterly 46 (2005), pp. 553-576. Rury's assessment of the state of educational history is not, however, universally shared. See the exchange among historians from schools of business, theology, law, journalism, medicine, and education in "Interchange: History in the Professional Schools," in The Journal of American History 92 (2005), 553-576. The participants of this commentary did note important differences in their work from that of scholars teaching in university departments of history. Yet, the depiction of the state of affairs that educational historian Jonathan Zimmerman offered did not seem all thatdifferent from the views offered by the other historians who work in professiona schools.

II.

Rury's starting point is to consider the similarities and differences between educational history on the one hand and the other similarly situated fields that he refers to as disciplinary history, namely the history of science, legal history, and economic history. There are, he points out, a number of commonalities among these disciplinary historians. The majority of these scholars, although a number of them have studied history or even received a degree in history, have completed their academic preparation in the professional fields in which they work. Another similarity is that for the most part these disciplinary historians teach in schools and departments in these professional fields rather than in departments of history. And finally, these scholars report that to varying degrees they have had to confront doubts from traditional historians about the value and rigor of their brand of disciplinary or professional history.

Yet there is, Rury argues, an important difference between historians of education and the other disciplinary historians he considers in his essay. He argues that most disciplinary historians believe that there is a strong connection between the issues about which they study and write and the professional field to which they belong. Educational historians, on the other hand, seem to emphasize the distance between their work and the educational professions. It is not that these scholars do not study educational issues. As Rury sees it, they focus their attention on a host of such subjects. The problem is that the issues that educational historians most often explore are broad in nature and tell us more about the larger culture and its practices than they do about the various realms of educational work, such as teaching, testing, curriculum development, and teacher education to name but a few. In other words, the close connections that exist between the history of law and other disciplinary histories and the concerns of practitioners within these professions are not to be found between educational historians and professional educators in related, non-historical fields. He goes on to wonder whether in fact educational historians can change the focus of their work and provide the same assistance to teachers, policy makers, and researchers that other disciplinary historians offer to scholars within their fields.[5]

A distinguishing feature of the work of these disciplinary historians, according to Rury was their penchant for introducing new con-

[5] Ibid., pp. 572-573.

ceptual frameworks and methodologies that challenged longstanding, virtually taken-for-granted and outdated assumptions within their fields. In this vein, he points to the role that these disciplinary historians have played in introducing the methods of social history to their respective fields. Rury goes on to note that it was the grounding of revisionist educational historians in social history that enabled them to contribute to the revitalization of their field during the late 1960s and early 1970s. Educational historians may be able to play a similar role in today's world of educational research and practice. As Rury sees it, the majority of educational historians hold positions in schools and colleges of education where their work brings them into contact with a range of issues that are important to the broad field of education to which they might offer their particular insights. Such issues as teacher certification, testing and assessment, religion and education, academic achievement, and youth culture to name a few are subjects that he believes would benefit from the perspective that educational historians might offer.[6]

III.

There is a strong utilitarian orientation to the discipline of history in the United States that would support a research agenda for educational history along the lines that Rury suggests. This functional outlook was evidenced in some of the first historical accounts about America that were penned during the seventeenth and eighteenth century to promote travel to the new world and ultimately settlement. Later accounts during the nineteenth century offered narratives to promote nationalism and Western expansion and support for the Federal Union. It was during the first half of the twentieth century that historians became more directly involved in the public policy arena. Their activities included among other things writing in favor of progressive era social reform, propagandizing in support of the allied cause in World War I, participation in World War II military intelligence work, and advising government agencies during the years of the cold war on international affairs.[7]

These efforts became more institutionalized with the emergence during the 1970s of the fields of public history and policy history. The work of public historians in government agencies that address such policy issues as defense, economic regulation, abortion, and employment

---

[6] Ibid., pp. 574-593.
[7] Vinovskis, Maris A., History and Educational Policymaking (New Haven: Yale University Press, 1999), 3-47.

discrimination would suggest that policy history would play an important influence within the field. As it turned out public history has achieved a degree of recognition and status within the broader field of history. It is less clear that this has been the case for policy history.[8] Julian Zelizer has noted in this vein the division of opinion among historians about the state of policy history. Some see it as about to emerge as an important specialty area within the field of history. Others, however, are less optimistic noting the small number of history departments that offer programs in policy history, the absence of regular conferences as well as professional organizations in policy history, and the infrequent appearance of articles on policy history in the principal journals in the field.[9] There are a number of explanations for why policy history has not emerged more forcefully as a field of specialization. Historians, it seems, tend to be skittish about using their expertise to undertake what would probably be the central task of policy history, namely studying the past to derive lessons for the present or for making predictions about the future.[10] Beyond that, however, the decade of the 1970s saw the emergence of social history as a dominant focus for historians coupled with a diminished interest in what might have been the most appropriate terrain for the study of policy, political history.[11] At the same time, it has also been the case that those who work in public policy do not readily turn to history for guidance.[12]

IV.

There is something of a model for reorienting educational history in the direction that Rury suggests in the field of educational policy studies. The designation goes back to the mid-1960s and represents to some degree an extension and modification of the social foundations movement of the 1930s. Like its earlier counterpart, educational policy studies represents an interdisciplinary designation for exploring educational issues from the vantage point of such disciplines as sociology, political science, anthropology, philosophy, and history. What can distinguish it at least in some quarters from the social foundations of education is the less explicit commitment of its practitioners to using their scholarship

[8] Graham, Hugh Davis, "The Stunted Career of Policy History: A Critique and an Agenda," in The Public Historian 15 (Spring, 1993), 16-17.
[9] Zelizer, Julian E., "Clio's Lost Tribe: Public Policy History Since 1978," in Journal of Policy History 12 (2000), 369.
[10] Vinovskis, pp. 239-242.
[11] Graham, pp. 29-31.
[12] Vinovskis, p. 241.

to promote social reform and change. Where those associated with the social foundations of education, at least in its earlier days, were unabashed reformers who saw the task of the schools as social reconstruction, contemporary scholars who identify with educational policy studies are less so. This reformist impulse is not absent from the field of educational policy studies. Yet, an important concern of those who affiliate with this area of study is with using its constitutive disciplines including educational history as lenses for developing and interpreting educational programs, policies, and practices.

Policy has for some time now been a popular topic among educational historians.[13] It is less clear, however, whether a focus on policy will connect the research of educational historians to the concerns of educators in anything approaching the way that Rury's disciplinary historians link their research to the professional fields in which they work. A 1995 collection of essays edited by Diane Ravitch and Maris Vinovskis points to the role that historical scholarship can play in helping policy makers recognize the historical roots of many of the issues that they mistakenly assume are new and novel. They are careful to note that such an awareness does not provide specific recommendations for resolving immediate policy dilemmas. Yet, it can, they believe, provide some helpful direction for contemporary policymakers.[14]

A recent volume of essays from a 2007 conference at Brown University on the role of history in educational policymaking explores the same terrain as the earlier work but is more guarded and cautious in asserting the connections. There are a range of essays contained within the volume. Some explore issues in the distant and not so distant past such as civic education and school segregation but leave the connection to current policy questions up to readers to make. Other essays, however, are more explicit in their linkages and offer readers historical accounts of the development of a number of policies over time including Head Start, No Child Left Behind, and standards-based reform and the

---

[13] See for example, Warren, Donald, "The Federal Interest: Politics and Policy Study," in Historical Inquiry in Education: A Research Agenda. ed. John Hardin Best (Washington, D.C: American Educational Research Association, 1983), pp. 158-179; Tyack, David & Cuban, Larry Tinkering Toward Utopia: A Century of Public School Reform (Cambridge: Harvard University Press, 1995); Kaestle, Carl F., "Federal Education Policy and the Changing National Polity for Education, 1957-2007," in To Educate a Nation: Federal and National Strategies of School Reform, ed. Carl F. Kaestle & Alyssa E. Lodewick (Lawrence: University Press of Kansas, 2007), pp. 17-40.

[14] Ravitch, Diane & Vinovskis, Maris, "Introduction" in Learning from the Past: What History Teaches Us About School Reform ed. Diane Ravitch & Maris Vinovskis (Baltimore: The John Hopkins University Press, 1995), pp. x, xiv.

patterns of conflicts and agreements surrounding them.[15] What is left unclear in these essays however, are the connections between educational history and educational policy making.

There are as it turns out several historiographical essays in the volume that explore this issue. In her essay, Tracy Steffes argues that the penchant of policymakers to want to generalize from the past to the present as well as to make predictions about the future on the basis of the past represents a misapplication of historical scholarship. History can, she goes on to say, help us in understanding the past, but not in those ways. Rather, its contribution among other things is to help us to frame more appropriate questions about the past, to challenge our taken for granted assumptions about the present, and to discover the often invisible influences of the past on the present.[16]

Jack Dougherty takes a more pessimistic view. While history and policy enter into his work, he notes that it is not all that easy to fit these two enterprises together. While historians focus on the past and are concerned with what has happened, policy makers look to the future and are interested in what will happen. A second reason for the uneasy relationship is their differences as to the purposes of history. Historians examine the past with the intent of learning about that time and place while policymakers assume a more functional outlook and are concerned about how to use their knowledge of the past to promote current policy objectives. Finally, historians wish to understand the past while policymakers are more concerned with taking action to bring about change. Any collaboration between these two fields, he concludes, would be a daunting effort that would require practitioners in both domains to make fundamental changes in the ways that they work.[17] One leaves this volume with the sense that there well may be valuable connections between the work of historians and policy makers. What is less certain, however, is how those linkages might be used to enhance the role that educational history can play in the broader field of educational research

---

[15] Wong, Kenneth K. & Rothman, Robert eds., Clio at the Table: Using History to Inform and Improve Education Policy (New York: Peter Lang, 2009). To gain a sense of the range of ways in which these essays offer a historical perspective on policy see the contributions by William Reese, Anne-Lise Halvorsen and Jeffrey Mirel, Elizabeth Rose, Gail Sunderman, and Margaret E. Goetz..

[16] Steffes, Tracy L., "Lessons from the Past: A Challenge and a Caution for Policy-Relevant History" in Clio at the Table: Using History to Inform and Improve Education Policy ed.Kenneth K. Wong & Robert Rothman (New York: Peter Lang, 2009), pp. 263-282.

[17] Dougherty, Jack, "Conflicting Questions Why Historians and Policymakers Miscommunicate on Urban Education" in Ibid., pp.251-262.

and practice. Resolving that uncertainty requires something of a different approach.

V.

A way that we propose to narrow the gap that Rury argues exists between educational history and educational policy, is with a strategy that brings together historical and ethnographic methods to form what can be called an ethnohistorical lens for examining the cultural practices of schooling.[18] The epistemological links between history and anthropology are in principle quite strong. Yet, the two disciplines have for much of the twentieth century pursued distinct and different methods of inquiry - archival research for the historian and ethnographic fieldwork for the anthropologist. In the case of the US, this separation began to lessen in the period following World War II as increasing numbers of anthropologists began to respond to emerging demands from both the state and civil society for knowledge related to areas of the world in which the nation had new strategic, economic, and political interests and involvements.

American anthropologists soon found themselves taking leading roles in many universities in the organization of area studies programs in which groups of scholars in different fields were brought together under one roof for the purpose of creating knowledge about less known but increasingly important national settings. The result was to establish under the rubric of area studies a group of new fields that encompassed the methods and research of a number of different social science disciplines. These new groupings included political scientists, economists, historians, and sociologists with their focus on such topics as modernization, nationalism, and colonialism. Also included in these new disciplines were anthropologists whose ethnographic methods of face-to-face observations coupled with their knowledge of indigenous languages enabled them to extend the research agenda of area studies to include explorations of villages as "authentic traditional" bounded entities, connected to national cultural, economic, and religious networks.[19] It is at this point that history and anthropology began to establish connections

---

[18] Levinson, Bradley, A.U. & Sutton, Margaret, "Policy as/in Practice—A Sociocultural Approach to the Study of Educational Policy," in Policy as Practice: Toward a Comparative Sociocultural Analysis of Educational Policy ed. Margaret Sutton and Bradley A.U. Levinson (New York: Ablex Publishing, 2001), pp. 1-22.

[19] Cohn, Bernard, An Anthropologist Among the Historians and Other Essays (New York: Oxford University Press, 1987).

that would pave the way for what has become a mutual interaction between these two disciplines.

We believe that two factors provided the impetus for this interaction between history and anthropology. There was the growth and diversification of anthropology during the 1960s that extended its focus beyond the study of indigenous culture to include research on urban, industrialized societies and such modern institutions as medicine and education. And during the following decade there was the emergence of cultural studies that among other things identified additional "others" for many social scientists including anthropologists to direct their attention, namely Blacks, ethnic minorities, women, and the urban poor.[20]

One of the major effects of these disciplinary changes was that the ethnographic methods based on participant observation and open ended interviews ceased to be the singular hallmark of anthropological inquiry. They were embraced by other social science disciplines in their efforts to explore the human story. At this point, the ethnographic look, which started with a gaze focused on the "exotic other" as part of the non-Western cultural and distant geographical world was transformed into an inward look into the "otherness" that characterized industrial modern and developed Western societies.

As a result, the clear definition of ethnography as a construction of the present as observed in the field versus the historical construction of the past as uncovered in archives becomes attenuated. Ethnographic work now came to feed historical constructions of the past and saw the impact of policy making as social and cultural production in the present.[21] Advancing this connection was the growing popularity of social history among educational historians. As Bernard Cohn describes this movement, it was history from the "bottom-up." Its subject was the study of the masses, the deprived, the exploited, and other excluded groups that more mainstream historians at the time saw not so much as protagonists but as passive objects for study. These groups, classes, or categories (women, the lumpen-proletariat, Blacks, ethnics and the dispossessed) began under the influence of social history during the decade of the 1970s to enjoy more attention. Accompanying this focus was the use of new sources including oral traditions, the study of marginalia, folklore, public celebrations and rituals, through the utilization of different kinds of records to explore past and present characteristics and life

[20] Ibid.
[21] Sutton and Levinson, Ibid.

patterns of the life of excluded groups. Cohn argues that this historical perspective, as a new kind of social history, has set the stage for a dialogue between historians and anthropologists that has made historical research receptive to ethnographic methods.

His model for this link between history and anthropology is the research and writing of ethnohistorians whose studies of indigenous populations in North America, Africa, Australia, and Oceania were written from a native point of view. The great contribution of ethnohistorians, according to Cohn, was their efforts to reconstruct what they saw as the distorted accounts of these indigenous, often non-literate peoples produced by European intellectuals and colonizers. Their sources for this new and what they saw representing a more accurate narrative, were the oral traditions of these populations that they gathered through ethnographic fieldwork and participant observation.[22] It is this effort bringing together these two documentary sources, one historical and the other anthropological and ethnographic, that we look to for what we see as an ethnohistorically informed research agenda for the history of education.

VI.

One of the first attempts at bringing history and ethnography together to explore issues of educational policy was Louis Smith and his colleagues' second look during the mid-1980s at the student-centered, Kensington Elementary School. Fifteen years earlier, Smith had studied the establishment of this progressively oriented school in the conservative Milford School District. The original research involved both a narrative account of the creation of this school and a description of its innovative features as well as an effort to develop a broader theory of innovation and change that had the potential to be generalized to other educational settings.[23] In the follow-up study Smith and his colleagues undertook an examination of the development of the Milford School District in an attempt to situate the creation, growth, and ultimate fate of the Kensington School in a historical context. Relying largely on board of education minutes, newsletters, school annuals, other district records, and interviews, the resulting narrative traced the evolution of the district from 1914 until the end of the decade of the 1970s, paying particular attention to the

[22] Cohn, Ibid.
[23] Smith, Louis M. & Keith, Pat M., Anatomy of Education Innovation: An Organizational Analysis of an Elementary School (New York: John Wiley and Sons, 1971), pp. 2-17.

important political conflicts affecting key school personnel. Their intent in developing this account was to describe the role that the Kensington School played in this history and to incorporate that history into their more general model of educational innovation and change.[24]

Writing in the mid-1980s Smith and his colleagues noted that despite what they saw as the similarities between the methods of historians and ethnographers, there had been very little previous research that sought to link these two approaches together. Although they did not begin their study as historians but rather as ethnographers, they found themselves drawn to historical research in order to explain the importance of the district and its development in the life of the Kensington School. It was, they claimed, their historical study that enabled them move conceptually from a study of innovation in one school to frame a broader theory of innovation and change in American public education.[25]

Rubén Donato's recent examination of the struggles of a subgroup of Hispanos or Latinos of Spanish origin in Southern Colorado between 1920 and 1963 to expand their educational opportunity is a good example of how educational historians can use this ethnohistorical approach. Looking at the experiences of Hispanos in four Southern Colorado school districts, Donato examines the interplay between patterns of discrimination, segregation, and acceptance that mediated the schooling of children in these communities. His account employed an array of sources that historians traditionally rely on including state and school district archival records, school board minutes, superintendents' reports, census reports, and high school and college yearbooks, In addition, he conducted a large number of ethnographic interviews of former teachers, administrators, students.

Donato focuses his attention in this study on the access that Hispanos had to the public schools, their treatment within the schools, and the ultimate impact on their lives and careers. He argues that the key factor that accounted for any educational success that these children enjoyed was the degree of autonomy that Hispanos experienced in their relations with Anglo populations in directing their schools and more generally their communities. His study not only provides a historical account of this struggle for equal educational opportunity but draws the implica-

[24] Smith, Louis M., Dwyer, David C., Prunty, John J., & Kleine, Paul F., Innovation and Change in Schooling: History, Politics, and Agency (New York: The Falmer Press, 1988), pp. 1-24.
[25] Ibid., pp. 25-41, 65-75, 258-283.

tions for contemporary policies regarding the education of Latinos.[26] In concluding his essay Donato highlights a point that we have made earlier in this essay that educational historians have been reluctant to connect their research with matters of educational policy because as they see it "such analyses abandon the stance of detachment that helps them deal with the past on its own terms."[27]

One group of researchers who have not been bothered by concerns about the need for detachment has been curriculum historians. Their studies of curriculum change and reform have provided a popular venue for connecting history to the development of curriculum policies and their implementation into actual school practice.[28] One of the authors of this essay, Barry Franklin, has focused his research on such case studies since the mid-1980s. His most recent work, which he is completing with one of his doctoral students, explores the reorganization of a large, comprehensive urban high school with an enrollment of around 1500 students into a number of smaller learning communities each enrolling approximately 300 to 400 students. The sub-title of the grant that funded this research, "the history of a curriculum reform" addresses what they are attempting in this study, namely to situate the notion of smaller learning communities, which has become in recent years, a very popular and trendy reform policy, in its historical context. They are doing this to explain why a host of stakeholders in this school and its surrounding community have embraced this reform model and once having done so how they have put it into practice. Much of the research is ethnographic in nature and involves in-depth interviews of various stakeholders; participant observation, including classroom observation, attendance at meetings, and simply conversing with school personnel in the staff lounge; and the review and examination of a variety of archival documents, including grant applications, school district reports, curriculum materials, and memoranda of various sorts. The goal in this portion

---

[26] Donato, Rubén, "Hispano Education and the Implications of Autonomy: Four School Systems in Southern Colorado, 1920-1963," in Harvard Educational Review 69 (1999), pp. 117-149.
[27] Ibid., p 143.
[28] Kliebard, Herbert M.& Franklin, Barry M., "The Course of the Course of Study: History of Curriculum," in Historical Inquiry in Education: A Research Agenda, ed. John Hardin Best (Washington, D.C.: American Educational Research Association, 1983), 138-157; McCulloch, Gary, The Secondary Technical School: A Usable Past? (London: The Falmer Press, 1989), pp. 22-26; Franklin, Barry M., "Curriculum History and Its Revisionist Legacy," in Rethinking the History of American Education ed. William J. Reese & John L. Rury (New York: Palgrave Macmillan, 2008), pp. 223-243.

of the research is to explain this reform in terms of the lived experiences of the various stakeholders.

There is, however, another dimension to this research that is clearly historical and involves placing this reform in the longer life of the school and in the school's place over time within the school district and the community. Here the research relies on the examination of an array of primary source documents that address both the history of the school and history of the reform itself. They believe that such an approach will not only inform readers about the history of a particular school reform. It will offer them information about the trajectory of reform efforts that will prove helpful to policy makers in their work in understanding not only smaller learning communities but the reform process itself.

This examination of smaller learning communities is part of a larger collection of case studies entitled *Curriculum, Community, and Urban School Reform* that Franklin has undertaken using an ethnohistorical approach. One such study, for example, explored the implementation of late 1990s reform efforts in New York City and Detroit sponsored by the Annenberg Foundation. Here Franklin used ethnographic methods, particularly interviews, to examine the role that intermediary organizations played in both cities in sponsoring and implementing different school-based reforms for addressing low academic achievement among economically disadvantaged students in urban school systems. Such interviews enabled him to describe how a number of stakeholder organizations in both cities conceptualized the problems facing urban schools and then to consider how these organizations framed and implemented polices to address them. The data obtained from these interviews were particularly helpful in allowing him to identify how the agreements and conflicts among these stakeholders advanced and retarded reform initiatives. He then examined an array of archival documents, particularly newspaper accounts and various reports, to construct a historical narrative that linked this reform to a longer history of efforts of urban schools and communities to address post-World War II demographic and economic transformations and associated patterns of racial discord.

Another case study in this volume examined the development and implementation a policy initiative of Britain's New Labour government, Education Action Zones (EAZ). Introduced in 1998 and continued through 2002, the program brought together clusters of usually fifteen to twenty-five schools located throughout England in areas of social and economic distress with the intent of raising academic standards and enhancing the social inclusion of the population. The EAZs were partnerships involving schools, local education agencies, parents, community groups, and private sector agencies and were funded by a combination of direct government support and business contributions. The study employed ethnographic methods, particularly interviews, to look at the introduction and implementation of the EAZ initiative in the schools of a borough of London given the pseudonym of North Upton. The account paid particular attention to the economic and social conditions facing the borough and its schools, the conflicts surrounding the introduction of the EAZ initiative, the changes that the EAZ program brought to the schools, and the impact of the initiative on student achievement.

The study also included a historical account of the origins of New Labour's reform agenda, including its recommendations for the nation's schools, and the connections between those reforms and the post World War II transformation of the British economy. Relying largely on an array of archival documents, this section of the study focused its attention on the transformation of the Labour Party into its more politically moderate counterpart known as New Labour, the embrace of "third- way" thinking under the leadership of Tony Blair, the relationship between the reform views of New Labour and the previous Conservative government under Margaret Thatcher, and the emergence of New Labour polices for reforming the nation's schools. [29]

The explorations of the links between history, anthropology and ethnography and the rich approaches that this perspective can produce, continues to be part of the debate in both historical and social sciences circles.

For us, it is this interplay between these distinct research methodologies—one for reconstructing the past and the other for interpreting the present— that we see as a way of connecting the work of educational historians to contemporary issues of educational policy.

[29] Franklin, Barry M., Curriculum, Community, and Urban School Reform (New York: Palgrave Macmillan, 2012).

On the Use and Abuse of History of Education - Different uses of Educational history in Sweden

Esbjörn Larsson

> The person who cannot set himself down on the crest of the moment, forgetting everything from the past, who is not capable of standing on a single point, like a goddess of victory, without dizziness or fear, will never know what happiness is. Even worse, he will never do anything to make other people happy.[1]

With these words, from his essay On the Use and Abuse of History for Life, the German philosopher Friedrich Nietzsche tries to envision the situation of someone who is burdened by history. As the title of his essay postulates, Nietzsche had an ambivalent relationship towards history and his historical thoughts go well beyond the text in question.[2] Nietzsche's philosophical writings about the meaning of history have had a great influence on many scholars in different academic disciplines. The French historian and philosopher Michel Foucault derives for example his concept of genealogy from Nietzsche's way of interpretating history.[3]

In this article I will concentrate on how Nietzsche's essay may help us to understand how history is used. By utilizing Nietzsche's three kinds of attitudes towards history – a monumental historical method, an antiquarian historical method and a critical historical method – I want to pinpoint different trends within the field of Swedish educational history.

---

[1] Nietzsche, Friedrich, On the Use and Abuse of History for Life (Sioux Falls: NuVision Publications, LLC, 2007 [1872]), p. 10.

[2] On the Use and Abuse of History for Life was one of Nietzsche's early works and his thoughts on history developed further along with his authorship. For an extensive analysis of Nietzsche's relationship towards history, see for example Pletsch, Carl E. "History and Friedrich Nietzsche's Philosophy of Time" in History and Theory Vol. 16 No 1 (1977), pp. 30–39.

[3] Foucault's use of the essay On the Use and Abuse of History for Life can be found in Foucault, Michel "Nietzsche, Genealogy, History", in The Foucault Reader: an Introduction to Foucault's Thought ed. Paul Rabinow (Penguin Books: Harmondsworth 1986 [1971]), pp. 93–97. Foucault's interpretation is however not undisputed. His, as well as other postmodernists' use of Nietzsche as a predecessor of disunity, has been criticized in Ken Gemes' "Postmodernism's Use and Abuse of Nietzsche" in Philosophy and Phenomenological Research Vol. 62, No. 2 (2001), pp. 349–354.

I will focus on three different areas – the use of history within the public sphere, non-academic organizations devoted to history of education and historical research on education.

It seems that Nietzsche's concept of monumental history as a historical method that makes use of grand stories has much to say about how history is used within the public sphere. Likewise Nietzsche's description of the antiquarian historical method as a vivid interest in anything old shows a great resemblance with the historical interest displayed in some non-academic historical writings. The critical historical method, on the other hand, is described as a way to take away the veil of the mysteries of life. In many aspects the critical approach can be seen as the essence of academic research.

The Grand History of Education

The monumental approach to history can be seen as synonymous with the history of big events. According to Nietzsche, a grand history may help people to escape the trivialities of ordinary life. By linking the challenges of today with the heroic deeds of the past, history can be a useful tool for the resourceful man.[4] Such thoughts may sound alien and almost fascist to our modern ears,[5] but by a closer look one can discover that much of our everyday historical knowledge is structured in a perspective of progress and big events.

The common description of the development of the Swedish educational system is a good example of a monumental history perspective. In Sweden the year 1842 and the School Act that imposed obligatory elementary schooling, is frequently considered as a milestone on the road towards an educational system with equal opportunities for all citizens.[6] The Swedish historian Lars Petterson has however pointed out

[4] Nietzsche (2007 [1872]), pp. 40–50.

[5] The Nazi movement's use of Nietzsche was analysed as early as 1940. Although much of Nietzsche's ideas correspond to ideals found within the Nazi faith, such as "a transvaluation of all values, the sanctity of the will to power, the right and duty of the strong to dominate, the sole right of great states to exist, and a renewing, a rebirth of German and European society", it would be a great exaggeration to say that he cleared the way for the national socialists in Germany. Brinton, Crane "The National Socialists' Use of Nietzsche" in Journal of the History of Ideas Vol. 1, No. 2 (1940), pp. 148–150. Quotation on p. 149.

[6] That this picture still prevails can be noticed in one of the more widely used university text books on history of education in Sweden. Although the text book does not deny other explanations, it stresses that the introduction of obligatory elementary school education should be seen as "an early striving towards a more democratic form of government" ["en tidig strävan efter ett mera demokratiskt styrelseskick"] Richardson, Gunnar, Svensk utbildningshistoria: skola och samhälle förr och nu 7th rev. edition (Lund: Studentlitteratur 2004 [1977]), pp. 55–59. Quotation on p. 58.

that this was hardly the case. The Swedish elementary school established in the mid 19th century was generally a school whose main purpose was to discipline the poor people of Sweden. Therefore the obligatory elementary schooling act of 1842 should rather be seen as a way to control the lower classes of society by creating a segmented school system.[7]

When Petterson depicts this embellishment as a kind of "Everyday Hegelianism", he draws support from the British historian Herbert Butterfield. In this argumentation Butterfields concept of Whig history – the tendency to arrange historical facts in a way where the present becomes the aim of historical change – is crucial. The result of Whiggism is often that historical actors are ascribed to have the same intentions as those that guide us today. Consequently every historical change can be interpreted as a teleological step towards the world we live in.[8]

Despite the similarities between Butterfield's and Nietzsche's ways of viewing this kind of history, they hardly agree on how we should relate to grand history. Butterfield rather sees Whig history as bad craftsmanship. The historian should not act as a judge or try to present history in an orderly fashion. Instead it is the historian's task to highlight any contradictions by a close attention to empirical details.[9] Nietzsche on the other hand points out the potential of the monumental historical method. The great deeds of the past may inspire visionaries of today.

---

[7] Petterson, Lars, Frihet, jämlikhet, egendom och Bentham: utvecklingslinjer i svensk folkundervisning mellan feodalism och kapitalism, 1809–1860 [Freedom, equality, property and Bentham: trends in Swedish popular education between feudalism and capitalism, 1809–1860] (Uppsala: Studia historica Upsaliensia 1992), pp. 161–167; Petterson, Lars "Pedagogik och historia: en komplicerad förbindelse" in Kobran, nallen och majjen: tradition och förnyelse i svensk skola och skolforskning ed. Staffan Selander (Stockholm: Myndigheten för skolutveckling 2003), p. 362. A corresponding development in France and England is discussed in Ringer, Fritz K. "On segmentation in modern educational systems: The case of French secondary education, 1865–1920" and Simon, Brian "Systematisation and segmentation in education: The case of England" in The rise of the modern educational system: Structural change and social reproduction 1870–1920 ed. Detlef K. Müller, Fritz K. Ringer & Brian Simon (Cambridge: Cambridge Univ. Press 1987).

[8] Butterfield, Herbert, The Whig interpretation of history (London: G. Bell and sons 1931), pp. 30–31; Petterson (2003), pp. 362–366. A similar criticism of a liberal history of education can be found in Green, Andy, Education and state formation: the rise of education systems in England, France and the USA (London: Macmillan 1990), pp. 27–32.

[9] Butterfield (1931), pp. 70–72. Butterfield has later been criticized for being to simplistic on this point. This criticism pinpoints the fact that Butterfield tends to see history as something that can be simply extracted from the historical sources, without the intrusion of theory. See for example Wilson, Adrian & Ashplant, T. G. "Whig History and Present-Centred History" in The Historical Journal Vol. 31 No. 1 (1988), pp. 5–10; Sewell, Keith C., "The 'Herbert Butterfield Problem' and Its Resolution" in Journal of the History of Ideas Vol. 64 No. 4 (2003), p. 600.

What Butterfield criticizes as the glorification of historical progress, Nietzsche views as an important political tool. According to Nietzsche the great risks with the grand history lies in the possibility that interest in history might come to predominate and thus to suffocate the longing for change and renewal.[10]

Examples of grand or monumental history are multiple, especially in contexts outside the academic sphere. A colourful example, in the field of history of education, is educational materials put together by the Swedish teachers' union: the film Steps towards the future – a film about the development of the teacher profession.[11] Already in the choice of the title it is obvious that the film will tell a story of progress. Like a staircase, history teleologically takes us to the society of today. The purpose of the film is to give a background to the development of the teacher profession from 1842 until the 1980's.

After a brief description of the early 19th century society, the viewer is confronted with a re-enactment of the education before the School Act of 1842. The teacher of that time is depicted as very strict and eager to use the rod if the pupils could not answer the questions given. The speakers voice tells the viewer that during that time anyone could be a teacher, even "the crippled, the old, poor people that could not earn their living by honest work".[12] But there were some proud teachers with a genuine interest in education. According to the film they were the ones that formed the first union of teachers in Sweden.

Despite the importance that is ascribed to the School Act of 1842, the film does not give a flattering description of the elementary schools that were founded as a result of this political decision. The teacher's salary was low and teachers lacked influence in the local school boards. The educational methods – mainly Joseph Lancaster's monitorial system – are described as harsh and almost inhumane. "But", as the speaker voice says, "all Swedish children attended school".[13]

Although the facts presented are mainly undisputed, there is much to be said about how the story is told. The monitorial system used in the early elementary schools may seem brutal by modern standards,

---

[10] Nietzsche (2007 [1872]), pp. 44–50.

[11] Steg mot framtiden – En film om läraryrkets utveckling (Stockholm: Lärarförbundet 1991).

[12] The quotation is translated from Swedish. The original is as follows: "krymplingar, åldringar, fattigjon som inte kunde göra rätt för sig genom hederligt arbete". Steg mot framtiden (1991), m. 03:02–08.

[13] Steg mot framtiden (1991), m. 4:45–6:52. The quotation is translated from Swedish. The original is as follows: "men alla svenska barn gick i skolan". Steg mot framtiden (1991), m. 6:47–52.

but in the first half of the 19th century it was considered as an educational breakthrough that revolutionized school education.[14] To depict it as a makeshift solution that was eventually abandoned stands out as an example of reductionism.[15] The same goes for the statement that the School Act of 1842 led to that all Swedish children started to attend school. As previous studies have emphasized, a large portion of the Swedish children attended school long before the School Act and it took many years before every child in reality secured an education.[16]

The film presents the picture of a school that slowly improved, often due to the hard work of the unions organizing elementary school teachers. The heroes of this struggle are quoted and presented as important for the progress.[17] To describe historical development in this way – as the struggle between reformers and reactionary forces – is a common way to write history in the Whig tradition and it also permeated many of the educational history surveys produced by The General Elementary School Teachers' Association during the 20th century.[18]

Concerning the 20th century, two important changes are stressed in the film: the abolition of corporal punishment and the introduction of a nine-year compulsory school that replaced the elementary schools as well as the grammar schools that catered for the educational needs of the educated classes. Despite the fact that these changes did not take place until after the Second World War, they are both issues that are addressed throughout the film.[19] This can also be seen as a kind of

---

[14] Monitorial education was mainly used in elementary schools in Sweden during the 19th century, but it was also used in a limited number of secondary schools. Larsson, Esbjörn "Klasser i sig och för sig: skillnader i växelundervisningens tillämpning för olika samhällsklasser i Sverige, ca 1820–1870" in Det mångsidiga verktyget: elva utbildningshistoriska uppsatser ed. Anne Berg & Hanna Enefalk (Uppsala: Opuscula Historica Upsaliensia 2009).

[15] According to the film, monitorial education was finally abolished due to the introduction of low paid female teachers. Steg mot framtiden (1991), m. 8:25–29. Although the arrival of female teachers may have contributed to the abolition of the monitorial system, this does not imply that Lancaster's methods were considered as an emergency solution when it was first introduced in the beginning of the 19th century.

[16] This fact has previously been discussed in Petterson, Lars, "1842, 1822 eller 1882? Vad är det som bör firas?" in Forskning om utbildning 4 (1991), pp. 22–27.

[17] See for example Steg mot framtiden (1991), m. 10:52–12:14, 13:30–57.

[18] The production of books on history of education within The General Elementary School Teacher's Association (Sveriges allmänna folkskollärarförening) has previously been discussed by Göran Sparrlöf in his presentation "Folkskolan i historieskrivningen – en sonderande undersökning" [The historiography of the elementary school – a probing investigation] at the Swedish Historians convention in Lund the 24–26 of April 2008.

[19] Corporal punishment is mentioned frequently when condemning out-dated educational methods throughout history, despite the fact that it was not abolished until 1957. Steg mot framtiden (1991), m. 2:46–3:13, 5:45–6:02, 22:16–38, 29:04–35. In a similar way recurrent references are made to the fact that all children were not given the same educational opportunities. Steg mot framtiden (1991), m. 6:20–30, 13:16–57, 28:04–29:02, 29:37–50.

whiggism, as the issues are portrayed in the light of their final solution. The result is that the viewer gets the impression that the decisions were almost predetermined.

The fascination for anything old

According to Nietzsche, the real dangers of being caught up in history do not lie in the monumental but in the antiquarian historical method. Instead of taking interest in great deeds of the past, antiquarian history focuses on the private and personal; it creates a sense of belonging and contentment.[20] In some ways this view appears to touch upon Karl Marx's characterizing of religion as "the opium of the people",[21] but with the great difference that Nietzsche does not see this effect as a problem. Nietzsche's aversion towards antiquarian history lies instead in that it puts preservation before renewal. The interest in history can then be a burden that threatens to poison our minds:

> Then we get a glimpse of the wretched drama of a blind mania for collecting, a restless compiling together of everything that ever existed. The man envelops himself in a mouldy smell. With the antiquarian style, he manages to corrupt even a significant talent, a noble need, into an insatiable new lust, a desire for everything really old. Often he sinks so deep that he is finally satisfied with that nourishment and takes pleasure in gobbling up for himself the dust of biographical quisquilien.[22]

In the same way as there are tendencies towards a monumental historical method within history of education, there has also been a vivid antiquarian interest. In Sweden it was very much personified by one of Swedish educational history's most prominent figures during the first half of the 20th century, Bror Rudolf Hall. Hall was born in 1876 in the parish of Hall on Gotland (Sweden's largest island). His father was an elementary school teacher and at the age of 22 Hall followed in his father's foot steps by taking a teachers exam. In the years to come he combined his work as a teacher with studies at the university in Lund. In 1911 he defended his doctor's dissertation about the 17th century Swedish bishop Johannes Rudbeckius as educator. Hall has gone down in posterity as

[20] Nietzsche (2007 [1872]), p. 52.
[21] Marx, Karl, Critique of Hegel's 'Philosophy of right', (Cambridge: 1970 [1844]), p. 131.
[22] Nietzsche (2007 [1872]), p. 25.

the founder of the Association for Swedish teaching history.[23] During his years as an editor for the association's script series he published no less then 76 volumes, mostly collections of source material. Hall died in Stockholm in 1950.[24]

Hall's desire to preserve is evident in the two lectures he held in the process of establishing the Association for Swedish teaching history in 1920.[25] In lectures at Uppsala in the summer of 1919, Hall pointed out four reasons for the importance of educational history. The first argument, which could be seen as a text book example of monumental history, was built on the importance of historical pedagogical words of wisdom. In a time that Hall considered as the "century of children and weak parenting" the "words of great educators" were crucial.[26]

Hall also emphasized a materialistic reason for promoting school history. In the struggle for public funding and increased teacher salaries, Hall saw historical studies as a key tool to show that the school system was important for the development of the country. In a similar way he also advocated the importance of showing that educational history was an integral part in the history of the nation. The fourth argument dealt with paying tribute to our predecessors. With the help of historical, studies, earlier generations could be honoured in a respectful and deserved manner.[27]

After this declamation, Hall discussed a more practical and urgent problem – the preservation of historical source material. With words of an approaching "natural disaster", Hall described how school archives were scattered like leaves in the wind. If nothing was done immediately, he foresaw a situation that could be compared with the destruction of the Ancient Library of Alexandria. Therefore he urged the boards of The General Elementary School Teachers' Association and The Friends of the Elementary School [Folkskolans vänner] to support the collection of his-

---

[23] Föreningen för svensk undervisningshistoria.

[24] Kaleen, Gustaf, "Hall, Bror Rudolf" in Svenskt biografiskt lexikon 17 ed. Erik Grill (Stockholm: SBL 1967), pp. 775–777.

[25] Also these lectures were preserved and later published in the 75th volume of the association's script series. Hall, B. Rudolf, Undervisningshistoriska önskemål: räddnings-, uppteckningś-, forsknings- och undervisningsuppgifter (Stockholm: Föreningen för svensk undervisningshistoria 1948). These documents as previously been used by Richardson in his essay on the establishment of the association. Richardson, Gunnar, "ÅSU-seriens tillkomst" in Årsböcker i svensk undervisningshistoria under 75 år (Uppsala: Föreningen för svensk undervisningshistoria 1996).

[26] The quotations are translated from Swedish. The original is as follows: "barnens och föräldraslapphetens århundrade" and "uttalanden av uppfostringskonstens stormän". Hall (1948), p. 47.

[27] Hall (1948), pp. 47–48.

torical source material from Swedish schools.[28]

The second lecture was held during the following year, when the Association for Swedish Teaching History was formed. Once again Hall stressed the importance of honouring the striving for better education among past generations. With the help of education, the Swedish people had left darkness and barbarism. Nothing was more important than the history of this educational success. Just like the previous year, Hall also emphasized the urgent task of saving historical source material.[29] That preservation was one of the main objectives of this mission is shown in the following:

> Each of you should in your own town become an eager scholar and collector on history of school and learning and not let any opportunity slip away. We should remember that every brick, every pointer and every rod of correction in a school house have been a witness and a help in the development of the Swedish breed until its current spiritual and moral standings. Therefore every line in a school book, every page in a record of examination should be preserved for the good of research.[30]

The quotation shows a way of treating history that is both monumental and antiquarian at the same time. It is obvious from this that for Hall the history of schooling should be written as a success story. In that respect Hall's view on history is whiggism in its purest form.[31] On the other hand he also shows an antiquarian's fascination for the details of history. It was not enough to write educational history in the brightest of colours as there was also a need to preserve and exalt every remnant.

Irrespective of how one feels about Hall's way of using history, no one can deny that the Association for Swedish teaching history has contributed much to Swedish history of education. Despite the fact that this association has never been an academic society the many volumes

---

[28]Hall (1948), pp. 48–51.

[29] Hall (1948), pp. 53–55.

[30] The quotation is translated from Swedish. The original is as follows: "Var och en i sin stad bör vara en skol- och lärdomshistorisk forskare och samlare som inte låter ett enda tillfälle gå sig ur händerna. Vi ska minnas att varje tegelsten, pekpinne och färla i ett skolhus varit vittne och behjälpliga till det svenska släktets frammarsch till dess nuvarande andliga och sedliga halt samt att varje rad i en skolbok, varje sida i en examenskatalog bör bevaras och komma forskningen till godo." Hall (1948), p. 55.

[31] A similar interpretation of Hall's publications within the association's script series can be found in Broady, Donald "Försvarstal för bildningstanken" in Meddelanden från Forum för pedagogisk historia. Nr 1 (Stockholm: Lärarhögskolan i Stockholm 1991), pp. 10–14.

of source material and other texts published by Hall and his successors remain useful for researchers .[32] But there is a great difference between this way of collecting, preserving and retelling the fragments from the past and scientifically based historical research. The Swedish historian Jan Lindegren describes the difference:

> To unreflectively retell the past is of little use. Even if one could gather all and everyone's stories it should not be more than the past in all its variety and incomprehensibility. History however is making things comprehensible; history is analysing the past. To make such an analysis the historian partly needs a perception of reality as such, partly needs a perception of the social reality which is to be studied. What the need requires is an elaborate ontology and an overall theory of human society, its development and dynamics. Only then, relevant questions can be asked and meaningful responses be obtained.[33]

With these words it is time to focus on the last of Nietzsche's typologies – the critical historical method.

---

[32] Lars Petterson stresses that many of the people who have published source materials as well as writings about the Swedish school system within the association's script series, have been retired teachers or headteachers. A similar characterisation of the script series as a forum for local history was made by Gunnar Richardson in the early 1980's. Richardson's article was later questioned by the board of the association for not acknowledging the fact that academic scholars had also contributed to the script series. The later fact has also been stressed by the current editor of the script series that has pointed out that no less then twelve of the 182 volumes published between 1920 and 1996 have been dissertations. Petterson (2003), p. 359–360; Richardson, Gunnar, "Är pedagogikhistorien bortglömd?" in Tvärsnitt (1980:3), p. 40; "Debatt om utbildningshistoria" [reply by the board of the Association for Swedish teaching history and repartee by Gunnar Richardson] in Tvärsnitt (1981:1), pp. 45–46; Nordström, Stig G., "ÅSU-serien under 75 år: ämnesprofil, finansiering och produktionsformer" in Årsböcker i svensk undervisningshistoria under 75 år (Uppsala: Föreningen för svensk undervisningshistoria 1996), p. 20.

[33] The quotation is translated from Swedish. The original is as follows: "Att oreflekterat återberätta det förgångna hjälper oss föga. Om man så samlade alla och allas berättelser skulle det fortfarande inte vara mer än det förgångna i hela sin mångfald och obegriplighet. Historia däremot är begripliggörande; historia är analys av det förgångna. För att kunna genomföra en sådan måste historikern dels ha en uppfattning om verkligheten som sådan, dels ha en uppfattning om den konkreta sociala verklighet som studeras. Först utifrån en genomarbetad ontologi och en helhetsteori om det mänskliga samhället och dess utveckling kan relevanta frågor ställas och först då kan meningsfulla svar erhållas." Lindegren, Jan, Varat, staten och diket: tre historieteoretiska uppsatser (Uppsala: Opuscula historica Upsaliensia 1988), backside cover.

The need for critical history

What Nietzsche labels as critical history is synonymous with the kind of scientifically based history that has developed since the late 19th century.[34] Although Nietzsche saw this method as an important tool to be able to break free from the past, he also saw the emergence of scientifically based history as alarming. What worried him was that the search for scientific truths might question the way we look at the world. He also questioned what would become of the world if every mystery was solved and all questions were answered.[35] According to Nietzsche such a world had a gloomy future:

> All living things need an atmosphere around them, a secret circle of darkness. If this veil is taken from them, if people condemn a religion, an art, a genius to orbit like a star without an atmosphere, then we should no longer wonder about their rapid decay and the way they become hard and barren.[36]

The impact of scientifically based history since the days of Nietzsche has however proved that his misgivings were highly exaggerated. Historians have regularly tried to question and revaluate current perceptions about our past, but with no greater effect on the public.[37] This is painfully evident when it comes to Swedish history of education. Despite the fact that historical research, especially in the last twenty years, has given us new information about public education, the whiggish comprehension of the year 1842 still prevails.[38] Apparently it is hard to accept that the elementary schools that evolved in the 19th century were never intended to give the Swedish population equal educational opportunities.[39]

Notwithstanding this lack of impact within the public sphere there have been some important changes within history of education during the 20th century. A closer look at these changes may help to explain why

[34] With regard to the critical historical method Nietzsche's essay can be understood as a criticism of the apprehension of continuity among many of his contemporaries. Ausmus, Harry J. "Nietzsche and Eschatology" in The Journal of Religion Vol. 58 No. 4 (1978), p. 349; Larsen, Jesper Eckhardt "ikke af brød alene...": argumenter for humaniora og universitetet i Norge, Danmark, Tyskland og USA 1945–2005 (København: Danmarks Pædagogiske Universitetsforlag 2007), p. 42.

[35] Nietzsche (2007 [1872]), pp. 57–63, 99–105.

[36] Nietzsche (2007 [1872]), p. 103.

[37] That teacher trainers as well as politicians continue to use history of education to promote their own agendas has previously been discussed in Depaepe, Marc "A Professionally Relevant History of Education for Teachers: Does it Exist? Reply to Jurgen Herbst's State of the Art Article" in Paedagogica Historica Vol. 37:3 (2001), pp. 639–640.

[38] See for example Richardson (2004 [1977]), pp. 55–59.

[39] Petterson (2003), pp. 362–366.

Nietzsche's dystopia has not yet arisen.

It is important to remember that Swedish history of education has never been an autonomous subject at Swedish universities and has never been possible to get a PhD in History of Education in Sweden. Instead, historical studies of education have been conducted in various disciplines such as Education, History, Economic History, Political Science, Church History and History of Ideas.[40] It is therefore difficult to write a comprehensive historiography on the history of education in Sweden. In the following discussion I will concentrate on the developments within the two major disciplines that as been involved in the historical studies of education – Education and History.

According to the Swedish sociologist of education Donald Broady, history of education was considered as an important element within Education and especially Teacher Education in Sweden until the end of the Second World War. Since then, Education changed from being a broader subject that could be considered as a part of humanities as well as general social sciences, towards a subject that primarily dealt with issues related to behavioural science and psychology. Consequently history of education, as a university discipline, was marginalised and pretty much left to non-academic historians such as retired teachers or headteachers.[41]

The developments within Education can however not be seen as the starting point for non-academic history of education in Sweden. As pointed out by the Swedish historian Bengt Sandin, the non-academic element within history of education was also considerable before the Second World War. The previously mentioned formation of the Association for Swedish teaching history played an important role during that time. Together with the General Elementary School Teachers' Association the Association for Swedish teaching history stood behind many of the books about history of education published during the first half of the

[40] Richardson, Gunnar, Smedberg, Staffan & Lönnström, Paul, Utbildningshistorisk forskning: problem, källmaterial, metodik (Uppsala: Acta Universitatis Upsaliensis 1984), p. 9.

[41] Broady, Donald & Larsson, Esbjörn "Utbildningshistorisk forskning vid svenska lärosäten och bildandet av en nationell forskarskola i utbildningshistoria" in Vägval i skolans historia (2007:2–3), p. 3. Broady claims social science traditions such as structuralism and system theory were not widely used within Swedish educational research until after the Swedish educationalists Urban Dahllöf's and Ulf P. Lundgren's introduction of the frame factor theory in the late 1960's and the early 1970's. Broady, Donald "Det svenska hos ramfaktorteorin" in Pedagogisk Forskning i Sverige (1999:1), pp. 116–118. This picture of the developments within Education at Swedish universities is somewhat supported by Richardson who claims that efforts within the field of history of education have not been seen as a requirement for a professorship in Education since the early 1950's. "Debatt om utbildningshistoria" (1981), p. 47.

20th century. The teachers' association also funded a lot of publications issued by the Association for Swedish teaching history.[42]

If we turn our eyes towards the academic historians we can see that the interest for historical studies of education was even lesser within History than in Education. The Swedish historian and historiographer Ragnar Björk has shown that if studies about the universities are excluded, history of education was near to non-existent within the discipline of History before the 1960's.[43] The main reason for this was that History until then was almost synonymous with political history. With the breakthrough of Social History in the mid 1960's History opened up towards a number of fields. From then on it was also possible to follow education studies within the discipline of History.[44]

The lack of a critical history of education, within the Swedish universities, is accordingly partly due to the late awakening of interest in history of education. Another reason was that a majority of the studies produced during the 1960's and 1970's lacked more elaborate theoretical perspectives. According to Sandin there was, with a few exceptions, a very limited interest in theoretical aspects within Swedish studies in history of education before the 1980's.[45] That the early 1980's could be considered as a kind of turning point, is demonstrated by the fact that the Swedish historian Gunnar Richardson published several articles questioning the value of theorizing the historical studies on education at this time.[46]

How this shift of perspectives came about and what influenced it is however not jet fully analyzed. As seen in Sandin's doctoral dissertation (1986) the renewal of Swedish history of education during the 1980's seems to have drawn at least some support from the radical

---

[42] Sandin, Bengt, Hemmet, gatan, fabriken eller skolan: folkundervisning och barnuppfostran i svenska städer 1600-1850 (Lund: Arkiv 1986), p. 12–14. For the funding of the Association for Swedish teaching history's script series, see Nordström (1996), p. 18.

[43] One of the first historical dissertations in the field of history of education in the 1960's were Richardson, Gunnar, Kulturkamp och klasskamp: ideologiska och sociala motsättningar i svensk skol- och kulturpolitik under 1880-talet [Cultural struggle and class struggle : ideological and social conflicts in Swedish educational and cultural policy in the 1880's], (Göteborg: Department of History 1963).

[44] Björk, Ragnar, "Utbildningsforskning som historisk analys", in Forskning om utbildning: en antologi ed. Staffan Selander (Stockholm: Symposion 1992), pp. 331–341.

[45] Sandin (1984), p. 19–20. This description of the field also finds support in Gunnar Richardson's inventory of Swedish history of education during the 1970's. Richardson (1980), pp. 35–40.

[46] See Richardson, Gunnar, "Behövs en strategi för utbildningshistorisk forskning?", Historisk tidskrift (1981:2), pp. 142–143; Richardson, Gunnar, "Om den påstådda bristen på konflikter och om frånvaron av moralisk indignation: ett genmäle till Dan Ch Christensen" Historisk tidskrift (1983:1); Richardson, Smedberg, & Lönnström, (1984), pp. 76–78.

revisionism that started in America in the beginning of the 1960's.[47] The direct impact of American research on Swedish history of education however still needs to be researched. In Sandin's thesis the revisionists are primarily used as a stepping stone and the more substantial theoretical influences are derived from Michel Foucault and the Italian philosopher and revolutionary Antonio Gramsci.[48] The influences from European theoretical traditions are also stressed by Petterson claiming that the new critical theory within history of education in Sweden was derived from German scholars and foremost from the Frankfurt School.[49]

Since Sandin's dissertation, the use of theory as well a critical perspective has become comme il faut within Swedish history of education.[50] As Petterson tries to summon up the results of the radical revisionist movements' impact on Swedish history of education during the 1980's and 1990's, he is nevertheless uncertain about its long term effects. In the beginning of the 21st century he feared a kind of post-revisionist reaction to the revisionist movement. In his view there had been a tendency towards a more eclectic view on theory as the more structural aspects had to stand back for a more vivid interest in personal history and history of events.[51] Whether Petterson's prophecy will come true remains to be seen. There are however Swedish critical studies within the field of history of education. One quite recent example is Johannes Westberg's dissertation Förskolepedagogikens framväxt: Pedagogisk förändring och dess förutsättningar, ca 1835–1945.[52] Westberg

---

[47] The so-called radical revisionist movement was initiated with Bailyn, Bernard, Education in the forming of American society: needs and opportunities for study (Chapel Hill: The University of North Carolina Press 1960). For more on its developments, see for example Katz, Michael B., "The Origins of Public Education: A Reassessment", History of Education Quarterly, Vol. 16, No. 4. (Winter, 1976); Herbst, Jurgen, "Beyond the Debate over Revisionism: Three Educational Pasts Writ Large", History of Education Quarterly, Vol. 20, No. 2. (Summer, 1980).

[48] Sandin (1984), pp. 21–25, 33-38.

[49] Petterson (2003), pp. 369–370.

[50] Among dissertations contemporary to Sandin's, Englund, Tomas, Curriculum as a political problem: changing educational conceptions, with special reference to citizenship education (Lund: Studentlitteratur 1986), Florin, Christina, Kampen om katedern: feminiserings- och professionaliseringsprocessen inom den svenska folkskolans lärarkår 1860-1906 = [Who should sit in the teacher's chair? : the processes of feminization and professionalization among Swedish elementary school teachers 1860-1906] (Umeå: Umeå Universitet 1987) and Johansson, Ulla, Att skolas för hemmet: trädgårdsskötsel, slöjd, huslig ekonomi och nykterhetsundervisning i den svenska folkskolan 1842-1919 med exempel från Sköns församling (Umeå: Pedagogiska institutionen 1987) can be mentioned.

[51] Petterson (2003), pp. 370–371.

[52] Westberg, Johannes, Förskolepedagogikens framväxt: pedagogisk förändring och dess förutsättningar, ca 1835-1945 [The birth of early childhood education: Pedagogical changes in Swedish early childhood care and education programs, 1835–1945] (Uppsala: Acta Universitatis Upsaliensis 2008).

challenges two wide spread understandings of childhood education. The first of these concerns the changing views on children and the concept of childhood.

Previous studies of childcare and education have stressed that the way children were looked upon changed during the last decades of the 19th and first decades of the 20th century. Children went from being viewed as mainly an economical asset to being valued more on a romantic and emotional level. This development has thus been regarded as a condition for the introduction of early childhood education in kindergartens during the first half of the 20th century. By analysing sources that originate from the infant schools that preceded the kindergartens, Westberg shows that a romanticized view of children was already in place by the first half of the 19th century. Despite the fact that the infant schools were designed to teach very small children to read and write they were nevertheless built upon the notion that children should be treated as children. The education suitable for children was described as "mild education".[53]

The other widespread "truth" that is questioned in Westberg's thesis is that of the importance of great educators for educational change. In previous studies of early childhood education, scholars have emphasized the importance of pedagogical reformers such as Friedrich Fröbel and Maria Montessori. Westberg on the other hand demonstrates convincingly that these ideas played a limited role in the introduction of early childhood education in Sweden. The change towards early childhood education was not caused by the arrival of new ideas. Instead there were changes within other parts of the educational system as well as new economical and organizational conditions for individual infant schools, day nurseries and kindergartens that resulted in these changes.[54]

Obviously, a scientifically based history of education has much to offer anyone who is interested in a better understanding of how our educational systems emerged. Although new knowledge might threaten to overthrow our perceptions, it should not prevent us from seeking new wisdoms. The very aim of historical research is to question and sometimes overthrow established narratives.[55]

---

[53] Westberg (2008), pp. 37–42.
[54] Westberg (2008), pp. 109–110, 127–139, 162–182.
[55] The need for more educational history that questions old perceptions is also highlighted in Depaepe, Marc "Demythologizing the Educational Past: An Endless Task in History of Education" in Historical Studies in Education/Revue d'histoire de l'éducation Vol. 9 No. 2 (1997), pp. 208–233.

Concluding remarks

In this article I have discussed how the three historical methods described by Nietzsche in the late 19th century can still be used to capture ways in which history – in this case history of education – is being used (or abused). As shown in the examples presented, the different kinds of history often overlap, which make them more like analytic categories than mere representations of empirical observations. This is especially true when it comes to monumental and antiquarian historical methods.

The seemingly uncomplicated interest in historical details is often supported by a grand story about the development of the current educational system. If we take these stories for granted and use them as starting point for our studies, our research runs the risk to be reduced to only a crossword puzzle. No important new knowledge can come out of such studies and our task is limited to filling out the blanks.

The critical history approach however, stands out as a method that can hardly be combined with the other two. Unlike Nietzsche, I have argued in favour of a critical or a scientifically based history. Such an argument might seem self-evident, but the examples in this article prove it is not that obvious. A more critical history of education is a quite new phenomenon in Sweden. We still have to fight against common conceptions that mistrust the result of scientifically based studies.

History is too often used to exalt progress and to glorify our present accomplishments. To prevent this, we always have to fend against the monumental or the grand history by challenging what is considered as common knowledge. On the other hand, we also have to be on the lookout for tendencies towards an antiquarian history. In the search for an objective history, it is easy to get caught up in empirical data. But by simply ridding our texts of anything that is not an undisputed fact, we will get a kind of history that lacks the potential to explain. The challenge of the historian lies instead in the use of the critical method. To scrutinize without tampering we need to balance both the demand for objectivity and the need for theoretical awareness.

History of education matters – if the past is present

Harry Haue

Why do subjects in the schools look like they do, and how has the relationship between them developed? And how has the purpose of education changed over time? These are the fundamental questions, which are addressed in this article in order to further to develop a dialogue between tradition and innovation. My first point is that the history of any subject is an important part of its didactical potential. Therefore, it is imperative for the historians of education and the teachers in the school to know this history. My second point is that it is important to analyse the aim-formulations of education, first of all because it is the crucial argument for content and form of the education and secondly because it is possible in these formulations to disclose the society's expectations of the purpose of education. In this article I shall focus on the development of the subject of history at the upper secondary level, and the normative aim in the general rules: *'almendannelse'* in Danish, *Allgemeinbildung* in German or *general education/liberal education* in the Anglophone world.

My theoretical assumption is that educational development since the Eighteenth Century can be comprehended as a communication between different systems in the way the German sociologist and philosopher, Niklas Luhmann, perceived it. According to this theory, society can be seen as a social system in which several subsystems exist, and among them is the school. If we regard the school as a social system, and the subjects as subsystems, the existence of those subjects will depend on their communication with other subjects and the school, science and society. In order to survive, these subjects must engage in a self-referential communication. Sometimes the subject must close its borders and sometimes open them for the adoption of new scientific developments and social innovations.[1]

---

[1] N. Luhmann. Soziale Systeme. Grundriss einer allgemeinen Theorie, Frankfurt am Main 1987.

My field of discussion is the subject of history at the upper secondary level in Denmark. With the reform of the Danish gymnasium in 2005, the subject of history was changed in a more radical way than had been the case in earlier reforms. In fact, it is not too far-fetched to argue that the 2005 reform in the subject of history amounted to a paradigmatic change. I shall illustrate this point further, and discuss the following parts of the changes of the subject in the general branch of the gymnasium, and try to explain the role that the history of education plays.

History and Civics

Since 1903, Civics has been a part of the subject of history; however, this supplement had been discussed since the Duke of Augustenborg as head of a commission in 1795, proposed a new curriculum for the grammar school. Instead of mainly focusing on Greek and Latin, the new school, inspired by developments in Germany, should include mathematics, natural sciences, modern languages and a number of disciplines connected to history and vernacular Danish teaching. One of these proposed subjects were Civics, which it was proposed, should contain a number of topics: The rights and duties of the citizens, constitutions of different states, the social hierarchy and the most important trades. However, those modern proposals were not implemented, mainly because of wars and recessions. In the Nineteenth Century however, Civics came to be thought of in connection with national history. After 1864, it was not possible to imitate the German way of treating Civics, especially after the loss of the duchies Schleswig and Holstein, but rather the French model, which was seen as a model for the implementation of Civics in 1903.[2]

When the Liberals succeeded the long reigning Conservative party 1901, there was space for a change in curriculum and Civics became a part of the history teacher's obligation, which should take up to ten per cent of the lessons. The content of Civics was the function of the main social institutions, the constitution and the main content of actual legislation. The development of the social sciences after the Second World War had an impact on secondary education, and in 1968 it became possible for the students to choose an optional subject of social science, which included a thread to civics. The reason for this was due

[2] H. Haue: Didactics of History and educational Policy in Denmark. Five Lectures, (Odense 2007), p. 22.

to structural inappropriateness, which had the consequence that those students who had chosen the optional subject and therefore were taught in a separate class, still had to learn civics as well when attending history lessons. The history teacher had to teach the 'experts' as well as the beginners in civics in the same class. This construction was untenable and was consequently changed in connection with the 2005 reform when a new independent subject of civics was created. The history teachers may have relieved themselves of a problem, however at the same time they lost twenty per cent of their classes to the new obligatory subject of civics. The subject of History was structurally taken back to its Nineteenth Century insular position, though at the same time it was prompted to collaborate in interdisciplinary work with civics and other subjects. This rather fundamental change of the subject of history was possible especially because the history teachers were not inclined to defend civics a part of their subject. Perhaps they were not sufficiently conscious of the history of their subject, and they did not take part in – at least not in time - a self-referential communication to maintain the status quo, and it was possible for the teachers of social science to gain hegemony in the discourse. After the reform, social science became a powerful subject as it was taught as a compulsory minor subject, civics, and a popular optional subject at a high level.[3]

Danish national history and world history

The modern Danish gymnasium was created in 1850. The school could no longer restrict itself to the classical languages, but had to incorporate natural sciences and modern languages, (German and French). This was in line with the 1795 ideas of the Duke of Augustenborg. English however, did not become part of the curriculum because it was regarded as a subject, which could not develop the pupils' formal qualifications. In other words, it was curiously not seen as a subject, which could contribute to the development of the student's '*Allgemeinbildung*'; general character development or formation.

Concerning the subject of history, it was changed and upgraded requiring that the nation's past should have higher priority. Danish history was then separated from world history with the argument that history in the schools should act as an important tool of the nation-building project. The Danish Society of the Freedom of the Press, formed

[3] H. Haue "Den historiske baggrund for fagenes nuværende placering" in: E. Damberg (red.) Fagdidaktik – mellem fag og didaktik. En konferencerapport, (Odense 2005), p. 141.

in 1835, arranged a competition for writing the best textbook on Danish history. C. F. Allen's book, which was the winner, was used for the next two generations or more in the grammar schools. Allen's goal was to prompt love of the country amongst the students. This nation-building idea was practiced in most European countries, and marked a change from the use of universal history in the late years of Enlightenment. According to this concept, history teaching had a universal approach and intended to encompass the history of all humankind. However, and this was especially the case for smaller countries, if the national history was to have a proportional place in the teaching of history, it would not be possible to give it a proper national preference and therefore it was deemed necessary to put more emphasis on this part of the subject. The demand for more emphasis on the national history was an answer to a demand from history teachers at the school level, the history department at the university and the majority of the politicians. The teachers and professors of the classical languages opposed this pressure only to a certain extent. Some amongst these felt that it was not acceptable to privilege the history of the nation's possible roots in a Viking past to the heritage of Roman history.[4]

From the 1840s onward, it became normal to separate national and world history in school lessons and to use different books. This differentiation between national and world history also inspired the teachers to develop a different didactical ethos. Love of the fatherland was not just a question of historical knowledge, but presupposed a special empathic treatment of national victories and defeats, and not least, the special qualities of the Danish people. If the teaching of history was to contribute to the nation building process, it was imperative to engage the pupils and convince them of the validity of certain values. If this objective was to succeed, the history teacher had to develop a new didactic of history. It is therefore reasonable to assume that the nation-building obligation contributed to the teacher's reflexions on new pedagogical concepts, and in the second half of the Nineteenth Century they could seek inspiration in the Danish Folk High Schools where the revival movement practiced a 'constructivist-like' education with emphasis on the narrative rendering of the past and dialogue. In these schools for adult farmhands, the history of the Danish people was an important subject. This pedagogical and didactical experience is an important heritage,

[4] H. Haue: Almendannelse som ledestjerne, (Odense, 2003), s. 198, H. Haue "Historical consciousness and Culture of Students in Denmark" in: Yearbook. International Society for History didactics (2006/07), p. 45.

which continues to have some impact on the Danish school system, Another continuing influence is the revivalists critical attitude towards the erudite school, which they labelled as "schools of death" due to their rote learning pedagogy. This picture has been propagated for more than 150 years, but as mentioned above, this could not be true in relation to the teaching of the history of the fatherland, and further research will probably prove that the epithets 'dead/black' about all grammar school teaching is exaggerated.[5]

Since 1850, each new reform made a distinction between world history and Danish history, the later often connected to a short view of the other Scandinavian countries. For example in 1960, the mandatory text did not mention Danish history separately, but used the concept of the history of the Nordic countries. The reason for that might have been the strong collaboration between the Nordic countries in the first generation after the Second World War. However, in 1971 it was emphasized that one of the topics before 1930 should contain the history of Denmark and the Nordic countries, but in the 1988 reform there were no references to the history of the other Scandinavian countries. One reason for the abandonment of the Nordic history approach might have been Denmark's membership of the EEC from 1973.

When preparing the reform of 2005, the Ministry of Education issued an instruction, which was to be the foundation for the work of all subject committees. Each was to include a representative from the universities, who was supposed to know the main lines of development of the subject.[6] In the instruction for the subject of history, it was furthermore stressed that the history and culture of Denmark should be accorded special attention, and the right wing political parties then in power frequently expressed this point of view. Nonetheless, the instruction gave no indication of the fact that Danish history should be thought of separately. The committee, however, had a discussion on this matter and agreed on formulating a rule that each national topic always had to be treated in a global perspective, and visa versa, each topic in the history of the world should be related to a contemporary development in Denmark. This was a paradigmatic decision. The main argument was 'globalisation'. As the national economy, cultural life, social conditions and policy decision to a growing extent were influenced by decisions made in Brussels and Washington, it made little sense to uphold the separate

[5] H. Haue: Didactics of History (Odense 2007), p. 43-45.
[6] As a teacher of history didactics and educational history at university level I was elected member of the committee.

treatment of national and world history in the classroom. Critics, mainly the discourse of the right wing politicians, accepted that the integration of national and world history was appropriate in contemporary history, but were not convinced that it was expedient when teaching about earlier periods. However, the committee's decision had an immediate impact on the editing of textbooks. Since the implementation of these new rules, contemporary history as well as earlier history is organized according to the integration concept. In the committee the pre-national way of thinking in universalistic perspectives in history writing and teaching was an inspiration for the new way of combining national and world history. The new rules corresponded to the cosmopolitan ideas of the Enlightenment. In a pre-nationalistic society of multi-ethnic countries, it was natural to perceive the history of the state as part of a broader concept, which at least included the different states of Europe and the colonies. Today the conditions are not that different – mentally as well as structurally – and we can therefore use this history of education to be inspired to cope with the challenges of globalisation.[7]

Synchronic and diachronic

These two Greek concepts were introduced into the mandatory text in 2005. In this case the committee was inspired by historical conceptions: The mandatory text in connection with the reform of the old grammar school in 1775, didactical considerations from 1841 and a paper reflecting the debate among history teachers in 1976. In 1775 the two terms were used, I believe, for the first time in Denmark, and research in the most used textbooks form the end of the Eighteenth Century confirm that they were written in correspondence with them. At the end of the books, there was a table, wherein the synchronic dates were to be written in the horizontal columns and the diachronic main events were to be entered in the vertical columns. The intention was that the students each Saturday should re-read the entries and be given time to consider the connection between the vertical and the horizontal placed information. In an article written in 1841 by well-known Danish history teacher and researcher Caspar Paludan-Müller, on the subject of history education, he stressed that the combination of the synchronic and the diachronic way of teaching history was the best precondition for the development of the students understanding of universal history.[8]

---

[7] www.uvm.dk the general rules.

[8] H. Haue: History of didactics, (Odense, 2007), p. 15.

For the next hundred years or more, the two Greek concepts were seldom used. However, the two concepts next appeared in relation to history teaching in 1976. At that time, Danish history teachers were engaged in a great didactical debate. The reason for that was the reform of 1971, in which the subject had changed fundamentally. Until then the chronological reading had been dominant. In 1971 however, under influence from the students' rebellion in 1968, the new rules prescribed that students should only work with three to five items or periods before 1930, and there were no requirements for knowing anything about the developments between Rome at the time of Augustus, the Vikings and the industrial revolution. The reasons for the reform of history teaching were threefold: a) It should first of all prevent students using too much time on acquiring superficial knowledge about a great number of more or less unimportant events, b) The students should develop their methodological competencies instead. c) By toning down chronology it was possible to let the students have more participation when choosing items and which of them should be object for examination.

The methodological competences could be used in other subjects and naturally in life as well. The key word was training of the student's critical sense. A majority of history teachers protested against giving up the chronological reading, and the board of history teachers union at the upper secondary level felt inclined to form a new unofficial programme for the teaching of history. Their considerations were published in a special issue of the unions' magazine with the title: *History teaching in the future. A discussion paper. Diachronic and synchronic, 1066 and 1984*, which became an important part of the discourse. After many years of oblivion, the two Greek key-words were used again. In an interview with one of the members it was said the Italian economist Carlo Chipolla had inspired them, and they had not been taken from the rules of 1775 or indeed the article from 1841. However, Chipolla does not mention either synchronic or diachronic in his economic history. It is more likely however, as suggested by another member, that it was inspired by structuralism as it was used in the contemporary teaching of literature. Ferdinand de Saussure' linguistic programme developed around 1900, used the two Greek terms, and argued that the synchronic way of thinking must be dominant to the diachronic way of analysing languages. This science discourse might have been important. I asked my respondent why they reused the two concepts, and the answer was that the 1970s was a time when all values were open for discussion and abolition. The old chronological way of teaching history did not meet the requirements of the day, and therefore a new construction had to be developed, and in order to cope with this complex question, it was necessary to find concepts that could reduce the complexity to manageable entities. This mirrored the way that the 1970s became a transition-period from the industrial age to the age of a knowledge economy in Western Europe. In this period of fundamental transitions the members of the board must have felt the need for new constructive guidelines. The didactical solution was to combine the profound study of items with 'la longue durée' in the sense of Ferdinand Braudel. The dominant discourse was school based, but at the same time many university teachers supported the idea of punctual research-oriented synchronic treatment of a specific item, for example the impact of the crusades in different parts of the world in connection with an outline of history of the Middle Ages.[9]

However, in 2005 the inspiration came from 1775 as well as 1976 and for the second time the principle of a synchronic and diachronic approach to the past was used in a mandatory text. As the 1976 programmee marked the transition from the industrial to the information society, the 1770s was a time with a similar dramatic transition from agriculture to industry. In these late modern years of transition from information society to knowledge economy, the use of the two key words was widely accepted as meeting the requirements of the day. Recently those two concepts have also been introduced into history teaching in the Danish primary school.[10] This is another example of the impact of educational history by implementing old elements of history teaching when coping with new challenges.

Interdisciplinary work

The 2005-reform made interdisciplinary work mandatory. At least ten per cent of the lessons became committed to interdisciplinary work, which was enabled by a new structure. In turn this allowed all subjects to be able to co-operate. This was a didactical revolution, although since then many teachers complained about too many meetings and the difficulties arising over when history should co-operate with for example mathematics or biology. However, the new interdisciplinary teaching has some obvious advantages: hence it is possible to work on the fringes of the subjects, not only inside the well-established content of

[9] Ibidem, p. 81.

[10] Ibidem, p. 77. In order to develop reasonable connections between the teaching of history in the primary and the secondary school, I became member of both committees.

subject matter. Because of this, the subject of history has been challenged by the interdisciplinary work with other humanities subjects, the natural sciences and social sciences, and consequently had to define new subject-borders. In order to cope with this new situation the history teachers have to develop new didactical proceedings. Additionally, the authorities have given the subject of history a special responsibility in relation to the interdisciplinary work, such as the key position of developing the student's sense of unity across the sciences. This concept of the omnipotent role of history teaching has many forerunners. The famous Danish-Norwegian poly-histor, Ludvig Holberg, expressed similar views in 1732 in his *Historiæ Universalis*, and C. Paludan-Müller had the same notions in 1840s. The point was made many times later on for example in the 1880s and in the beginning of the Twentieth Century. In many ways History at the beginning of the Twenty First Century draws on conceptions from for example the poly historical Eighteenth Century approaches to teaching. In order to illustrate this point it is necessary to look at the development of disciplinary teaching in Denmark, at the upper secondary level. Going back to the Eighteenth Century, much of the education was interdisciplinary for several reasons. Apart from the last two years in the grammar school, the class had the same teacher in all subjects, often encompassing Greek, Latin, History, Religion and Mother Tongue and now and then some lessons in what ws called, *'Sfaerica'* or the natural sciences. In the Nineteenth Century during four reforms of teacher education at the university, the teacher became even more of a specialist teacher, who had one main subject and one or two minor subjects. From 1883, pedagogical and didactical supplementary education was required. The specialisation of teacher education was a function of the development of differentiation in several sciences and during the second half of the Nineteenth Century the borderlines between the subjects became clearly marked. The paired subjects of a specialist teacher were normally chosen from the same faculty, such as English and German, History and Geography, Greek and Latin and Mathematics and Physics. The mandatory texts never mentioned the cooperation between the subjects as desirable, and in the pedagogical literature it was seldom discussed.[11]

In the 1970s interdisciplinary work became a higher priority, however, since the reform in 1960, the upper secondary school had un-

[11] H. Haue: Didactics of History (Odense, 2007), p. 77.

dergone a process of specialisation, in which the students had several optional subjects and were therefore placed in different classes during each school day. Whilst specialisation was seen by many as the answer to the growing complexity of late modern society, the social complexity could also be addressed through interdisciplinary work. This posed a dilemma for politicians and educationists alike. The left wing parties wanted interdisciplinary organization of youth education, which should also be integrated with vocational education. The right wing parties did not want to integrate the gymnasium and the vocational training schools and had serious doubts concerning the blessings of the compulsory co-operation between subjects. For many years, the debates between these two points of view were outspoken. However, around 2000 the complexites of late modern society became so striking that obviously a compromise had to be made. In 2003, the parliament unanimously passed a new law for a reform of upper secondary education in Denmark, which introduced a structure that enabled all subjects to co-operate, and demanded that ten per cent of the lessons should be organised as interdisciplinary teaching. This was a revolution and naturally an enormous challenge for the teachers, who had to build teams and reflect upon core values of their subject in relation to two or three other subjects and to discuss a number of practical solutions. This situation resembles in some ways the conditions in the Eighteenth Century, but only to a certain extent. In the Eighteenth Century, the subjects were diverging and in the Twenty First Century, they appear to be converging. In the first period, the teacher was a generalist and in the latter a specialist. However, apart from these not negligible differences, there are also similarities. In both periods there was a need for a dialogue between different subjects in order to cope with social changes. Compared to the Nineteenth and most of the Twentieth Century, the Enlightenment and the postmodern era had weaker boundaries in relation to the sciences as well as between nations. Therefore there are good reasons to compare the history of education of 1795 and 2005. Research in the history of education is the only way to utilize educational experiences in order to avoid ignorance and misuse of the past. It is equally important to make this research known in the public.

Allgemeinbildung

The reform of the grammar schools in 1850 introduced '*almendannelse*' as a new overall purpose of education. The concept was a translation of the German *Allgemeinbildung*, which was developed by J. H. Herbart and W. von Humboldt in the beginning of the Nineteenth Century within the context of philosophical idealism. This concept was used in the German speaking world and the Nordic countries, and is still normative for the Danish gymnasium, whereas Sweden changed to an Anglo-American way of thinking about curriculum, where the concept is not used. In 1946 a national education committee decided not to recommend the further use of '*almendanning*', and one of the arguments was that this concept had not prevented Germans from supporting Hitler, and it was characterized as an exaggerated romantic German heritage. However, in Denmark '*almendannelse*' is still the overriding goal for the teaching in the gymnasium, although there has been an ongoing debate on its content and function. This very fundamental concept in Danish educational development does not exist in English and is difficult to translate, but 'general character development' would indicate the principal substance. In the latest research '*almendannelse*' has been defined as:

> An education, which comprises the common (*almene*) parts of the sciences and disciplines that society needs so as to develop the students' personal authority to reflect over their relationship with their fellow human beings, nature and society.[12]

The concept therefore consists of two parts: the selection of materials and purposes of learning. The concept is broad, but may not contain everything; for example in 1850 Hebrew was not included in the new collection of disciplines with the reference that it did not belong to general cultivation. On the other hand in 1988 general aspects of computer science were accepted as being a part of the student's general formation. The subject matter shall be presented in a way as to strengthen the students' ability to reflect. It is also important to note that '*almendannelse*' is singular, on the contrary to the plural 'competences', and thereby indicates a holistic education. The concept can be conceived as a *formula of contingency* in the sense that Luhmann uses the concept, which facilitates communication about a difficult communicative subject matter by reducing complexity; in other words a linguistic frame for understanding and operating in a complex reality.[13]

---

[12] H. Haue. Didactics of History, p. 43. See also: H. Haue. Algemeinbildung – ein deutsches Begriff im dänischen Gymnasium (Odense, 2008), p. 8.

[13] N. Luhmann: Das Erziehungssystem der Gesellschaft (Frankfurt am Main, 2002), p. 82.

The 1850-reform corresponded to the idea of the existence of a holistic culture and therefore the students needing to have a common curriculum, which contained: the classical languages, natural sciences, modern languages and subjects like history, religion and the mother tongue. This was a very ambitious curriculum, and in the next two decades parents and teachers complained that the students were overburdened with thirty-six lessons a week and several hours of daily homework. At the same time natural scientists wanted more lessons for their own subjects at the expense of Latin. The classical philologists could not accept this, and in 1871 the Gordian knot had to be cut by the creation of a two-tier gymnasium, a reform inspired by developments in Sweden and France. The two-tier gymnasium was a challenge to the idea of a holistic culture, and some doubt was expressed as to the appropriateness of still using 'almendannelse'. The gymnasium was to educate two different types of students; one with a classical and the other with a natural sciences option. Those in favour of the two tier solution argued that a more complex society demanded a more complex school, where the students should have a choice corresponding to their interests and abilities. His Majesties Inspector, a respected classical philologist, had to accept the political decision, but he avoided using 'almendannelse' in the new general rules. However, the concept was used as before the reform, and thereby indicated an approval of the students' ability to acquire 'almendannelse' on the basis of different curricular contents. In a reform in 1903 a third tier was added to the existing two, based on modern languages. In the goals paragraph the term 'almendannelse' was reinstated and the argument that the gymnasium should not give the students a common culture, but offer them the opportunity to form their own culture within a broader curricular framework, won general acceptance. In the debate on the development of the Danish gymnasium the majority accepted the more expansive concept. However, a suggestion to incorporate vocational subjects in the gymnasium was rejected with the argument that commercial correspondence and book-keeping did not contribute to the development of the students 'almendannelse'. The argument was substantiated by the fact that those subjects functioned as a preparation to specific trades and therefore they could not contribute to the students' 'general character development'.

The debate in the first half of the Twentieth Century was concerned about the nature of 'almendannelse'. Critics argued that it was an old-fashioned concept, which had a conservative influence on the development of the gymnasium. In 1960 the reform committee had a profound discussion of the content and function of 'almendannelse'. The background was that social developments and new scientific knowledge had to be part of the curriculum. The solution was a more differentiated and more outspoken scientific education and, as so often during the last century, the agenda focussed around whether 'almendannelse' could and should be used as the over-riding goal for teaching in the gymnasium. Instead of 'almendannelse' it was perhaps better to use the term, 'general humanistic orientation'. However, the committee ended up with the conclusion that 'almendannelse' was expansive enough to comprise the new more differentiated and scientific education. In order to create a comprehensive understanding of the connections between the subjects it was decided to introduce a book on the history of European ideas, which all students should read in relation to their work with the specific subjects. In reality this solution had only a cosmetic function but served as a pretext for the maintenance of an imagined unity of the education. One of the members of the committee, a professor of French, refused to accept the new school subject of Social Science on the grounds that it did not sufficiently contribute to the students' 'general character development'. From 1963 the classical line was abandoned, but it was still possible for the students after the first year to choose Latin and Greek as main subjects. Challenges from late modern society led to a reform in 1988, which gave the students the opportunity to choose among a number of new subjects and then to follow their interests and compose exactly the kind of education which they thought they needed. The reform weakened the gymnasiums 'bildung-character' by taking into account the many individual preferences, and thereby came to emulate the Anglo-American curriculum model, where each student's freedom to choose combinations of subjects is considered important. However, the implication was that the pupils of a class more than had been the case previously only had a limited number of subjects in common, while in the remaining time they followed various optional subjects. For this reason it was only possible to establish interdisciplinary cooperation between the common subjects mostly history and Danish. This further atomizing process was criticised during the 1990s and a new, more 'bildungs' orientated discourse became hegemonic. In 2003 a very large Parliamentary majority passed a new law regarding upper secondary education, where the most substantial innovation was the decision for all pupils to have virtually all courses in one class. It then became possible for all subjects to cooperate, and for ten per cent of the lessons, interdisciplinary work became compulsory. The main purpose was to ensure that central problems in a complex world could be treated in school as this would often require more than one subject to find an answer. Earlier the growing complexity was met with more subjects and more choices for the students.

The reform, which was implemented in 2005 solved the challenge of complexity in a radically different way. Through this development a number of subjects established by the former reform were not longer important. The answer to complexity was interdisciplinary work. In 2002 one of the central issues in the educational debate was the question: Could the purpose of education after such a radical reform still be '*almendannelse*'? Some felt that the answer was no, because the concept was too old fashioned to cope with the new challenges. Another argument was that Denmark was one of very few countries in the world to use '*almendannelse*', which made it difficult to compare the Danish gymnasium to those of other countries. Therefore it was better to restrict the goal, as before 1850, to 'preparation for further studies'. In this connection it was pointed out that '*almendannelse*' was not just considered old fashioned but also difficult to define. Others advocated for the maintenance of the concept because the reform expressed exactly the idea of 'general character development'. At this crucial point my dissertation was published.[14] In this book, I undertook an archaeological research on the function of the concept in Danish upper-secondary education 1770-2000. Before I had the opportunity to defend my thesis, I was invited to address teacher union members and the Minister of Education and to give an outline of the impact of the concept on educational development. A few days later the Minister of Education invited me to her office in order further to elaborate on the concept in relation to the reform text, which was then drafted. Then I was called to the parliamentary committee on education, and have reasons to believe that our discussions confirmed their determination to maintenance the use of '*almendannelse*' as the goal for education in the Danish gymnasium. [15] My 600 pages dissertation was reviewed in the newspapers and was out of print within a couple of months. When the Ministry of Education came to formulate the paragraph dealing with the purpose of the education, I was consulted. In the following years there was a general consent to the appropriateness of this goal for education at the upper-secondary level. However,

[14] H. Haue. Almendannelse som ledestjerne. En undersøgelse af almendannelsens funktion i dansk gymnasieundervisning 1770-2000 (Odense, 2003). A shortened edition appeared in 2004. Almendannelse for tiden – en ledetråd i dansk gymnasieundervisning (Odense, 2004)

[15] H. Haue. Allgemeinbildung. Ein deutscher Begriff im dänischen Gymnasium (Odense 2008), p. 221.

critics have pointed out that praxis in many cases does not correspond to the intentions of the overall goal; this however, is also an old story.

Conclusion

Educational history matters. This article has shown that knowledge of history of education has had some impact in the latest reform process concerning the Danish upper-secondary school. In the case of the subject of history substantial elements and principles were inspired from earlier general rules and debates. It was therefore important that the committee was aware of this heritage. As to the normative goal for the upper-secondary education, there are god reasons to believe that research in the development of '*almendannelse*' may have contributed to its maintenance. One of the most important tasks is to give the curriculum studies a historical perspective, because knowledge of a subjects' history is an important part of its didactical development. It is equally important that research in history of education focuses on continuity in order to describe the strongest elements in a tradition, because they may deserve special attention in situations where a rupture is emerging. Therefore it is important that the researcher of history of education communicates on a scientific as well as on a popular level, and makes the past present.

The Uses and Abuses of Contemporary University History in Denmark

Else Hansen

Universities and other institutes of higher education are central to a society's intellectual development, both through teaching and research. The role of universities is not static in society but open to debate subject to, amongst other things, shifting attitudes towards the importance of knowledge, research, higher education and the relationship between the private and public sectors. This means that not only the present condition of universities, but also their history is important in understanding both the contemporary role they play and how this may develop in the future.

The history of universities should be primarily regarded as the written accounts we find in historical publications and also yearbooks, which describe the conditions of the universities as they once were. Historical works are usually founded upon academic study of sources and other materials, which can shed light on the history of universities. Anniversary literature typically contains contributions, which openly stem from the authors' recollections as participants in the earlier phases of the university's history.

Alongside such university history is the more or less commonly or lay understood senses. These are the opinions relating to past events formed by individuals and groups. Popular conceptions such as these are often based on interpretations of recollection and experience but not necessarily with a basis in historical studies of the source material. These popular conceptions of the history of universities is most often communicated anecdotally or as an undocumented aside in an unrelated context where the intention is to comment on the present using historical allegories rather than to understand the past.

History is interpreted in relation to contemporary events

The past can be used as a precedent for present initiatives. The History of Universities contains – like other historical subjects – examples of history being used and influenced by events contemporary to the historical analysis. When history is employed in that way, it is rarely source-based, but is instead, based upon experience and recollection which fit the actually relevant interpretation. An example of this from my current research on Danish University Policy 1945-1975, concerns the understanding of and utilisation of the history of the inception of the Faculty Law.

The Faculty Law fixed the internal, organisational structure of the universities and was ratified by the Danish Parliament in 1970. With the introduction of this law, all teachers (rather than simply professors) and students were given considerable influence over the internal running of the universities. Until then, only the professors influenced research and teaching policies – a privilege which they guarded jealously. The expansions of the 1960s brought an increased number of students and teachers who were not professors.

During the 1960s, there were criticisms of professorial privileges over research and teaching from many sides. Many politicians wanted universities to be more open to the needs of society, graduates were to be better equipped to meet the challenges of the job market and their research should address pressing social problems such as the developing countries and the mass media. The central administration wanted better opportunities to influence (control) the universities, which were becoming steadily more expensive to run due to their constant expansion. Last but not least, the new lecturers who bore a larger part of the new teaching burden wanted more influence over the running of the universities. The conservative academic mandarins, however, stood in the way of these demands.

An Education Ministry committee worked on these problems between 1962 and 1968, without reaching a consensus. The committee's report contained no less than six minority statements. This was first and foremost an admission that there was no agreement over the proposed changes. There were also large areas of disagreement between the representatives of different universities. However the report did show that there was a desire for change for example, concerning the competence of the rector in matters of research policy.[1]

Both lecturers and students expressed disappointment that the report did not contain any suggestions concerning an increased influence for their respective groups. Lecturers held meetings and framed resolu-

[1] Universitetsadministrationsudvalget af 1962: Betænkning II om den højere undervisnings og forskningens administrative organisation. (University Administrations Commitee 1962 - Motion II referring to higher education and research administration. Betænkning, 475, Copenhagen 1968)

tions. Students occupied university buildings and demanded the establishment of a Student Council in every subject area. The Rector of Copenhagen University was among the committee's minority. He wanted to introduce a new policy directive, which would rely upon a broader mandate than just professorial votes. He also wanted to see a broader range of opinions represented in the Faculty Direction. The committee's work had shown that the new structure he sought would not be achieved by conventional means – in a committee the rectors of other universities and higher educational institutions could obstruct his proposals. With this in mind it was no surprise that he supported the student movement as fully as his position allowed him. By the end of the following year, the demands of the students had become the demands of Copenhagen University, voted in by a narrow majority in the Chancellery and sent to the Ministry of Education where a bill of law was formed along the same lines.

Not only would the rector have a widened area of responsibility and the institutes would be larger with an elected leadership, but also what was remarkable about the new Faculty Law, was that the professors would no longer be in a privileged position. The teaching groupings at the universities would be integrated and lecturers and professors would participate in leadership matters on an equal footing. The students would have 50% of the seats in the Student Council and in the case of financial bodies the students would hold 33% of the seats. The right wing parties in parliament, who held the majority and formed the government at the time, passed this law. Conversely the Social Democrats and the left wing voted against as they wanted to secure the students a greater influence in the running of the universities. The student protests of the late 1960s were the factor which brought about the changes in the running of the universities which had been desired for so long by everyone but the professors. The Faculty Law had, however, been adopted by a right wing government.

As soon as the law was passed, the newspapers' interpretation of events gave the students all the responsibility for the new leadership structure. What had happened, according to them, was that the faculties and politicians had allowed themselves to be "pressurized" by demonstrating students into passing the new law. In this way, criticism not originating with the students themselves became invisible. In addition it was not made clear that conditions had been criticised before

1968.[2] During the 1970s there was an increased polarisation of opinion at the universities. Many students expressed ever-sharper criticism of university policy, which increasingly took its lead from Marxist theory. At the same time the state introduced more control and administrative mechanisms. During the 1970s and 80s, the Faculty Law was constantly under discussion. Some were dissatisfied that critical students – often in collusion with large and small groups of lecturers – were, de facto, availing themselves of all the opportunities, which the law gave them. Others felt that the law did not give them enough influence and were strongly critical of the state and its reforms.

At the beginning of the 1980s, the Faculty Law was denounced in public debate as, "the result of the panic surrounding the student protests of the 1960s", [3] or simply as "the most important result of the student protests" .[4] The Faculty Law was, in fact, the result of a surprising alliance between right wing politicians and critical, activist students, both groups agreeing on the need for change in the leadership structure of the universities. All parties quickly forgot this alliance. The students got the credit – or the responsibility – for the law, which was changed in 1993.

The politician Bertel Haarder was a particularly harsh critic of the Faculty Law at the start of the 1980s. He represented the Venstre (economic liberal), which had been a party to the legislation in 1970, and was Minister for Education between 1982 and 1993. It is striking that, in debate, he never mentions that his own party was a supporter of the law. On the other hand, he never gives the student movement any credit for the law – perhaps that would be to admit the extent of their influence. Instead, he rails against something more diffuse, which he refers to as the 1960's ideology of "democratisation and popular meetings", and that "students and char ladies" have become equal members of university governing bodies.[5]

What was forgotten was that the student protest had been instrumental in abolishing the absolute dominance of the professors in universities in favour of a system which gave both non-professorial

---

[2] Dich, Jørgen S.: Universiteternes fremtid(The Future of Universities) in Berlingske Tidende, 20.3.1970.

[3] Meyer, Poul: Lapperier på universiteterne (Bodging at the Universities) in Jyllands Posten 22.3.1984.

[4] Asmussen, Kaj: "Guldhornsromantik i styrelsesloven" ("Golden age romanticism and the Faculty Law") in Aarhus Stifttidende 4.1.1986.

[5] Brøndum, Chr: Forskere om politisk misbrug af styrelsesloven(Researchers on the political abuse of the Faculty Law) in Berlingske Tidende, 22.2.1981.

teachers, other university employees and students influence in the running of the university. The power vacuum left by the professors was partially filled internally but also allowed for a greater degree of state intervention under the new system. In the 1970s, the political climate of the universities became increasingly polarised with a strong left-wing student movement on the one hand and ever more stringent state control on the other. It was against this background that it was expedient to make the Faculty Law synonymous with the Student Protests, and to therefore stress that, if the law were repealed then the critical students would disappear with it.

It was only on the occasion of the 40th anniversary of the student protests that a serious account of the student movement in Denmark first appeared. The study examines the Danish students, their motives and organisations closely but does not address the developments in state administration of the universities. This study questions, not least, the student movement's internal organisation, motives and trends, thus providing a more nuanced insight into the student movement which until now had been based on recollection and politically influenced assessment as described above.[6]

However, student protests and the abolition of professorial privileges can still be seen as a clear improvement in conditions at the universities, and terms from the debate over the introduction of the Faculty Law can still be used to separate the "good" and "bad" guys. This occurred with the launching of the website "Research Freedom" which is home to to an animated and high-level discussion of the changes in the running of the universities, which is currently in progress. I shall emphasise that the blog is characterised by serious and scholarly contributions, but I would like to draw attention to the original name (and current URL) of the blog which is "Professorial regime", apparently because it associates with the overthrow of the old governing forms in the universities which many still remember and which gave such widespread influence to lecturers and students. The problem today is not the "professorial regime" but a technocratic political regime. The new, and heavily criticised, conditions at the universities have not, as yet, had a name coined for them with as much symbolic value as "The Professorial Regime", which stems from the period of student protest and which relates to the increased influence wielded by students on the internal conditions of

[6] Jensen, Steven L.B. og Thomas Ekman Jørgensen: 1968 - og det der fulgte: studenteroprørets forudsætninger og konsekvenser (1968 and what followed: The student protest and its concequences) (Copenhagen, 2008).

the universities. The name of the blog was changed after a brief debate where, amongst other things, it was pointed out that "the professors had less power than ever before" and that the current problem should be dubbed "admin regime."[7] This example has not been used to discredit this excellent blog but to show how the history of universities can be used to underscore current conflicts.

The two examples of how the student protests in 1968 have been used in order to make sense of later developments at the universities show how history can be used to cast perspective on present. This is not necessarily built on a foundation of academic study, but rather upon one of subjective interpretation based on actual events or possibly recollection of the events in question.

Major reforms and historical interpretation

More general references to history can be observed when new political reforms are presented. It is at such times that Education Ministers can be heard to say that the particular reform in question is the first or biggest since a given precedent.

This happened when the Faculty Law was presented to parliament in 1969. The minister for education explained that, with the introduction of the constitution in 1849, no new legislation concerning the universities had been introduced; instead the existing conditions had been maintained with rules enacted by royal decree and not through parliament. This would in 1970 be corrected by the introduction of specific legislation, which would regulate the conditions within higher education. That the universities were now submitting to legislation was seen as one of the greatest advantages of the Faculty Law. With this historical interpretation, the right wing Minister of Education identified closely with the activist students' rhetoric. The students called the previous governing structure at the universities, "the professorial regime" with a historical nod to the "ancient regime" which preceded democracy and the constitution. The minister underlined the antiquated state of the universities in society by claiming that only they were unlegislated for. Whether this was a correct assessment, I am unable to judge. I can however, mention that as late as 2007 a debate about new legislation concerning baptism took place. It was to replace a previous law from 1828![8]

---

[7] <http://redfriforsk.blogspot.com/2007/01/om-bloggen-forskningsfrihed.html> [visited 31.03.2008]

[8] <www.folkekirken.dk> [visited 1.4.2008]

The responsable minister, Helge Sander, presented his reform plans for the universities accompanied by the observation that this reform was the biggest since 1479; the year of Copenhagen University's foundation. The 2003 reform strengthened the universities' leadership dramatically and placed the universities' upper administration in the hands of committees with a majority of member recruited from outside the academic world. The reform, therefore, changed established administrative systems, but when the reform is presented in context of previous reforms, it becomes an example of the use of history in highlighting a contemporary innovation rather than comparing it to previous reforms.[9]

In both these examples of large-scale reforms being launched amongst historical references, academic studies and publications concerning the history of universities in a longer perspective have been published to set the particular events in the context of this perspective. After the student protests Ole B. Thomsen published his "The University of Civil Service Studies" in 1975, in 1979 Olaf Pedersen published his "Studium Generale" and in 2007 Jens Erik Kristensen published "Ideas for a University" with an introduction by Jens Erik Kristensen.[10]

In their forewords, all three works make reference the contemporary political situation at the universities. In the 1970s, the student protests and in 2007, the University Law of 2003. In "Studium Generale", Olaf Pedersen reminds the reader that student's demands for greater influence over their study conditions "belongs to the agenda of the long term history of universities"; in fact, since the 11th century in Bologna.[11] The reason for examining "The University of Civil Service Studies" and the foundation of 1788 benefiting Copenhagen University is, according to author Ole B. Thomsen, that within the foundation can be observed the structure for university study that was valid until the end of the 1960s. He asserts that a long-term historical view is required

---

[9] Aarsland, Line: I dialog med Sander (A dialog with Sander) in Universitetsavisen 5, 2002. Pedersen, Lars Nørgaard: Minister: Universiteter skal tilpasse sig erhvervslivet (Minister: The university must adapt to the commercial sector) in Jyllandsposten, 16.3.2002.

[10] Pedersen, Olaf: Studium generale (Copenhagen, 1979) / The first universities: studium generale and the origins of university education in Europe (Cambridge University Press, 1997). Thomsen, Ole B.: Embedsstudiernes universitet: en undersøgelse af Københavns universitets fundats af 1788 som grundlag for vores nuværende studiestruktur. (Vocational university: an investigation of the university charter of 1788 as a basis for our present curriculum) Vols I og II (Copenhagen, 1975). Ideer om et universitet: det moderne universitets idehistorie fra 1800 til i dag (Ideas for a University: the modern history of universities from 1800 to the present), ed.by Jens Erik Kristensen (Aarhus, 2007).

[11] Olaf Petersen: Studium Generale. 1979, page 9-10.

in order to understand what was changed after almost 200 years in the 1960s and 70s. The introduction to "Ideas for a University" from 2007 is titled simply "The University Law of 2003 as a departure point". It points out a paradox, that the classic ideas behind a university are maintained as a goal but are abandoned in practice in that the meaning of autonomy shifts from institutional autonomy, to that which the author calls operational autonomy i.e. the freedom to fill the preset political parameters. In contrast to the two books from the 1970s, this book is not a unified publication but a collection of translated texts on the ideas behind universities.

Whilst Olaf Pedersen merely comments on contemporary conditions on the basis of his research, it is more explicit in the case of Ole B. Thomsen and Jens Erik Kristensen that they are dealing with a reaction to the contemporary political conditions in the university sector. Researchers have wanted to create a deeper historical understanding of the actual reforms and thereby contribute to a qualification of the debate.

Anniversary literature and the formation of identity

The Jubilee Commemorative Books is a very important literary grouping in the Danish history of universities, which has not yet been referred to. These make up the largest literary grouping in the History of Universities as even the newest of the "traditional" Danish universities is now over 25 years old and has published a jubilee book.[12]

Jubilee books should first and foremost create an identity, the identity of the university itself, not least the people, who have worked there for longer or shorter terms. This story should be told properly, with all the event lines leading up to the jubilee and making it worthy of celebration. As Rector Carl F. Wendel described in his foreword to Aarhus University's 50 years Jubilee book from 1978:

> "It is a natural occupation at the time of a jubilee, to see what has been achieved and by whom...Just as with the university's very existence this book reminds us with good reason, memory and witness of the debt of gratitude we

[12]Aarhus Universitet 1928-1978, ed. by Gustav Albeck (Århus, 1978). Københavns Universitet 1479-1979 (Copenhagen University 1479 1979) 14 volumes with Leif Grane et. al. (Copenhagen, 1979-2005). Boje, Per og Knud J.V. Jespersen: Frugten vokser frem. (Pastures new) (Odense, 1991). Oldenburg, Peter Ditlev: Glimt: glimt fra nordjysk universitetshistorie gennem 40 år: AalborgUniversitet fylder 25 (Glimpses from Northern Jutish University History over 40 years: Aalborg University at 25.) (Aalborg, 1999). Aarhus Universitet 1978-2003, ed. Ingeborg Christensen (Aarhus, 2005).

> owe those far-sighted and energetic people who have co-operated in the creation of Aarhus University and the many who have helped them."[13]

The publication commemorating 500 years of Copenhagen University is far more detailed, consisting of 14 volumes rather than the 50 or 75 year jubilee books for Århus, which restrict themselves to one volume. Despite their size, the two jubilee books are constructed in the same way. This is with general paragraphs on the running of the university and the research and teaching situation whilst individual departments are dealt with in separate volumes or chapters authored by the department's own members who do not necessarily have any comprehensive knowledge of subject or faculy history, the relevant source material or historical presentation.

The 1991 jubilee book from Odense University is the work of only two authors, two historians who have shared their study period between them. It gives a less detailed insight into the individual departments' development, but a more unified presentation of the university's history. On the occasion of Aalborg University's silver jubilee in 1999 a collection of interviews by a journalist were published. These covered important aspects of the university's history as described by those who had taken part in the events.

One can find a wealth of concrete information concerning conditions at the universities, their economy, research and teaching contained in jubilee books. The books seek to create a shared understanding of just how "we" have come to be where we are. This means that past disagreements are downplayed and presented as resolved. The alternative to presenting past disagreements as irrelevant and resolved is to look into the conflicts, describe the elements of which they consisted and their consequences in the long and short terms. This is to risk uncovering things, which have been deliberately forgotten.

Roskilde University Centre

Roskilde University Centre was founded in 1972, partly as a necessary relief for Copenhagen University - hence the proximity (30 km) to Copenhagen - and partly as a new university where new theories of teaching, teamwork and course length could be tried out. In addition to this, the new Faculty Law and a relatively strong student movement meant that the students at Roskilde University Centre gained a greater influ-

[13] Rector's foreword. Carl F. Wandel. Aarhus Universitet 1928-1978. 1978.

ence over the structure of their studies than students had traditionally had. The free study boundaries were exploited to pursue studies, which were compatible with Roskilde University Centre's unofficial motto: "a university working for working class interests" which were studies with a background in Marxist theory.

Scared, the government and parliament responded, several times, by threatening to close Roskilde University Centre. A large number of students were given notice of impending expulsion and, for a while, an external rectory was set up. It finally became clear that the ambition of, "a university working for working class interests", would have to give way to budgetary directives from the Ministry of Education and demands were made for the closure of several departments at Roskilde University Centre, the internal historical viewpoint of the university changed quickly.

The historical viewpoint had previously focused on the contemporary conflicts between left-wing students and lecturers and, non left-wing lecturers, the administration and the government and their insistence on a broad intellectual spectrum of study. This focus now shifted to show Roskilde University Centre as a reaction to the "Professorial Regime", and to rigid and tradition bound universities. Instead of looking at the student protests of the 1970's, there was a robust dismissal of the harsh criticisms levelled at Roskilde University Centre by the right-wing press at the conditions there. The conflicts of the 1970's came to be seen as a question of the opposition between Roskilde University Centre's just and reasonable goals and the unreasonable interference and demands of the ministry and a witch-hunt in the right-wing press. Boel Jørgensen, rector at Roskilde University Centre 1978-1988, has explained that this new approach was first actualised when she deliberately emphasised the relaying of positive stories from Roskilde University Centre.

Only the editorship of the annual information bulletin for new students was remiss in discovering that the university had a new story to tell. As late as 1980 there were armed Sandanista guerrillas on the front cover. This resulted in harsh internal criticism and was the last of its kind.

Whilst other universities had published one book to mark jubilee years, Roskilde University Centre's silver jubilee, in 1997, resulted in no less than three books being published. The least official of the three was that published by the Students Council, which contained a feature on the early history of Roskilde University Centre, partly made up of essays by a prominent student activist, who had been employed as a lecturer throughout its history. This book told the history of Roskilde University Centre according to the new historical viewpoint which had dominated since the 1980's. However, the conflicts, which had resulted in the departure from the original historical narrative, were not described.[14] Another jubilee book – edited by the rector and therefore very official – contains a series of personal recollections from all periods of Roskilde University Centre's history which are described by the participants themselves and based on their personal experiences. This type of book gives space to different historical perspectives without them necessarily conflicting.[15]

The third book had only one author, yours truly. I had disobeyed the most important commandment of writing a jubilee book – namely to write a book which reflected everyone's experience and which everyone could feel justified by.[16] I had, with a basis in the archive material, discovered that the historical viewpoint at Roskilde University Centre had changed radically and I presented this as one of my most important conclusions. I pointed out that Roskilde University Centre had moved from one strategy to another in a process whereby the ideas and events of the 1970s were not denied; they were merely interpreted in a new way. This includes, for example, the unusual teaching methods at Roskilde University Centre such as problem-orientated group projects. This was justified in the 1970s as an excellent approach to completing studies in the interests of the working class, later this changed to the justification that it gave students skills essential to competing in the job market.

That there were three jubilee books shows a university, which had not reached a consensus over its history.

History as a starting point for change

Above, we have shown how university history has been used to create a specific understanding of contemporary conditions. History however, can be used as a starting point for change. An example of this can be seen in the University Commission of 1935-43. The Commission was intended to work on administration and teaching policy at Copenhagen University. It was this commission whose latest version of administration policy had triggered the student protests in 1968. Only four of the fourteen mem-

---

[14] Nielsen, Jens Chr., Niels Hasselgaard Jensenius, Henning Salling Olesen: Utopien der slog rod. RUC – radikalitet og realisme (The Utopia that took Root. Roskilde University Center. Radicalism and Realism.) (Roskilde, 1997).

[15] RUC i 25 år, (Roskilde University Center at 25) ed. by Henrik Toft Jensen et al. (Frederiksberg, 1997).

[16] Else Hansen: En koral i tidens strøm. RUC 1972-1997 (A Coral in the Stream of Time). (Frederiksberg, 1997).

bers of the commission were from the university. The others were from political parties and from the central administration, and even at this stage they had a strong influence on conditions at the university. What is worth mentioning here is that the commission collected historical accounts as a basis for its work with university conditions – also in the case of students' economies. The commission would reform, but after historical precedent.[17]

If we fast-forward to 1967, the picture is somewhat different. "The Plan Sketch" was a blueprint for the development of the institutes of higher education up to 1980. The greatly increased intake of students and the rise of the computer have made it both possible and necessary to plan according to statistics and prognoses. I would not call prognoses history. However, prognoses from 1967 were projections of the preceding conditions and development in gymnasiums and the tendency to apply for higher education. In that sense, the immediate past was used in planning. Whether this constitutes a use of history is open to debate.[18]

The latest reform in 2003 was launched as the greatest reform since 1479, the year of Copenhagen University's foundation. This historical precedent is the only one contained in the reform. Instead of taking a position based on historical precedent the minister emphasised that, in the future, universities should follow the needs of the market and Danish universities were to be able to compete internationally. The global argument was to be decisive.

The uses of the History of Universities

I want to conclude, that there has been no supply of or demand for the history of universities in the last 40-50 years. The planning and development of reform has been based on statistics and prognoses and later on the case for globalisation. The continuation or repudiation of university tradition has not occupied a prominent place in the debate and has not, therefore, resulted in a demand for studies and reflections in university history. The administration of universities by the state has not led to a demand for historical study or reflection on its role

The literature concerning the history of Danish universities is dominated by the anniversary publications and it is through these that university

[17] Betænkning afgivet af Universitetskommissionen af 1935. 1. Del. 1936. 5. Del. 1943. (Report from the Committee for Education 1935).

[18] Planlægningsrådet for de højere uddannelser: Skitse for udbygningen af de højere uddannelser i tiden indtil 1980 (Planning Council For Higher Education: Sketches for developments in higher education for the period ending 1980). (Copenhagen, June 1967).

history has primarily been used, to shape identities for institutes, faculties and people. Anniversary publications can be excellent but they do not, nor do they attempt to, set the universities in the context of societal development encompassing state politics, intellectual development or sociological changes in student teacher relations. Therefore, the history of universities has only been lightly dealt with in a methodical way. There seems to have been a degree of academic reserve and hesitation when addressing this subject. A whole generation of historians has been influenced by the polarised university culture of the 1970's in which many were active participants. The lack of will to research the subject may be a result of too many historians believing that they know the subject all too well from their own student days. In addition to this a historian of universities will inevitably end up writing his or her own history – unless they deliberately choose an earlier period – and must write about former colleagues and teachers, to take sides in conflicts which might not be regarded as settled by all participants.

The books which together form the field of study of the history of universities – and there are more than I have referred to here – each has its importance and relevance. Despite this, I would postulate that we lack a Danish University History. The characteristics of the present sources are those of individual works without reference to each other. The driving force behind many of the works is the desire to sketch current or recollected conditions rather than to address broader academic questions.

In 1968 when so much changed at universities throughout the western world, The Committee for Academic Cooperation suggested that an institute for research into political questions concerning higher education should be set up.[19] The Committee for Academic Cooperation wanted to create a better basis for future reform, as they felt that the contemporary reforms were being built on untried foundations. I have not found evidence of any serious discussion of the matter. At Copenhagen University, an institute of University Pedagogic Method was founded, which produced the previously mentioned book by Ole B. Thomsen. But we still lack a Danish research centre which deals with the ideas, politics and history of universities. This is in contrast to Sweden where the – much maligned – University Chancellery has supported research of

---

[19] Rigsarkivet: Undervisningsministeriet, 3. afdeling, 1. kontor, Journalsager 50-0-7/68 (pk.271) "Udtalelse fra AS efter konferencen den 21/3-68". 1968.03.21. (National Archives: Ministry of Education 3rd Dept, 1st Office. Files 50-0-7/68 (pk.271) "Statement by AS after conference of 21/3-68")

universities since 1972. From 1992-97 there was another independent research body concerned with higher education.[20]

I have given examples of how history has been applied – or denied – to create a particular picture, which can accompany a contemporary proposal or perception. Events and periods in university history have been used by politicians to assist their latest proposals or opinions but there have been several examples of unsustainable generalisations and interpretations which – consciously or not – look selectively at the events they refer to. Several jubilee books do not have a collected narrative of their university's history but intentionally have fragmented snapshots provided by multiple authors whose experience and opinions mirror the widest possible spectrum of the readership and which therefore strengthens rather than challenges the existing collective identity.

University history has not been produced exclusively by academic critique of sources relating to aspects of the past but by a contemporary use of history where individual elements are highlighted in order to show contemporary conditions in a certain light. The many examples of the application of university history in the context of contemporary events shows that historical studies are produced whether or not they are academically grounded. It is strange that all sides are apparently satisfied with the existing historical interpretations, which recollection and political relations have resulted in. It is my contention that any sign of critical, thorough and source-based research is lacking and should be sought. It would not necessarily mean that the history of universities be utilised more precisely. However, it would hopefully mean that it will be easier to challenge unsupported interpretations.

[20] Forskning om forskning i Norden. (Research on Research in Nordic Countries) Ed. by Stefan Björklund. TemaNord 1994:530.

Politics and Educational Historiography: Criticizing "Civilization" and Shaping Educational Policies in Latin America

Marcelo Caruso

The discourse of social sciences postulates the distinctive character of a knowledge shaped by methodical rigour and objectiveness. Western societies assume that knowledge in a "scientific" context develops as a differentiating process from "interested" and biased forms of knowledge production. In particular, the question of a "politicization" of science has become a topos in scholarship dealing especially with dictatorships and ideological dominance in the brief 20th century. The accusation of "politicization" suggests the irruption of an alien logic of action into the process of knowledge production, leading to a contamination of "good" scholarship in the context of the social sciences. The critique of this fundamental belief of Western science has been a recurrent subject of critical approaches to the social sciences. Yet the possibility of a certain politicization of scholarly work simultaneously leading to a more professional and differentiated standard of scholarship has rarely been addressed.

In the following, I will propose this focus in dealing with Latin American educational historiography. As a particular form of scholarship within the "social sciences", educational historiography is certainly affected by changing manifestations of zeitgeist and different waves of theoretical and historiographical work. Discourses on the educational past – as with all discourses in the social sciences – not only display versions of past forms of education, socialization and learning, but are also informative with regard to the preferences, commitments, and intellectual orientations of their producers. However, the sense of the term "politicization" alluded to in these pages is more profound than a general connection between prevalent ideologies and intellectual preferences. The very object of educational historiography changed in the 1970s in this region, and criticism of founding categories of narratives concerning the educational past was conceived of not as a mere exercise of scholarly argumentation, but rather as a political act to change the sense of educational activities. The privileged relationship of a renewed educational historiography in Latin America to politics seems to have been both a characteristic of a regional culture of scholarship and a distinctive attempt to assess the relevance of the *raison d'être* of this discipline.

I will present my argument in two parts. First, I will proceed with the emergence of a Latin American historiography of education from the late 19th century onwards, in order to delineate the founding narratives used by liberal intellectuals at that time. I will briefly sketch the crisis and collapse of this narrative as a political act related to the social and political uprisings of the 1960s and 1970s. In a second section, I will address a specific, more explicit, process of "politicization" of educational historiography: the numerous links between policy-makers with outstanding political responsibility and researchers in the history of education in the case of Argentina after the end of the last dictatorship (1983). The possibility of educational historiography being a specific form of politicization of educational knowledge will be assessed in the concluding comments.

Even though the last section focuses on Argentina, there are good reasons to treat Latin American educational historiography beyond national boundaries. The intricate links between their national histories, the common language of the Hispanic American republics and the easy understanding between Portuguese and Spanish readers and speakers are only some basic factors in a broadly common trajectory. Moreover, the long tradition of exchange between universities, the Latin American reach of student movements throughout the 20th century, and the similar conditions of academic work at universities and research centres suggest a crossing of paths of development in educational history in the region.

Old political ties: The emergence of educational historiography in Latin America and its crisis.

As early as the first scholarly works on the subject, regional similarities across countries are evident. Imbued in a spirit of republican order – even Brazil, until 1889 formally an "Empire", had to deal with the irruption of modern politics after independence –, Latin American countries went on to establish a Western-type of general school system that was meant to be compatible with their notably advanced liberal constitutions. Moreover, schools were intended to bridge the blatant disparities between the progressive formal principles of the constitutional order and the disappointing inequalities and injustices of real life. Elementary schools were meant to help produce a healthy and 'tameable' politicization of the local populations within the new polities. Historical knowledge of the educational past emerged in the middle of this construction of schools as eminent tools of progress. It is not surprising that these first works resulted from the quills of clearly political men and not as a derivative of the existence of institutions for teacher education, as in the German-speaking countries during the 19th century.[1] The first short reconstructions of the educational past were clearly embedded in political discussions concerning the legacy of liberal policies.[2]

One leitmotiv of these narratives was to show the cultural break with the colonial past. The question of "spiritual independence" that was meant to follow political independence pervaded all analysis and considered school policy to be a crucial field in this undertaking.[3] The rupture between colonial and independent times certainly structured the chronology and the narration of founding works such as the history of higher learning in the Province of Buenos Aires published in1868 by the Argentinian José María Gutiérrez (1809-1878), in the comprehensive educational history of Brazil between the "discovery" and the end of the empire written originally in French in the 1880s by the Brazilian José Ricardo Pires de Almeida (1843-1913), and the account of the introduction of Lancasterian schooling in Chile and South America authored by the Chilean Domingo Amunátegui Solar (1860-1946) and published in 1895.[4] All these works stressed the educational implications of independence and the fertile soil of the new age for the "advancement" of education in spite of backlashes and notorious deficiencies. None of the three authors were schoolmen, but scholars in the real meaning of the word. Gutiérrez and Amunátegui were both well-known writers who became presidents of the University of Buenos Aires and the National University in Santiago de Chile respectively. As for Pires de Almeida, he was a member of the Brazilian Institute for History and Geography, a

---

[1] Daniel Tröhler, "Lehrerbildung, Nation und pädagogische Historiographie. Die 'Geschichte der Pädagogik' in Frankreich und Deutschland nach 1871," Zeitschrift für Pädagogik 52 (2006): 540-554.
[2] Lucas Alamán, "Compañía Lancasteriana," in Diccionario universal de historia y geografia (Mexico: Tipografía de Rafael/Librería de Andrade, 1853), 467-472; Miguel Luis Amunátegui and Gregorio Víctor Amunátegui, De la instrucción primaria en Chile. Lo que es, lo que debería ser (Santiago: Imprenta del Ferrocarril, 1856).
[3] Gernot Volger, "Zwischen Tradition und Moderne. Lateinamerikas spanisches Erbe als Entwicklungshemmnis," Archiv für Kulturgeschichte 82, no. 1 (2000): 211-226.
[4] José Ricardo Pires de Almeida, histoire de l'instruction publique au Brésil (1500-1889). Histoire et legislation (Rio de Janeiro: Leuzinger Ed., 1889); Domingo Amunátegui Solar, El sistema de Lancaster en Chile y otros países sud-americanos (Santiago: Imprenta Cervantes, 1895); Juan María Gutiérrez, Noticias históricas sobre el orijen y el desarrollo de la enseñanza pública superior en Buenos Aires (Buenos Aires: Imprenta del Siglo, 1868).

prestigious research organization in the country.[5] Briefly, the main motive of these intellectuals in their incursion into educational history was the nation- and state-building role of educational history, including some democratic connotations and a drive towards laic positions against the Catholic Church.

Evidently, educational historiography was unable to emerge at that time in the field of teacher education. The first institution for teacher training in the region, established in Santiago de Chile in 1842, did not foresee a course in educational history for teachers. Its founding director, the Argentinean exile Domingo Faustino Sarmiento (1811-1888), today an educational leader still referred to as *padre del aula* (Father of the classroom) in his country, did not include it in the curriculum of this institution.[6] Until the end of the 19th century, a teacher's education did not imply any particular interest in educational history. Even existing works on educational history were often mere translations of French works into Spanish, and not the outcome of any specific historiographical tradition.[7] Only in the 1930s and 1940s did scholarly works on the educational past mushroom, including both more positivistic approaches, relying solely on sound archival work,[8] and more theory-oriented research.[9]

In general terms, the founding works of Latin American educational historiography displayed the pervading power of a narrative of progress and civilization coined in the 19th century that I will refer to as the liberal narrative on civilisation and barbarism. This leitmotiv of the elite discursive production certainly had many versions combining different explanatory factors and social and cultural values. More racial approaches certainly existed and shaped educational realities at the end of the 19th century in many countries. However, the more powerful version of this narrative of civilization and progress was definitely the liberal one. This was the version that superseded the relatively short heyday

[5] Moysés Kuhlmann Jr., "Raízes da historiografia educational brasileira (1881-1922)," Cadernos de Pesquisa, no. 106 (1999): 159-71, here 160-62.
[6] Domingo Faustino Sarmiento, Educación común en el Estado de Buenos-Aires (Santiago de Chile: Imprenta de Julio Belin, 1855), 66-70.
[7] Alexandre Daguet, Manual de pedagogia seguido de un compendio de la historia de la educación (Santiago de Chile: Cervantes, 1889); Jules Paroz, Historia universal de la pedagogía (Gerona: Paciano Torres, 1889).
[8] Only as an example from a vast field of research: Antonino Salvadores, La instrucción primaria desde 1810 hasta la sanción de la Ley 1420 (Buenos Aires: Talleres gráficos del Consejo Nacional de Educación, 1941).
[9] An outstanding and pioneering work was undoubtedly Fernando de Azevedo, A cultura brasileira: Introdução ao estudo da cultura no Brasil (Rio de Janeiro: Serviço Gráfico do Instituto Brasileiro de Geografía e Estatística, 1943).

of more racist approaches, lasted well into the middle of the 20th century and was even embraced by "anti-systemic" forces such as Marxism and anarchism. Closely in tune with the founding republican and liberal myths of the Latin American republics, this narrative could be summarized in exemplary fashion in Sarmiento's formulations. An ardent liberal who was elected as the Argentinian president in 1868, he became famous in the region after the publication of his powerful work *Civilización i barbarie, vida de Facundo Quiroga i aspecto físico, costumbre i ábitos de la República Argentina* (Civilization and barbarism, life of Facundo Quiroga and physical description, costumes and habits of the Argentine Republic, 1845). In his passionate writing, Sarmiento addressed a constellation of problems common to all new independent polities in the region. After the breakdown of the old colonial order in the first decades of the 19th century, the liberal and modernizing project of republicanism had to face traditional identities, the unbroken influence of the Catholic Church and the persistence of colonial patterns of meaning and political action. The new rights conceded to free blacks, to the Indians and even to the urban white populace, displayed above all in the adoption of a general male adult franchise,[10] were both a promise to be fulfilled and a challenge to be faced. Elite discourse in the middle of the 19th century emphasized the necessary cultural transformation of all popular classes, after they had been fairly confident in their inherent republican qualities. Of course, this enormous task of inventing a new political culture and guaranteeing obedience under republican and liberal conditions was supposed to be achieved mainly by an extension of modern schooling. This work of "civilization" had to encounter the resilience of "barbarism" that the popular classes still embodied.[11] The outcome of this discourse was especially ambivalent: While celebrating liberal principles of wide political participation and a generous, somewhat inclusive modernization, Sarmiento rejected the idea that the real, existing popular classes could be permanently raised to achieve the required grade of "civilization".

Whereas, in his early work, he outlined the political conflict between forces of civilization and barbarism, he continuously returned to this leitmotiv and made it more precise in later essays and books. Regarding the Indios and the gauchos, but also commenting on the failure of the new republican elites, his view remained adamant, "because no

---

[10] Caruso, Marcelo, "Literacy and Suffrage. The politicisation of schooling in postcolonial Hispanic America (1810-1850)." Paedagogica Historica 46, Nr. 4 (2010): 463-478.

[11] Sarmiento, Domingo Faustino, Barbarei und Zivilisation: das Leben des Facundo Quiroga (Frankfurt a.M., 1845/2007).

one feature of our national character is attractive. We have no morals, no institutions or active government, no traditions or customs, we have only barbarism".[12] He envisioned a civilized future for Argentina, in which a demographic change would come after the regime changed to independence. This future society would abandon the practice of dispersing a scarce population and focusing on livestock as the basis of wealth to be reshaped by a massive immigration of rational Northern Europeans, living a more urban, organized form of life and cultivating a new type of religiosity akin to Protestantism. However, this promising future had to deal with the menacing persistence of barbarism as an agrarian economic and social structure. Sarmiento was not even completely confident regarding the efficacy of immigration as a factor inconsistently transforming the habits and culture of the local population. If the children of the immigrants were to grow up under the dominant structures marked by big properties and barbarian intercourse, "they will be absorbed in the barbarism of their new fatherland". They would adopt our habits and they would become "blond gauchos with blue eyes" as had already occurred with German and Irish children.[13] An additional factor, namely schooling, had to counteract these tendencies and would be able to create a new political culture of popular participation and civic responsibility, as in his strongly admired Massachusetts: "Only strong public schooling would impede the children of the Basques, Italians, and Spaniards from rejecting the industrial habits of their parents and then decaying into the barbarism of our masses".[14] In this vein, even progressive plans for inclusive and more or less "democratic" schooling envisioned a thorough acculturation of whole populations, a rejection of their collective identities, and a loss of the legitimacy of popular and traditional cultures. Although Sarmiento's diagnosis referred to the specific situation of the Argentine provinces, similar oppositions of "civilization" and "barbarism" related to the task of schooling emerged even in the 20th century.[15] On the whole, the idea that modern schooling represented a justified cultural colonization of backward local cultural patterns affected blacks in

---

[12] Sarmiento, Educación común en el Estado de Buenos Aires, 78. My own translation, MC.
[13] Ibid., 76.
[14] Ibid., 79.
[15] For Brazil, see Marta Maria Chagas de Carvalho, "L'histoire de l'éducation au Brésil: traditions historiographiques et processus de renovation de la discipline," Paedagogica Historica 36, no. 3 (2000): 909-33, and Lilia Moritz Schwarcz, The Spectacle of the Races: Scientists, Institutions, and the Race Question in Brazil, 1870-1930 (New York: Hill & Wang, 1999). For Colombia, Alejandro Alvarez Gallego, ...Y la escuela se hizo necesaria. En busca del sentido actual de la escuela (Bogotá: Cooperativa editorial magisterio, 1995).

Brazil and Cuba, Indios in Bolivia and Peru as well as the white poor in the Argentine pampas. The slogan of those introducing the Swedish exercises to Bolivian schools at the end of the 19th century summarises very concisely the hopes and dangers inherent in the task of modern schooling in the region: "Let's transform our indios into young Swedes!"[16]

The first professional works on educational history in the 20th century showed a varying acceptance of this leitmotiv.[17] The discourse on civilization indeed acquired a more theoretical turn with the dominant representations of "development" (*desarrollo*) in the 1950s and 1960s. The logic of eliminating subaltern and traditional realities remained, now under the label of "underdevelopment" (*subdesarrollo*). Only in the 1960s was the civilization narrative to meet fierce opposition in the field of education. The work of the Brazilian Paulo Freire (1921-1997) and the invectives against modern schools by the Mexico-based German scholar Ivan Illich (1926-2002), among other critics, led to a radical critique of the enterprise of civilization and to a reassessment of the educational reality in the region. The expansion of the existing schooling was no longer credited with any redeeming power regarding the situation of the subaltern. Moreover, schooling itself seemed to be a central mechanism in producing and reproducing the chronic injustice characteristic of the region. In this light, the progressive Sarmiento became only one chapter in a long history of repression and exploitation that discourses in other fields such as liberation theology and critical sociology brought into the universities and middle classes. However, the spread of the model of military dictatorships as a remedy for widespread unrest, strongly supported by the United States in alliance with local elites, interrupted the transfer of these critical impulses of the educational discussion to the field of the history of education.

Nonetheless, above all in the 1980s, critical assessments of the educational past as an explicit revision of the narrative of civilization appealed to the audiences of the mass universities. The role of schooling as a promise of political modernity accompanying the emergence of the new polities in the early 19th century was now critically reassessed. The consolidation of national systems of education at the end of the 19th cen-

---

[16] Françoise Martínez, "¡Que nuestros indios se conviertan en pequeños suecos! La introducción de la gimnasia en las escuelas bolivianas," Bulletin de l'Institut français d'études andines 28, no. 3 (1999): 361-86.

[17] Azevedo, A cultura brasileira; José F. Martínez Díaz, Historia de la educación pública en Cuba (Pinar del Rio: Imprenta Casa Villalba, 1943); Octavio Méndez Pereira, El desarrollo de la instrucción pública en Panamá (Panamá: Imprenta de la Paz, 1915); Salvadores, Instrucción primaria.

tury, traditionally praised as the outcome of wise decisions only counteracted by the greed of the elites, the opposition of the Catholic Church, or the fear of popular movements, now became a chapter in a longer history of oppression and informal colonization. The chronic failure of school expansion and pedagogic reform towards a more democratic and inclusive school system was no longer deemed a dysfunction. Now it was also the logical result of imported technologies of knowledge and power deeply rooted in modern schooling.

It is very difficult to bring the rich strains of historiography developed from the 1980s onwards under a common label. However, all national historiographies seemed to have found particular theoretical approaches to re-elaborate the inherited versions of the past.[18] Whereas in Brazil a Marxist approach to Foucault's work heavily shaped a renewed historiography of education focusing on the schooling of the subaltern, the impact of critical ethnology on the national myth of *mestización* can be defined as a salient feature of the most innovative part of Mexican historiography. In the Colombian case, a different reading of Foucault's work, heavily relying on the epistemic-structuralist approach, questioned the old narrative of liberal progress being hindered by a reactionary Catholic orthodoxy. Of course, not all historians in these and other countries embraced such historiographical innovations and engaged in radically criticizing the discourses on the educational past. However, the impact of the liberal legacy of the 19th century has consistently been questioned and pervaded not only scholarly discourses, but also the imagery of the past held by the educated middle classes and teachers. It was under the influence of these new historiographies that studies of the educational past were available to a relative large group of students, with the multiplication of universities, the creation of departments of education, and the relatively consistent introduction of educational history into the curricula of these institutions.

New ties: Educational historiography and educational policies in post-dictatorial Argentina (1983-2011)

While Latin American historiography of education has shown direct and explicit ties to political projects since its emergence and consolidation, the case of Argentine historiography after the last military dictatorship

---

[18] I developed the following argument in more detail in: Marcelo Caruso, "Abstand Von 'Zivilisation'. Supranationale Umwelt und aktuelle Entwicklungslinien lateinamerikanischer Bildungsgeschichtsschreibung," Jahrbuch für Historische Bildungsforschung 14(2009): 323-47, here 337-41.

(1976-1983) has brought these old political ties to a new, more explicit level of entanglement. In the following, I will describe some developments in the field of Argentine historiography of education not only as a field being shaped by the politics of a given time, but rather as forming versions of the past that have enforced and justified current strategies in the field of educational policy.

In the first half of the 20th century, scholarly versions of the educational past were published. These works tended to be traditional in their outlook, positivistic in their methods and more or less liberal in their interpretations.[19] In the middle of the century, a Catholic historiography emerged, emphasizing colonial education before independence, a time in which the dominance of pure Catholicism was uncontested.[20] Although divergent in their interpretations, both historiographical tendencies developed in an educational context heavily shaped by the law of 1420 on common, laic and free primary schooling, issued in 1884. Liberal-conservative forces dealing with the Catholic Church in a kind of Argentinian *Kulturkampf* had adopted this law. Although envisioned 'only' as a federal law, affecting the schools of the federal capital city of Buenos Aires and the sparsely populated "national territories", and leaving the development of mass education of the provinces to their respective governments following explicit provisions of the national constitution from 1853 onwards, the law nonetheless proved influential for the school policies of the federal states. In 1905, the adoption of a complementary law allowed for the establishment of "federal" schools, patterned after the principles of the law 1420, in the provinces. In order to avoid conflict with the distribution of competences in the field of educational policy established by the national constitution, these schools in the provinces could only be established if the provincial governments applied for the foundation of these schools.

---

19 Juan P. Ramos, Historia De la instrucción primaria en la República Argentina (1810-1910), 2 vols. (Buenos Aires: Jacobo Peuser, 1910); Porfirio Fariña Núñez, El maestro de Sarmiento. Ignacio Fermín Rodríguez (Mendoza: Dirección General de Escuelas, 1937); Juan Probst, La instrucción primaria durante la dominación española en el territorio que forma actualmente la República Argentina (Buenos Aires: Facultad de Filosofía y Letras - Instituto de Didáctica, 1940); Juan Balzasar Maciel. El maestro de la generación de Mayo (Buenos Aires: Universidad de Buenos Aires/Instituto de Didáctica, 1940); Salvadores, Instrucción primaria; Alfredo Estévez, "La Universidad de Buenos Aires en la educación pública argentina. Documentos para su historia," Revista de la Universidad de Buenos Aires 2, no. 4 (1947): 441-60; Antonino Salvadores, Urquiza en la historia de la educación argentina (La Plata: Talleres Gráficos Olivieri y Domínguez, 1951).

20 Guillermo Furlong, Nacimiento y desarrollo de la filosofía en el Río de la Plata, 1536-1810 (Buenos Aires: Kraft, 1952).

In the following decades, the expansion of mass schooling in Argentina, which, together with Uruguay, was the most successful country in schooling a large part of its population within Latin America, continued successfully under the auspices of this law. Not only liberals, but also socialists, radicals, communists and even anarchists became fond of this act, mainly because it excluded the teaching of religion from the standard curriculum. The broad acceptance of this law as a progressive measure even affected the development of educational historiography. In 1934, for the celebration of the 50th anniversary of the enactment of the law 1420, the national council of education called for the submission of works on educational history covering the years preceding the adoption of the law. In these works, the difficult advancement of schooling both during the colonial and independent periods formed a contrast to the accelerated, albeit not general, expansion of primary schooling from the end of the 19th century onwards. The recurrent celebration of the Domingo figure, Faustino Sarmiento, reinforced optimistic views concerning the educational achievements of the national law. Although Sarmiento had retired when the draft for the law entered the congressional floor and also had little to do with the passing of the law, Argentinian liberals and leftists linked Sarmiento's passionate ideas concerning popular education to the law 1420, as if the former could only have been directly inspired by the latter. In sum, in the middle of the 20th century, a whole mythology of the progressive educational past had been consolidated, including Sarmiento, the law 1420 and the expansion of public schools. This liberal mystification even increased when the governments presided over by Juan Domingo Perón (1895-1974) introduced religious instruction into public schools. Faced with an increasing Catholic challenge from the 1940s onwards, Liberal, republican and even leftist circles considered reforms of this law as being essentially reactionary and incompatible with democratic politics.

The renewal of educational historiography from the 1970s onwards did not fundamentally affect the progressive imagery regarding the educational past while simultaneously articulating critical insights. This mythology remained the decisive context for a long time for discussions on educational history. Only after the end of the last military dictatorship (1983) did the field of educational history become fully reconstituted. First, new analytical approaches in the social sciences and the new cultural history gained more attention during the 1980s. Second, educational studies were established in all provinces with at least one chair of history of education in each university. Finally, the discipline of the history of education established itself more broadly and firmly with annual conferences from 1987 onwards, with the foundation of the Argentinian Society for the History of Education (SAHE in Spanish) in 1995 and the publication of the Argentinian Yearbook for the History of Education from 1996 onwards. In the following I will present four researchers who, on the basis of their historical work, have set new standards for the discipline, and contributed to reconfiguring the history of education, and at the same time have deeply influenced educational politics with their work. Their views on the history of education that became significant for the formulation of their positions in educational politics will be briefly sketched.

One of the perhaps surprising developments in the post-dictatorship development in the history of Argentina after 1983 was the cancelling of a number of appointments for university chairs that had been filled during the years of dictatorship under conditions of political exclusion. This break with the dictatorship stood in sharp contrast to the continuity of faculty members characterising the post-dictatorship development of Spanish universities and eventually led to a reconnection between many of the exiled scholars and public universities in Argentina. In the field of educational studies at what was by far the largest and most prestigious university in the country, the University of Buenos Aires replaced almost every faculty member during the subsequent years by new hiring committees. Ever since her appointment as professor of general educational history, Cecilia Braslavsky (1952-2005) has become a leading figure for a new history of education. Although her profile was more focused on teaching than on research, she had a major impact on formulating a new narrative of educational historiography.

Braslavsky had written her dissertation in Leipzig and had worked primarily with the theoretical and historiographical perspectives of Robert Alt. She was the second daughter of the famous activist for the Argentinian Communist Party and one of the founders of educational studies in Argentina, Berta Braslavsky (1913-2008). When her mother went into exile in Venezuela following the military coup of 1976, Cecilia seized the chance to go to the highly venerated (among Argentinian communists) German Democratic Republic (GDR) for her doctoral studies. The theme of the dissertation that dealt with the phases of the introduction and implementation of compulsory school attendance in Latin American countries, had strong traces of a Marxist teleological narrative of the educational development of mankind coined in the GDR. This narrative covered the consecutive stages in the development of modes of production from "primitive communism" (Urkommunismus) to "industrial capitalism". Her very popular course on the history of education at the University of Buenos Aires consistently displayed well-known motives of GDR historiography, such as the progressive character of the Reformation, a stress on the progressive albeit not fully "liberating" role of bourgeois pedagogy and the reconstruction of a specific educational history of the working class.

Braslavsky was not only a very successful and respected university teacher, she also led the section "education and society" at the *Facultad Latinoamericana de Ciencias Sociales* (FLACSO), a research position that supported pioneering work in graduate programmes of educational sociology and educational policy. Under her supervision, a large number of historical works in education were produced during the 1980s and 1990s. In FLACSO, she was the successor of Juan Carlos Tedesco, an educational researcher, who had begun a career as early as the 1980s as head of international organizations in education. Tedesco had also developed a profile as a strong social historian of education in the early 1970s. In 1970, he published a large monograph on the first phase of Argentinian schooling (1880-1900), where he, counter to the then-prevalent Marxist interpretations, argued that schooling in this phase was to be explained and analysed mostly "politically" as opposed to "economically." He also used neo-Marxist terms derived from the theory of the Italian Antonio Gramsci on cultural dimensions of society and politics in the theory of hegemony, and thereby gained a profile as a new kind of Marxist, that was not so bound up by the older Marxists distinctions between "basis" and "superstructure" In this way he combined the break of the cultural revolutionary movement of the late 1960s, and its new stress on politics, with a sophisticated historiographical approach.[21] Tedesco saw in the early expansion of the Argentinian school system after Sarmiento and the Law 1420 the emergence of a field of opportunities for upward social mobility and, on the whole, better chances for the middle classes and immigrants. This basic "democratic" tendency in Argentinian school history was even increased by the successful rejection of any attempt at introducing tracking between different strands of secondary education, especially those that would introduce a "second class" vocational secondary school.[22] According to Tedesco, the noticeable size and cultural level of the middle class in Argentina, as viewed against the

[21] Tedesco, Juan Carlos Educación y sociedad en la Argentina (1880-1945) (Solar: Buenos Aires 1970/1986), 17.
[22] ibid. 173f.

background of other Latin American countries, was mainly the outcome of expanding an "open," i.e. non-tracked, and solely academic, form of secondary schooling.

Although Tedesco had not published any work in the field of the history of education since the 1980s, his early historiographical work gained a unique model status, becoming a central reference point for many master theses in FLACSO, often supervised by Cecilia Braslavsky.[23] These theses addressed in historiographical terms an educational discussion of the time linked to perceived problems of the Argentinian school system. First, they referred to the problem of the long history of dictatorships and authoritarianism in Argentina. The last military dictatorship (1976-1983) had not only killed thousands of people, it had also established an authoritarian Catholic pedagogy in schools that had been dominant for many years. Second, they treated the problem of the cultural and social relevance of school knowledge. Cecilia Braslavsky was an adamant advocate of the actualization of school knowledge and she repeatedly diagnosed the current curriculum content as "outdated". Following a thesis coined by her mother Berta, she referred to this problem as the "emptying" of the school curriculum and linked it to the policies issued under the last dictatorships.

Tedesco and Braslavsky were in complete agreement regarding the shortcomings of the curricular content in school work. In this vein, they not only advanced a diagnosis of policy, they also made a theoretical argument against the diagnosis of the French strain of educational sociology which was very widely received in the 1970s (Bourdieu/Passeron, Baudelot/Establet), namely that modern school systems only aimed at reproducing inequality and existing power structures. Tedesco pointed out that scientifically produced and broadly disseminated knowledge was not only "ideological," – as its critics claimed – but was rather a pillar of societal participation: "The school of thought of social reproduction regards the curriculum as random and superficial knowledge, and on top of that a possession of the ruling class. But a great deal of this knowledge is not a product of a specific group or social class, but a product of relations between people and between man and nature. From this viewpoint the problem (of the school curriculum, MC) lies in the acquisition

---

[23] Alliaud, Andrea Los maestros y su historia: los orígenes del magisterio argentino. 2 vols. (CEAL: Buenos Aires, 1993), Gvirtz, Silvina Nuevas y viejas tendencias en la docencia (1945-1955) (Buenos Aires: CEAL, 1991), Pinkasz, Daniel, La formación pedagógica de los docentes de enseñanza media. Argentina 1930-1945 (Buenos Aires: FLACSO/CONICET, 1989).

of this knowledge, or to put it differently, in its distribution".[24] Through his discussion of the social significance of curricular content beyond the suspicion of its embedding ideological and power relations, Tedesco formulated the basis of a critical educational position in educational policy that strongly linked curriculum reform and democratization – primarily understood as distribution – of societal power. At that time, this position received the name "critical pedagogy of school content." Its primary goal was to work against the aforementioned "emptying of curricular content" in the school experience of the popular classes. By means of qualitatively improved school-work, this being better grounded scientifically, a decisive contribution could be delivered to the democratization of Argentinian society. Cecilia Braslavsky introduced this view into the writing of important master theses that combined curriculum history and sociology of the school curriculum. With the help of these arguments, Tedesco and Braslavsky formulated a kind of social democratic reform programme of better knowledge distribution that actualized the known motives of a "progressive bourgeoisie" and its pedagogy (Braslavsky), or rather the democratic development of the Argentinian school system from the end of the 19th century onwards (Tedesco) into the post-dictatorship reality.

Whereas different variations of a social-democratically transformed Marxism patterned the positions shared by Braslavsky and Tedesco, the historiography and political references of Adriana Puiggrós, the chair for Argentinian and Latin American History of Education at the University of Buenos Aires, was rooted in a critique of orthodox Marxism. The educational scholar Adriana Puiggrós is the daughter of a very famous historian, Rodolfo Puiggrós (1906-1980). In the 1950s he had undergone a rather unusual change of political affiliation from the Communist Party to the anti-Marxist and national-Catholic but worker-friendly Peronism. From then onwards, Rodolfo Puiggrós published extensively to prove that the Peronist movement represented a left-wing project. He was elected the rector of the University of Buenos Aires during the left-Peronist "spring" of the years 1973 and 1974. His daughter was also elected as the dean of the philosophical faculty by the left-Peronist dominated council. In the middle of a bloody conflict between the increasingly active left-Peronist urban guerrilla and the anti-communist, right-Peronist death caldrons, Adriana Puiggrós had to leave the country

[24]Tedesco, Juan Carlos "Elementos para una sociologia del curriculo escolar en la Argentina," in Braslavsky, Cecilia/Carciofi, Ricardo/Tedesco, Juan Carlos (eds.), El proyecto educativo autoritario. Argentina 1976- 1982 (Buenos Aires: GEL, 1982), 19.

and face exile in Mexico.

During the Mexican years, Puiggrós published two highly praised theses. These contained a historical critique of modernization in Latin America as imperialism and an analysis of alternative educational practices of political emancipatory movements in the history of this region.[25] Both works debated the above-mentioned dichotomy introduced by Domingo Faustino Sarmiento, "civilisation and barbarism."[26] Although Puiggrós initially characterized this dichotomy as a banner of the school systems of the "advanced bourgeoisie," she radicalized her view in her doctoral thesis. She characterized this opposition as being racist in its premises. She used the new possibilities of discourse analysis and used it to argue that, beyond Sarmiento's mapping of cultural forces, a silenced tradition of popular education and schooling existed. The groups working within this tradition carried it out in a semi-autonomous way, or at least in tension with the "official" school systems being established by the dominant classes in all Latin American countries.[27] In spite of her many references to Marxism in its Gramscian tradition, she fiercely criticised the traditional pedagogy of the Latin American left of Marxist tendency for continuing this liberal discourse, praising an abstract "working class" and disdaining the existing popular classes. In her view, Latin American Marxists were so entrenched in a Eurocentric view of societal development and civilisation that they were only able to focus on the deficits and shortcomings of the popular movements. Due to their neglect of the multi-cultural and agrarian realities of Latin America, Puiggrós called the orthodox socialist pedagogy along European lines a form of "neo-colonialism" that defined progress as the cultural elimination of the popular cultures. In this sense, Marxist pedagogies were equally as Eurocentric as the classical liberal narrative. In Puiggrós' view, the Marxists of the 20th century were the true followers of the liberals in the 19th century. She presented a great deal of evidence to support her claim from highly ranking Marxist and socialist intellectuals.[28]

It was clear for Puiggrós that the central problem of the Argentinian school system was not one of "distributing" knowledge, but rather

---

[25] Puiggrós, Adriana, Imperialismo y educación en América Latina (Mexico: Nueva Imagen, 1980), and Puiggrós, Adriana, La educación popular en America Latina. Origenes, polémicas yperspectivas (Mexico: Nueva Imagen, 1984).

[26] Sarmiento, Barbarei und Zivilisation.

[27] Puiggrós, Adriana, Sujetos, disciplina y currículum en los orígenes del sistema educativo argentino (Buenos Aires: Galerna, 1990), 79-88.

[28] Puiggrós, Adriana, La educación popular en America Latina. Origenes, polémicas y perspectivas (Mexico: Nueva Imagen, 1984), 165f.

of the relation between schools and social strata of the population unable to fit into the Eurocentric cultural arrangement. She dealt with this question on the basis of entirely new theoretical premises. She dedicated her work at the University of Buenos Aires primarily to investigating formal and non-formal pedagogical alternatives in Latin America. With her co-researchers, she produced a large data collection with over 4000 such examples of marginalized or alternative educational initiatives containing a wide range of proposals. The common feature of these remarkably different initiatives was her subordinated or alienated position in relation to the centralized, "normal", and state-organized educational system. Unions, teachers, child-education movements and reform educationalists of all types were the agents which Puiggrós elaborated on in order to "deconstruct" the still very positive and liberal view of the development of the national educational system.[29]

Under her leadership, and thanks to her inspiring work, the most ambitious project in the field of the history of education in Argentina emerged years later: the eight-volume *Historia de la educación en la Argentina* (published between 1990 and 1997) that thoroughly analysed the system of schooling between 1884 and 1983. This project also substantially contributed to the consolidation of new chairs of history of education in the provinces as places of genuine research. In a postscript written by some of the contributors to the last volume, Puiggrós and her co-workers stressed that the project "was carried out exactly at a moment in which our national government initiated a painful change in society, the economy and cultural affairs."[30] The reference was to the government of Carlos Menem, a right-wing Peronist, who, in the 1990s, pulled through a large programme of privatization, liberalization and opening of the economy under conditions of widespread corruption. An implicit background to her analysis was also the extent to which the former workers party, the Peronists, had chosen to follow such a programme. It is not strange that she began the volume on Peronism by citing her own withdrawal from the party.[31] In any case, Puiggrós remained true to her analytical endeavour to transform the liberal-Marxist narrative of the history of education in Argentina. She drew heavily on

[29] For the methodological framework see Puiggrós, Sujetos, disciplina y currículum, 14-24.
[30] Amuchástegui, Patricia et al. "Prólogo con epilogo," in Puiggrós, Adriana (ed.), Dictaduras y utopías en la historia reciente de la educación Argentina (1955-1983) (Buenos Aires: Galerna, 1997), 15.
[31] Bernetti, Jorge Luis/Puiggrós, Adriana, Peronismo, cultura política y educación (1945-1955) (Buenos Aires: Galerna 1993), 9.

new theoretical references such as Foucault and Lacan for a critical analysis of the purported "democratic" fruits of the liberal-conservative state-centred school development. However, she had to discuss it carefully so that she did not deliver ammunition to the advocates of privatization and the right-wing Peronists. From her viewpoint, for instance, Tedesco's praise of the democratic virtues of classical secondary education became a lack of curricular plurality, narrowing the path of educational opportunities for the lower classes. And where Tedesco often criticized vocational education and training systems as incomplete and "second class" education, she stressed the subordinate yet remarkable development of such educational institutions during the first wave of Peronism. She presented this policy as a kind of political and cultural recognition of knowledge and practices related to the industrial workforce and other popular classes.[32]

The work of a student of Cecilia Braslavsky, Mariano Narodowski, professor of history of education at the University of Quilmes (by Buenos Aires) and later professor of educational policy at the University Torcuato di Tella (Buenos Aires), also stood in tension to the liberal-cum-social democratic narrative of Argentinian educational history. He shared a certain affinity to the leftist wing of Peronism and collaborated with the teachers' union, as well as Puiggrós. In his critical work on the liberal modern era in education, he also had recourse to Michel Foucault's oeuvre in order to discuss the epistemological assumptions of modern schooling. He showed particular interest in *Discipline and Punish* and also worked on the theme of school discipline. His dissertation delivered in Brazil, *Infancia y poder* (childhood and power), was an all-round blow against the narrative of emancipatory modern pedagogy combining Ariès' thesis on the invention of childhood with Foucault's concepts of disciplinary institutions. His analysis brought to the fore what was at least an ambivalent picture of modernity.[33]

A result of his break with traditional educational historiography and his theoretical affinity to a Foucaultian power analysis was his research on the import of the Bell-Lancaster system of monitorial schooling in Buenos Aires in the early 19th century. Being a theme that Foucault himself had dealt with in *Discipline and Punish*, Narodowki showed a rare interest in the history of education before 1884, in which the mythical school law 1420 had been enacted. In an essay on Argentinian educa-

[32] Tedesco 1970/1986, ibid, 190-202 and 224-233; Bernetti/Puiggrós, ibid, 121f.
[33] Narodowski, Mariano, Infancia y poder. La conformación de la pedagogía moderna (Buenos Aires: Santillana, 1995).

tional historiography, he referred to the time before 1884 as the "dark side of the moon" – because it had never been brought to the attention of modern historiography since the 1970s.[34] He thereby problematized an epoch that had not been taken seriously since the first major works of liberal historiography. While Puiggrós had also criticized the institutional practices of the liberal-conservative era with Foucault, Narodowski rather placed the emphasis on the co-opting of pedagogy and educational knowledge through the modern state. He was fascinated by the history of these technicians and politicians of education and the absorption of their knowledge by a modern bureaucratic state for governmental purposes. In this vein, his sympathy for earlier anarchist and socialist concepts of education with a certain distance to the state was consistent. His last historiographical essays demystifying the state-centred school law of 1884 also continued in this line of discussion.

While the educational policy implications of these historiographical positions shall be addressed in the following section, it is not at all the aim of this analysis to suggest a process of simple linear links between educational historiography and educational politics. It will be shown that the positions already sketched in the historiography were activated in specific political contexts and also changed under different political conditions. By addressing the political place of the history of education is by no means to imply a mechanical transfer of knowledge of the past into a diagnosis of the present and a foreseeing of the future. However, certain positions in educational politics and political changes cannot fully be understood without this background in historiography.

To pinpoint this relationship, however, all aforementioned researchers had collected experience with party politics very early in their biographies. The left-wing Peronist Puiggrós did not leave her party until 1985. It was told about Juan Carlos Tedesco that he had been active as an advisor for the Radical Citizens Union, a social democratic grouping, not to speak of his early engagement with Trotskyist groups as a young man. Cecilia Braslavsky had also been engaged in a leftist social democratic party after turning her back on communism. Narodowski had been active on the leftist scene and for a while had an affinity to the left-wing Peronists. In addition to this, he had been active in the human rights movement and advised some members of the teachers' unions.

[34] Narodowski, Mariano, "El lado oscuro de la luna. El temprano siglo XIX y la historiografía educational Argentina," in Cucuzza, Rubén (ed.) Historia de la educación en debate (Buenos Aires: Miño y Dávila, 1996), 269-280.

Nonetheless, it was not until the 1990s that educational researchers were elected to the parliament and became ministers. The sphere of the educational ministries had until then been occupied mostly by lawyers, but this changed fundamentally and the protagonists of this article have all played an important role in this change.

The initial point was when Cecilia Braslavsky assumed the leadership of the curriculum department of the Argentinian educational ministry in 1993. This was by no means an easy time for the Argentinian school system. A comprehensive decentralization of the secondary school system was carried out in the context of the conservative-neoliberal government of the right-wing Peronist Carlos Saúl Menem, and due to a heavy cut in funding. With the new educational act of 1993, the ministry of education, an important actor for the liberal historiography of education, was defined as "the educational ministry without schools," but was still supposed to function as coordinator, evaluator and centre for controlling the curriculum. In a broader sense, this reform was unpopular. Through the new educational law, the heritage of the almost mythical act 1420 was devaluated quite substantially, and its dismantling at the same time symbolized the end of the double promise of egalitarianism and laicism. The abandonment of the traditional school system was with primary and secondary schools (seven and five years respectively) and its replacement with ten years of comprehensive schooling confused many and was never fully accepted.

Braslavsky became ardently engaged in the curriculum change. Indeed, this work was an evident continuation of her positioning with regards to the progressive role of schooling in modernity and her diagnosis that Argentinian schools suffered from the "emptying of curricular content." In the ministry of education, Braslavsky was responsible for the development of a rather ambitious framework for the national curriculum that she produced in collaboration with prestigious scholars from many countries. Technically this curricular framework was a masterpiece of the educational policies during these years.[35] In spite of this, and maybe not so surprisingly, Braslavsky experienced open hostility from the Catholic Church, mainly due to her rather extensive use of the concept of "gender" in the curriculum guidelines. Finally, the political leadership gave in to this pressure, and Braslavsky had to change the curriculum framework in more than one aspect.

[35] Braslavsky, Cecilia (ed.), Contenidos básicos comunes para la educación general básica (Buenos Aires: Ministerio de Cultura y Educación, 1994).

In the light of her earlier political positioning, this caused quite a stir. At the end of the day, she worked for a conservative-neoliberal government with a fairly bad reputation among the education-friendly middle classes. Suddenly, the formerly rather popular professor was labelled *persona non grata* and openly and harshly criticised by her former students. This situation worsened after her compromise with the Catholic Church. In the context, not only of the university, but also the organized educational history, the word used was of "betrayal", no matter how much Braslavsky tried to explain that she was not only working for the sitting government, but for the greater good of the public educational system in the country. The consistency of her participation with her historiographical position was never verbalised. Her stress on the importance of a general, radical examination of the content of the curriculum in the school system was an outcome of her historical insights into the "distribution problem" of relevant school knowledge in Argentinian schools.

Her hitherto close partner and colleague at the university, Adriana Puiggrós, openly criticized Braslavsky on the national educational political scene in the mid- 1990s. With the establishment of FREPASO, a coalition for various discontented political figures with a strong presence of highly disappointed leftist Peronists, Puiggrós found a political home again. Soon she was elected as a member of the constitutional assembly in 1994. Hereafter she was more than once elected member of the national parliament and was active there as a member of the committee for technology and research. Puiggrós was appointed minister of education in the province of Buenos Aires between 2005 and 2007, the largest school subsystem in South America. Today, she is still an ordinary member of the parliament, and is chairing the committee on education.

Her discussions with Braslavsky on topics such as the curricular framework, the heavy cuts in combination with decentralization and the role of teachers in the reform process took place in the national newspapers. Strong changes also followed in her argumentation in the context of the neoliberal reforms of the 1990s. Since 1997, a "white tent" has stood in front of the parliament, in the colours of the traditional uniforms of teachers and pupils in the public schools. This large party tent has been a visual sign of protest against poor teacher payment meant to mark discussions in educational politics for the following four years. In this context, Puiggrós strongly voiced the protest movement, positioning herself through the historiography of education in quite a new tone. Thus she wrote in the largest Argentinian newspaper in September 1997: "Sarmiento" – the subject of one of her critical studies on the history of education – "is a symbol of opposition. His portrait stands with a gagged mouth in front of the white tent."[36] Even though she continually showed the contradictions of Sarmiento, both in this and in other essays, especially his racist opinions on the majority of the "real existing population,"[37] she used his figure slyly in this context. The liberal Sarmiento, at the end of the day, seemed to be a powerful companion in the fight against neo-liberalism. Because of the widespread popularity and fame of the figure of Sarmiento the impact of this reinterpretation in the public arena should not be underestimated.

Puiggrós's engagement in day-to-day educational politics naturally proved to be more conventional than her critique from the viewpoint of historiography of the traditional educational system of Argentina and her stress of a "pedagogical alternative" had suggested. Especially remarkable was her strong support to counter the "neoliberal" "general school act" from 1993 that had put an end to the old structuring of schooling into seven years of primary and five years of secondary schooling. She argued on many occasions that these well-known categories found widespread acceptance, also among the popular classes. This old separation was – according to her argument – still associated with the old classical liberal ideals of equality that were under pressure from neoliberal thinking and now had to be defended. Naturally, Puiggrós kept a more open position than usual with regard to the "alternative." This was evident, for instance, in the establishment of an agency for the accreditation of informal vocational learning in the province of Buenos Aires. Generally, she never failed to acknowledge the crossovers between "education and work", a "forgotten" theme of the classical schools structure and one which she stressed in her historiography. In the aftermath of the financial crisis of 2001, she and her research group dared to carry out an oral history project on the practices of transmitting of work-knowledge in the industries and workplaces occupied and managed by the workers themselves during and after the crisis.[38] To see the whole picture, it is also important to follow the changes in her argumentation in the historiography of education. In a handbook on the history of Argentinean education for schoolteachers, the milder picture of Sarmiento and the progressive nature of the school system that came

---

[36] Puiggrós, Adriana, "Reformar con el apoyo en la gente," Clarin (Buenos Aires, 10 September 1997).
[37] Puiggrós, Adriana, De Simón Rodríguez a Paulo Freire. Educación para la integración iberoamericana (Bogotá: Convenio Andrés Bello, 2005), 52-53.
[38] Puiggrós, Adriana, La fábrica del conocimiento (Rosario: Homo Sapiens, 2004).

out of the 1420 Act clearly advanced new interpretations.[39]

As Braslavsky's profile was characterized by the continuity between the historiography of education and educational politics, and the political engagement of Puiggrós had no minor consequences for her historiography, the most surprising link between historiography and educational politics was the development of Mariano Narodowski – the Foucaultian among the students of Braslavsky. Like Puiggrós, Narodowski also has quite a long history of working with different teacher unions. However, his concern for the autonomy of the teaching profession vis-a-vis the state gave him the impulse, and not so much the issue of salaries and collective professional rights. In this vein, Narodowski carried out the risky operation of weakening the link between profession and state that had been established in the 1420 Act. In this framework he tried to present the history of educational thinking at Rio de la Plata as an increasing tendency towards a state-dependent form of thinking and his historiographical work aimed at picturing the insufficiency of this model in the face of new pedagogical challenges.[40] He followed his earlier findings on the conflict between teachers and the "first" state educators in the first half of the nineteenth century, namely the English missionary James Thompson and the Spanish teacher Pablo Baladía, both engaged by the state to introduce and organize the Bell-Lancasterian or monitorial system of education.[41] In addition, Narodowski saw an ongoing line between defining childhood as a state affair, the object of a dissertation of his which was highly esteemed in Latin America, and the emergence of "state specialists" in this domain, following the widespread acceptance and transfiguration of the School Act 1420. These "state educators" had basically posed the question of how this relationship could be improved by means of school reforms.[42] It adds to the analytical strengths of Narodowski to have seen the strategic role that the history of education had played in this context. The writing of a history of education was one of the "favourite strategies" of the state educators for achieving legitimacy. After the publication of the monumental *Historia de la instrucción pri-*

[39] Puiggrós, Adriana, De Simón Rodríguez a Paulo Freire.
[40] Narodowski, Mariano "Para volver al Estado. Del pedagogo de Estado al pedagogo de 1a Diversidad," Propuesta Educativa no. 8 (1997): 51-55.
[41] Narodowski, Mariano/López, Claudina, "El mejor de los métodos posibles: la introducciónde método lancasteriano en Iberoamérica en el temprano siglo XIX," in Camara Bastos, Maria Helena/Mendes de Faria Filho, Luciano (eds.), A escola elementar no século XIX. 0 metoda monitorial/mútuo (Passo Fundo/RGS: Universidade de Passo Fundo, 1999), Narodowski, Mariano "La expansión lancasteriana in Iberoamérica. El caso de Buenos Aires,", Anuario IEHS 9 (1994): 255-278.
[42] Narodowski, "Para volver al Estado," 53.

maria en la República Argentina (1910) written by the ministerial official Juan P. Ramos for the centenary celebration of the first independence movements, it was more or less impossible to think of school education as a public concern apart from the state.

Narodowski's counter-proposal was to suggest a type of educator with a distant relationship to the state in order to avoid co-opting and dependency. This opinion, which was built on his basic democratic views and Foucaultian analysis, did however have surprising effects: Narodowski became one of the most consistent and exposed defenders of a neoliberal educational policy, although he would himself probably deny this categorization. As early as in his critique of the state educator in the 1990s, he defended the idea of a "pedagogo de mercado" (educator of the market). He phrased this type as "an intellectual required by the market for his knowledge independently of all agents."[43] Narodowski also used the expression "fashion educator" (pedagogo fashion) without intending to characterize the market affinity as in any way superficial. He viewed this new figure positively on the basis of a societal "demand" for school education rather than state decrees. He fully realised that the services of these educators was of varying quality, but he defended this development as a step away from the old "normalizing" style of state education. For the new educator he also coined the market-oriented concept of "educator of plurality." And finally, he saw in the decline of the state educator an opportunity for the development of a true, politically autonomous form of educational research.[44]

After this positioning he dedicated himself to strongly quantitative empirical research in education, thereby making a clear break with Foucaultian epistemological preferences. He stated that the school system, even when publicly organised and financed, had become a gatekeeper for social inequality, and that state schooling was a false road to social justice in education. One of his main contentions was the introduction of educational vouchers as representing a stronger affinity towards the "demand" side in educational policy, i.e. the parents.[45] He continued his disbelief in the state and in the myth of the progressive character of the old, state-centred, educational acts. He did not altogether lose

[43] Ibid, 54.
[44] Ibid, 55.
[45] Narodowski, Mariano "Socio-economic Segregation in the Argentinian Education System: school choice without vouchers" in Compare 32 (2002): 181-191, Narodowski, Mariano "School Choice and Quasi-State Monopoly in Education Systems in Latin America: the case of Argentina," in Forsey, Martin/Davies, Scott/Walford, Geoffrey (eds.), The Globalisation of School Choice? (Oxford: Symposium, 2008), 131-44.

his touch for specific "leftist" agendas in the process, however. Pushing back the state could open up room in which to "give back the power to teachers and educators"[46] It is one of the most interesting examples of the political consequences of the history of education that his Foucaultian position turned into a sort of "state-phobia", to use a phrase from Foucault himself.

Whereas the political discussion of public education in the 1990s was strongly influenced by discussions and interventions shaped by Braslavsky and Puiggrós, recent years, after 2001, have witnessed the rise of Narodowski and Tedesco to become strong actors in educational politics. This happened in a political scene influenced by the financial breakdown of 2001 and the following instability and re-structuring of the economy and the welfare state. With the election in 2003 of Nestor Kirchner (1950-2010) as the president of Argentina, followed by his wife in 2007, left-wing Peronism experienced an unexpected revival after many had thought it dead and gone. Now national educational politics once again took hold of the myth of the 1420 Act, combined with a strong critique of the policies of the 1990s. While a close colleague of Braslavsky, the educational sociologist Daniel Filmus, was the national minister of education from 2003 to 2007, this office was then held from 2007 onwards by the fourth protagonist of this article, Juan Carlos Tedesco. Although he had combined views on the progressive nature of Argentinian school history and the "emptying of curricular content" with educational politics, he had not been an actor in discussions during the 1990s due to his work for UNESCO, with seats in Santiago de Chile and Geneva. He worked for the left Peronist government from 2007 to 2009, without himself being a Peronist. He found a fruitful terrain for his content-focused educational politics in times of educational standards, PISA-studies and regional evaluation studies.

His opponent in many respects was Mariano Narodowski. He was appointed as the leading candidate for the victorious liberal-conservative list for the parliamentary elections in 2007 in the city of Buenos Aires. Later he was appointed minister of education by the mayor of the town Mauricio Macri. After he took office, it was clear that the agenda now was radical change towards "demand", and "supply" in the politics of education was not so easy to impose. However, the strong protests of the

[46] Narodowski, Mariano (2006): Con la disolución de la asimetría se pierde la educación. Interview on the official site of the Argentinean ministry of education EDUCAR (viewed on the 15th of May 2007) in the url: http://portal.educ.ar/noticias/entrevistas/mariano-narodowski-con-la-diso.php.

teachers' union in the city led to the first fierce and public fight between the federal minister of education, Tedesco and Narodowski. In the end, Narodowski had to quit following a scandal regarding illegal surveillance activities in his ministry. In sum, the close connection between the historiography of education and educational policy also seem to characterise the new century and new presences confirm this tendency, such as the recent appointment of Silvina Gvirtz, another former student of Cecilia Braslavsky and the former editor of the Argentinian Yearbook of History of Education, as a minister in the Province of Buenos Aires shows.[47]

Concluding words

The links between historiographical arguments and political affiliations marking the field of the historiography of education surely shows the peculiarity of the institutionalization path of educational research in the country. The consolidation of educational studies at the universities always displayed a strong ethos of becoming active in educational and school reform work, and that on a political level. Students and the public did not only view a stronger emphasis on almost politically neutral academic work with suspicion, also scholars and university teachers somewhat disliked the alleged neutrality of scholarly work. Added to this were the relatively low salaries of the university faculty, in spite of a slight increase in the public universities in recent years. This obliged the scholars of education to take on additional work. However, this economic factor does not seem to have been decisive for the development described here, at least not for the four actors presented in this piece.

At any rate, no one-dimensional relationship between the historiography of education and educational politics can be traced in the profiles of these researchers and university professors in the area of the history of education. Specific narratives of school history, however, seem to deliver crucial resources for the formulation and legitimation of educational policies. These narratives can have different sources and references, be it the idea of the progressive development of the form of "mankind" imported from the GDR (Braslavsky), a critical analysis of modern society as a control society (Narodowski), or the different views of educational development in its relationship to the national state (Puiggrós, Tedesco). In view of the complexity of modern educational set

[47] This holds true in spite of the death of Cecilia Braslavski in 2005. To the very end she was convinced of the value of educational history for the improvement of schooling, at least in the sense of educational politics. See Braslavsky, Cecilia "The History of Education and the Contemporary Challenge of Quality Education for All," Prospects 35 (2005): 385-399.

tings, the reference to the past or, as Jürgen Schriewer would phrase it, the "externalization to history," seems to be a promising strategy gaining legitimacy when scholars face confusing and complex conditions.[48] When educational politics constantly stand under a demand for legitimacy, any reference to broader areas of reality such as "history", "science", or "tradition" can be an easily communicable way of advancing conflicting statements in the public arena.

However, this connection can naturally have effects in the opposite direction as well. As is shown by the case of the more than subtle shifts in the interpretation of Sarmiento and the traditional school system by Puiggrós, new constellations in educational politics can be a resource for reinterpreting the educational past. At the end of the day, as Foucault formulated it, history is always the history of the present. It is not clear whether this close connection between historiography and politics will continue in the educational field. This will depend on the quality of the political interventions of the actors who are or were active scholars in the field of the history of education. After viewing the last PISA results, and irrespective of the fact that certain improvements in schools may not be so closely connected to specific educational policies, the last two decades have not been a happy time for the educational system in the country. For instance, PISA has challenged the notion, more an assumption than a certainty, that Argentina has a "top position" within Latin America. Seen in this light, scholars of the history of education are by no means better ministers of education or holders of educational offices per se. For the history of education this is however only an advantage: the sub-discipline is widely popular within the field of educational studies, the positions are well-established in the university structure and the field seems to promise that this study can be an excellent preparation for other carriers.

[48] Schriewer, Jürgen "Vergleich als Methode und Externalisierung auf Welt. Vom Umgang mit Alterität in Reflexionsdisziplinen," in Baecker, Dirk et al. (eds.): Theorie als Passion (Frankfurt a.M.: Suhrkamp, 1987), 629-668.

Section 3

Educational historiography and the raison d'être of the history of education

History of Education in Germany: Historic Development – Results – Raison d'être

Carola Groppe

1. Introduction

In Germany, the history of education is a field of study that, though overlapping with educational science in some areas, cannot be confined to any one discipline. Research into history of education is conducted throughout many disciplines, such as the sciences of history, education, philology or sociology. The history of education is thus not defined through its relation to other disciplines but through its cognitive interest, which I believe can be summed up as follows: History of education focuses on the historical development of the relationship between the individual and society in its conveyance through processes of education and socialisation. Thus, it includes comprehensive study of socialisation in a historical framework, as well as the history of institutions, pedagogic professions, theory and discourse.

At the same time, questions of education and socialisation are a primary cognitive interest of the broadly differentiated discipline of educational science. Chairs of history of education were thus established mainly within educational science. The purpose of this paper is to outline the process of institutionalisation of the history of education, as well as the development of research in 20th century Germany. Resulting issues of the history of education within the scientific field and beyond will be discussed.

2. Historic Development

Within the current German scientific community, the history of education is considered part of the discipline of educational science. The German Society for Educational Science (DGfE – founded in 1964) has a department dedicated to the History of Education (founded in 1972, with approximately 300 members) among its 13 departments and 21 committees.[1] A lengthy process, the most important steps of which are outlined

---

[1] See http://www.dgfe.de/ueber/ (Zugriff 22.11.2010).

in the following chapter, preceded this institutionalisation of historical research within educational science.

2.1 Institutionalisation

The history of German educational science itself plays an important part. As late as 1800, matters of pedagogy were still considered part of theological and philosophical reflection[2] and as such the business of professors at faculties of arts and philosophy (Immanuel Kant had held a chair of logics and metaphyics at the philosophical faculty of the University of Königsberg[3] since 1770). A fundamental change only came about in the Weimar Republic.

As Immanuel Kant held a chair at the preparatory faculty ('Faculty of Arts') leading to professional studies at the faculties of theology, law and medicine, he and his colleagues were required to read a variety of materials intended to provide students with prerequisite common knowledge qualifying them for a university course. These materials included subject matter drawn from geography and anthropology. Such a preparatory faculty was necessary, as there were no norms for university access: students starting university had acquired vastly different qualifications through private education or attendance of grammar schools (with vastly different curricula). However, the process of increasing social and scientific appreciation of the philosophical faculty had started at the universities of Halle (est. 1694) and Göttingen (est. 1737) as early as the mid eighteenth century.[4] Through its connections to Britain, Göttingen had a certain international flair and became a university for the sons of nobility, gentry and bourgeoisie. They studied cameralism (science of administration), law or imperial history and, through their high social standing, brought prestige to the philosophical faculty.

Classical philology was among the disciplines that profited from these circumstances, achieving a prominent standing and becoming a field of study, teaching and research in its own right, rather than a mere preparatory subject. When the universities of Prussia were restructured

---

[2] See for example Immanuel Kant, „Über Pädagogik" (1803) in Immanuel Kant, Werke in zehn Bänden, Bd. 10, Schriften zur Anthropologie, Geschichtsphilosophie, Politik und Pädagogik, Teil 2, ed. Wilhelm Weischedel (Darmstadt, 1975), pp. 695-761.

[3] See on the function of the faculty of arts Walter Rüegg, Geschichte der Universität in Europa. Band 2: Von der Reformation zur Französischen Revolution 1500-1800 (München: CH Beck, 1996).

[4] See Hans-Ulrich Wehler, Deutsche Gesellschaftsgeschichte. Bd. 1. Vom Feudalismus des Alten Reiches bis zur Defensiven Modernisierung der Reformära, 1700-1815 (München: CH Beck, 1996), p. 294ff.

in the early nineteenth century, the universites of Halle and Göttingen served as models. After losing considerable territory in the Treaties of Tilsit in 1807, the state of Prussia was left with only two of its previous five universities: Königsberg and Frankfurt (Oder). The loss of Halle University was especially devastating. Wilhelm von Humboldt reopened this university again in Berlin on 16 August 1809 with the help of professors who had emigrated from Halle to Berlin. Furthermore, he completed the ascent of the philosophical faculty and, in connection with the reform of collegiate schools, declared it an equal faculty that championed the idea of universities as seats of study, science and research.[5] At the same time, the philosophical faculty took on a new kind of student body: prospective grammar school teachers. Despite these developments, pedagogy could not establish itself as a scientific discipline at universities during the nineteenth century. Prussian universities only required prospective teachers to study pedagogy during the so-called probation years (one-year internship with a one-year pedagogic seminar, added in 1890).[6] Pedagogy was a requirement only at training colleges and seminars for prospective primary school teachers.[7]

Nineteenth century concepts for a 'practical science' predated the academic establishment of pedagogy in the beginning of the twentieth century. This idea of a 'practical science' had been developed as a result of the development of primary schools, out of sheer practical necessity and due to career-strategic demands on the part of teachers. At the same time, philosophically rooted concepts of pedagogy as a science emerged, trying to establish educational science as an academic discipline.[8] However, it was only in the Weimar Republic that a Prussian-based development began to establish pedagogy as a scientific discipline taught at universities with its own chairs. The aim was for educational science to not only serve as a part of teacher training but also

---

[5] See R. Steven Turner, „Universitäten" in Handbuch der deutschen Bildungsgeschichte. Bd. III, 1800-1870. Von der Neuordnung Deutschlands bis zur Gründung des Deutschen Reiches ed. Karl-Ernst Jeismann & Peter Lundgreen (München: CH Beck, 1987), pp. 221-249, p. 227. Walter Rüegg, „Themen, Probleme, Erkenntnisse" in Geschichte der Universität in Europa. Bd. III. Vom 19. Jahrhundert zum Zweiten Weltkrieg (1800-1945) ed. Walter Rüegg (München: CH Beck, 2004), pp. 17-41, p. 18ff.

[6] See Hartmut Titze, „Lehrerbildung und Professionalisierung", in Handbuch der deutschen Bildungsgeschichte Bd. IV 1870-1918. Von der Reichsgründung bis zum Ende des Ersten Weltkrieg ed. Christa Berg (München: CH Beck, 1991), pp. 345-370, p. 348.

[7] See Titze, op. cit., p. 358.

[8] See Heinz-Elmar Tenorth, „Erziehungswissenschaft", in Historisches Wörterbuch der Pädagogik, ed. Dietrich Benner & Jürgen Oelkers, (Weinheim und Basel: Beltz, 2004) pp. 341-382, p. 353ff.

as a way of accompanying and leading the way for social and political change.[9] However, through the course of this development, it was not an empirical educational science but a humanistic pedagogy that was established. This humanistic pedagogy strived for legitimisation of the autonomy (as opposed to societal function) of pedagogy as well as the establishment and historical-normative foundation of norms and values for education through philosophical reflection.[10] Yet, humanistic pedagogy was by no means immune to an affinity with Nazi ideology during the Third Reich.[11] Beyond institutional attempts towards securing conformity, account should also be taken of an animosity towards liberalism and democracy as well as ideological irrationalism being exhibited by many in educational science.[12] After the end of World War II, humanistic pedagogy could initially re-establish itself as a normative science.[13] The introduction of a degree in educational sciences in the late 1960s created undergraduate courses which allowed for the differentiation of various subdisciplines. The foundation of a separate section for the History of Education within the German Society for Educational Science in 1972 points to this fact. The history of education has had an institutional basis since then, including its own media outlet, the *Jahrbuch für Historische Bildungsforschung* (Annual History of Education), first published in 1993. However, since 1990 the increasing importance of quantitative-empirical educational research and, in the aftermath of PISA, of school education and didactics, has turned the history of education into one of the endangered subdisciplines of educational sciences in Germany.

Other disciplines also deal with questions of the history of education. General history and German philology continue to contribute to the history of education through historical and discourse-historical research

---

[9] See Heinz-Elmar Tenorth, „Pädagogisches Denken" in Handbuch der deutschen Bildungsgeschichte, Bd. V 1918-1945. Die Weimarer Republik und die nationalsozialistische Diktatur ed. Dieter Langewiesche & Heinz-Elmar Tenorth (München: C.H. Beck, 1989), pp. 111-153, p. 116ff.; Carola Groppe, Die Macht der Bildung. Das deutsche Bürgertum und der George-Kreis 1890-1933 (Köln, Weimar, Wien: Böhlau, 1997), pp. 535-560.

[10] See Herman Nohl, Die pädagogische Bewegung in Deutschland und ihre Theorie (1933/1935) (Frankfurt am Main: Klostermann, 7. Aufl. 1970).

[11] See Heinz-Elmar Tenorth, „Erziehungswissenschaft in Deutschland – Skizze ihrer Geschichte von 1900 bis zur Vereinigung 1990" in Geschichte von Erziehungswissenschaft und Erziehungswirklichkeit ed. Klaus Harney & Heinz-Hermann Krüger (Opladen & Bloomfield Hills: Barbara Budrich 2006), pp. 133-173, p. 139ff.

[12] See Heinz-Elmar Tenorth, „Pädagogisches Denken", op.cit., p. 135ff.

[13] See Eva Matthes, Geisteswissenschaftliche Pädagogik nach der NS-Zeit. Politische und pädagogische Verarbeitungsversuche (Bad Heilbrunn: Julius Klinkhard, 1998).

into conceptual and intellectual history[14] and through the development of the educational system or family relationships[15]. However, these areas of research are not institutionalised within their disciplines.

2.2 Development of Research

The late institutionalisation of the history of education as a subdiscipline of educational sciences says nothing about the development of research. It must be noted that research into the history of education – as defined at the outset of this paper – was already being conducted within the disciplines of history, philosophy and German philology in the late 19th century.[16]

These works of research however served various purposes, one of which was educational political goals. On the basis of historical developments, humanistic pedagogy argued for the autonomy of pedagogy and the importance of its educational goals. When Herman Nohl (1879-1960), one of the most important advocates of humanistic pedagogy in Germany, wrote his manuscript *Die Deutsche Bewegung* (a compilation of his lectures known under that title since 1921) in 1939, he drew on research papers, some of which had been drafted as early as the pre-WWI era.[17] Nohl saw the "German Movement" in poetry and philosophy between 1770 and 1830 as a specifically German counter-movement to European Enlightenment, an expression of a special national spirit. The aim of his lecture was thus:

> to make this fact of the higher life within the German Movement transparent, in order to find, through study of the purport and internal cohesion of this spiritual constitution, the basis on which to found our intellectual confidence and inner unity of learning.[18]

[14] See for example Georg Bollenbeck, Bildung und Kultur. Glanz und Elend eines deutschen Deutungsmusters (Frankfurt a.M., Leipzig: Suhrkamp, 1994).
[15] See for example Gunilla Friederike Budde, Auf dem Weg ins Bürgerleben. Kindheit und Erziehung in deutschen und englischen Bürgerfamilien 1840–1914 (Göttingen: Vandenhoeck & Ruprecht, 1994).
[16] See for example Friedrich Paulsen, Geschichte des gelehrten Unterrichts auf den deutschen Schulen und Universitäten vom Ausgang des Mittelalters bis zur Gegenwart (Berlin, Leipzig 3. erw. Aufl.: Walter de Gruyter & Co, 1921).
[17] See Herman Nohl, „Die Deutsche Bewegung und die idealistischen Systeme" (1911) in Hermann Nohl, Die Deutsche Bewegung. Vorlesungen und Aufsätze zur Geistesgeschichte von 1770-1830 ed. Otto Friedrich Bollnow, Frithjof Rodi (Göttingen: Vandenhoeck & Ruprecht, 1970), pp. 78-86.
[18] Herman Nohl, „Die Deutsche Bewegung" (Die Göttinger Vorlesung, 1939) in Herman Nohl, Die deutsche Bewegung, op. cit., pp.87-230, p. 90. [translated by the author] „[...] diese Tatsache des höheren Lebens in der Deutschen Bewegung durchsichtig zu machen, um in dem Studium ihres Gehaltes und des inneren Zusammenhangs dieser geistigen Verfassung die Substanz zu finden, auf die wir unser geistiges Selbstbewußtsein und die innere Einheit unserer Bildung gründen können."

Nohls description of the "Pedagogic Movement" (1933/35) continues the thought: the pedagogic movement is part of the German movement.[19] Following demise in the nineteenth century[20], its historical task is to through a "new unity of cultural will", form a "'gestalt' [...] in which the concept of education may be fulfilled".[21] Pedagogically imparted "authenticity, increased responsibility [...], a will to conformation and allegiance" are the foundation for this, while at the sime time determining the choice of educational subjects: historic figures and works of the German Movement.[22] Nohl assumes laws of history, dividing eras into phases of rises, cultural peaks and demises, which only differ in their individual manifestation. Nohl confidently defines the purpose of the contemporary pedagogic movementas "a service, an active dedication to that which is timeless"[23]. Comparable attitudes towards the significance of history can be found in other advocates of humanistic pedagogy, such as Wilhelm Flitner (1889-1990). As late as 1967 he saw the western lifestyles of antiquity and the Middle Ages as "potent complexes of norms", which he systematically consults against the backdrop of their relevance to the "new world of the industrial era".[24] Eduard Spranger (1882-1963) sees basic categories of social life and moral orientation as ultimately not shaped historically but determined anthropologically. Historical manifestations are thus mere emanations of anthropological constants, identifying and illustrating them:

> For example, what family should and should not be, is in its quintessence already present in the mind. The same goes for the quintessences of other norms:

---

[19] See Herman Nohl, Die pädagogische Bewegung in Deutschland und ihre Theorie (Frankfurt a.M.: G. Schulte-Bumke, 7. unveränd. Aufl., 1970), p. 94.

[20] Nohl understands this to be the "social, moral and intellectual destitution of our people, which has befallen our minds due to the development of industry, cities, labour and housing conditions and the scientific enlightenment and development of specialised science. The subjects sense of self-worth was lost in the process." Herman Nohl, Die pädagogische Bewegung in Deutschland und ihre Theorie, op. cit., p. 3f. [translated by the author] die „soziale, sittliche und geistige Not unseres Volkes, die durch die Entwicklung der Industrie, der Großstädte, der Arbeits- und Wohnverhältnisse, aber auch durch die naturwissenschaftliche Aufklärung und die Entwicklung der Spezialwissenschaften über die Seelen hereingebrochen ist. In diesem Prozeß ging der Selbstwert des Subjekts verloren."

[21] Ibid., p. 90, p. 10. [translated by the author] „neue Einheit des Kulturwillens" [...] „Gestalt [...], in der sich der Begriff der Bildung erst erfüllt".

[22] See ibid., p. 79ff., quotation p. 92. [translated by the author] „Wahrhaftigkeit, Steigerung der Verantwortlichkeit [...], Wille zu Form und Bindung".

[23] Ibid., p. 219. [translated by the author] „Dienst, d.h. die tätige Hingabe an ein Objektives".

[24] Wilhelm Flitner, Die Geschichte der abendländischen Lebensformen. Vorwort zur 2. Auflage 1967 in Wilhelm Flitner, Gesammelte Schriften Bd. 7, ed. Karl Erlinghagen & Andreas Flitner & Ulrich Herrmann (Paderborn, München u.a.: Schöningh, 1990), p. 23, p. 27ff. [translated by the author] „lebendig wirksamen Normgefüge" [...] „neue Welt der industriellen Epoche".

> what constitutes moral power and morally justified obedience is already intuitively present in man's heart.[25]

Historical developments become a functional aspect of systematic problem definitions and solutions; they are not empirically researched but used selectively with normative intent. With regard to history, a history of pedagogic ideas, the 'great educators' and the normatively oriented analysis of specific eras were dominant. The history of education was by no means considered across its entire spectrum. This way, history loses its distinct explanatory potential of the formation and problems of educational institutions and pedagogic thought forms and thus its relevance as a critical corrective and medium for reflexion of current educational political decisions and developments of the field of pedagogy.

When educational sciences turned towards social science in the 1960s, the history of education freed itself from normative efforts and focused on themes of social sciences. New focal points were, among others, questions of socialisation and the development of pedagogic institutions.[26] These were approached through educational-statistical and sociological analysis. Besides an import of theories and methods from related disciplines, this initially also brought about a new self-image of a 'critical pedagogy'. In 1975, Ulrich Herrman defined the role of the research of the history of education as follows:

> If the purport of historical research is the elucidation of the past as the prologue to the present – thus identifying present constraints, opportunities and alternatives with regard to shaping the future – then the result must be a characteristic form and function of historiography relevant to the present and the future.[27]

---

[25] Eduard Spranger, Gedanken zur staatsbürgerlichen Erziehung (1957). (Bochum: Kamp, erw. Ausg., 1963), p. 45. [translated by the author] „Was z. B. die Familie sein soll und nicht sein sollte, das [...] lebt dem Kern nach gleichsam apriori im Gemüt. So ist es, dem Kern nach, auch für andere Ordnungen: was sittliche Macht ist und sittlich gerechtfertigter Gehorsam, das trägt der Mensch im voraus ahnungsweise in der Tiefe seiner Brust."

[26] See Dietrich Benner & Friedrich Brüggen, „Theorien der Erziehungswissenschaft im 20. Jahrhundert. Entwicklungsprobleme – Paradigmen – Aussichten" in Bildungsprozesse und Erziehungsverhältnisse im 20. Jahrhundert. Praktische Entwicklungen und Formen der Reflexion im historischen Kontext = Zeitschrift für Pädagogik, 42. Beiheft ed. Dietrich Benner & Heinz-Elmar Tenorth (Weinheim, Basel: Beltz, 2000), pp. 240-263, p. 249ff.

[27] Ulrich Herrmann, „Probleme einer Erziehungswissenschaftlichen Historik" (1975) in Ulrich Herrmann, Historische Bildungsforschung und Sozialgeschichte der Bildung. Programme – Analysen – Ergebnisse (Weinheim: Deutscher Studien Verlag, 1991), pp. 11–19, p. 17. [translated by the author] „Wenn der Sinn der historischen Forschung in der Aufklärung der Vergangenheit als der Vorgeschichte der Gegenwart liegt – mithin im Auffinden gegenwärtiger Zwänge, Möglichkeiten und Alternativen im Hinblick auf eine zu gestaltende Zukunft –, dann muss sich daraus eine charakteristische gegenwarts- und zukunftsbezogene Form und Funktion der Geschichtsschreibung ergeben."

The cognitive interest thus remained similar to that of older pedagogic historiography: History should enter into focus to the extent that it makes a – now critical – contribution to the solution of specific problems of the present day. This changed in the 1970s. Historical pedagogy, which had acted with a "strong focus on practice and profession" and a normative orientation, became an autonomous subdiscipline: History of Education, recognised by and connected with its related disciplines of history and sociology.[28] Studies into the history of education were presented, especially about the history of the educational system, analysing its structural development and participation in education, as well as its role in the greater context of developments in educational policy and society as a whole.[29] The ensuing years saw the publication of many papers on the history of education, usually focusing on questions of social history and history of everyday life about intergenerational relationships and processes of socialisation, as well as educational institutions and professions. The six volumes of the *Handbuch der deutschen Bildungsgeschichte* (Handbook of German History of Education) offered a first comprehensive overview of the subject.[30] This development was connected with an increasing pluralism of theories and methods, a wider range of sources and a departure from questions of practice-related action orientation.[31] Peter Vogel identifies three general areas of educational scientific research: educational science as empirical science, as practice-oriented science and as a reflective science. While the first area is concerned with empirical analysis of educational reality and theoretical interpretation of acquired results, the second drafts possible solutions to problems in educational reality that are appropriate to the findings of educational research and critically reviewed. The third area phrases and reviews the groundwork of educational-scientific research, i.e. central ideas,

---

[28] Heinz-Elmar Tenorth, „Historische Bildungsforschung", in Handbuch Bildungsforschung ed. Rudolf Tippelt (Opladen: Leske + Budrich, 2002), pp. 123-139, p. 123. [translated by the author] „stark praxis- und professionsfixiert".

[29] See for example Achim Leschinsky & Peter Martin Roeder, Schule im historischen Prozess. um Wechselverhältnis von institutioneller Erziehung und gesellschaftlicher Entwicklung (Stuttgart: Klett-Cotta, 1976); Detlef K. Müller, Sozialstruktur und Schulsystem. Aspekte zum Strukturwandel des Schulwesens im 19. Jahrhundert (Göttingen: Vandenhoeck & Ruprecht, 1977); Detlef K. Müller & Bernd Zymek [unter Mitarb. von Ulrich G. Herrmann], Sozialgeschichte und Statistik des Schulsystems in den Staaten des Deutschen Reiches 1800-1945 = Datenhandbuch zur deutschen Bildungsgeschichte, Bd.II, Höhere und mittlere Schulen, 1. Teil (Göttingen: Vandenhoeck & Ruprecht, 1987).

[30] See Christa Berg et al. (Eds.), Handbuch der deutschen Bildungsgeschichte, Bd. 1-6 (München: CH Beck, 1987-2005).

[31] See Heinz-Elmar Tenorth, „Historische Bildungsforschung", op. cit., pp. 123ff.

These developments may be positively interpreted as a process of emancipation and constitution of an independent field of research. The external perception of the history of education as no longer being a necessary part of educational science researching the pedagogical field may be problematic. This includes educational science itself. The transformation of the results of educational historical research into the horizon of reflection of other subdisciplines seems difficult, insofar as firmly historical thinking, in contrast to the approach of humanistic pedagogy, serves as a critical authority of categories and topics of research. While educational-historical research seems an integral, though marginal, part of pluralised fields of research within philology or specialist history and is thus rarely reflected upon, the history of education is deeply rooted in educational science and must deal with and convey its function and relevance within the latter. This creates an ambivalent situation: the development of the history of education as a discipline – its autonomisation from duties of legitimisation and the research achievements resulting from this autonomisation – leads to an obligation to justify its benefits to educational science. Due to the history of education being poorly institutionalisted and of little relevance in related disciplines, mention of referential sciences is largely obsolete. Within Germany, the history of education mainly has to face questions about the nature of its contributions, in its current constitution, to educational science, for example, why the history of education should not be entirely integrated into specialist history and which argumentative explanations there are for this problem area in the context of educational science. The first item concerns epistemological principles and questions of disciplinary history, the second item concerns aspects of discourse history and sciency policy.

3. Raison d' être

3.1 Epistemological Principles and Disciplinary History

In science, phenomena of crisis usually lead to self-thematisation, to "codifying all knowledge worth preserving" and to "taking stock of the state of development, alternatively to controversy about status and potential of the discipline".[32] Similar phenomena may be currently apparent in the discipline of the history of education (with this very book being a manifestation of them). In this context, the 14th annual issue of the *Zeitschrift für pädagogische Historiographie* (Journal of Pedagogic Historiography) in 2009 devoted its discussion section to the topic of "Learning from History (of Education)". On the one hand, the title indicates that the history of education is seen as being part of general historical research, thus going beyond the scope of educational science. On the other, the 20 short essays printed in the journal describe opportunities and problems of the history of education in the context of educational science.[33] While the first aspect refers to the potential of historical research to provide insights into contemporary problems in general, the second aspect refers to the question as to how the history of education contributes to educational science. I shall summarise some of the central theses of these essays and complement them with a suggestion of my own.

The essays point out the poor basis for interpreting empirical studies without a connection to history[34] and highlight the enlightening effect of historical analyses regarding problems of the present.[35] Further, the facilitation of alternative thought through historical perspective is discussed.[36] The possibility of dissociation of institutional structures and conventional thought forms through the history of education is emphasised, thus referencing an emancipatory process.[37] Furthermore, recurring points of legitimisation of twentieth century history of education are science-historically observed. It is noted that, despite significant chang-

[32]Heinz-Elmar Tenorth, „Erziehungswissenschaft in Deutschland", op. cit., p. 147. [translated by the author] „Kodifizierung des bewahrenswerten Wissens" [...] „Bilanzierung ihres Entwicklungsstandes, andererseits zu Kontroversen über den Status und die Möglichkeiten des Faches". For the turn of the century 20th century see Gunter Scholtz, Zwischen Wissenschaftsanspruch und Orientierungsbedürfnis: zu Grundlage und Wandel der Geisteswissenschaften (Frankfurt a.M.: Suhrkamp, 1991); Gangolf Hübinger, „Wertkollisionen im frühen 20. Jahrhundert. Die Kompetenz der Geisteswissenschaften zur Deutung sozialer Wirklichkeit" in Wissenschaften und Wissenschaftspolitik: Bestandsaufnahmen zu Formationen, Brüchen und Kontinuitäten im Deutschland des 20. Jahrhunderts ed. Rüdiger vom Bruch & Brigitte Kaderas (Stuttgart: Steiner, 2002), pp. 75-83; Carola Groppe, Die Macht der Bildung, op. cit.

[33] See Zeitschrift für pädagogische Historiographie 14, Heft 2 (2009), pp. 68-88.

[34]See Jonas Flöter, „Mit der Geschichte lernen!" in Zeitschrift für pädagogische Historiographie, op. cit., pp. 71-72, p. 72.

[35] See Edith Glaser, „Aus Bildungsgeschichte(n) lernen? in Zeitschrift für pädagogische Historiographie, op.cit., pp. 75-76, p. 75.

[36] See Eva Matthes, "Gedanken zum Stellenwert und zur Situation der Historischen Bildungsforschung im universitären Alltag" in Zeitschrift für pädagogische Historiographie, op.cit., pp.80-81, p. 80f.

[37] See Bernd Zymek, „Orientierung? Distanzierung!" in Zeitschrift für pädagogische Historiographie, op.cit., p. 88.

es in educational science, they barely differ at all, namely consisting in the emphasis on orientation and enlightenment. This phenomenon is perceived to be both eye-opening as well as disconcerting.[38]

In summary, the arguments and suggestions presented in the contributions take on the question as to the relevance of history to society and the collective and individual conscience in general. Drawing on historian Hans-Ulrich Wehler's work, contributions to the discussion argue that history can provide orientational knowledge but no knowledge that may be used to gain power or upon which to base decisions to offer solutions to current problems.[39] It prevents utopian certainty of salvation and spontaneous solutions and enables critical dissociation. According to Hans-Ulrich Wehler, it leads to a "sceptical, realistic judgement and understanding of problems".[40] The contributions go on to argue that the history of education provides the historical foundation for educational science's specific topics of research while at the same time subjecting the research findings to a historical review.

Like any other scientific discipline, educational science needs and possesses a historical memory. This memory is usually rooted within the disciplines themselves. However, it also overlaps with history, such as in the field of the history of science, but also in other subdisciplines, such as history of law or economics. History as a science of all that is historical is thus a reference frame for historical subdisciplines of other sciences. However, these historical subdisciplines also have specific functions within their respective sciences and are thus rooted both there and in history. While within the disciplines they historically reflect upon topics specific to those disciplines, within history they are part of a discipline-specific order which helps to treat the historical field in general and has structured it according to a disciplinary inner logic. In Germany, the history of education is not a subdiscipline of history in its own right – as opposed to economic history. One possible hypothesis is that the marginalisation of the history of education from educational science[41] may in part be due to history not establishing this field of research as a subdiscipline and thus not bringing it to attention.

---

[38] See Andreas Hoffmann-Ocon, „Orientierung oder Irritation durch Bildungsgeschichte?" in Zeitschrift für pädagogische Historiographie, op. cit., pp. 76-77, p. 76f.

[39] See Hans-Ulrich Wehler, Aus der Geschichte lernen? Essays (München: CH Beck, 1988), p. 12f.

[40] Ibid, p. 13. [translated by the author] „skeptischen, realitätsnahen Urteil und Verständnis von Problemen".

[41] See Marcelo Caruso, „Abdankung der Geschichte: Chancen der Fragmente" in Zeitschrift für pädagogische Historiographie, op.cit., pp. 69-70, p. 69.

As part of its function within the discipline, the history of education takes on certain responsibilities: it develops insights into the historic developments of both educational science itself and its objects of research (childhood, adolescence, school, family). It thus provides insights into the historical conditionality of its research topics and, on a meta level, into the historicity of its insights (through disciplinary and economic history).[42]

The history of education thus provides the basis for educational scientific research. However, I believe it also serves as a heuristic frame of reference to related disciplines, such as history, sociology or the philologies, by highlighting the historic development of the relationship between society and the individual in its communication through processes of education and socialisation. Due to its cognitive interest, it is also oriented in an interdisciplinary way, both in theory and method and also in its use of sources and bodies of knowledge. The history of education may highlight historical trends and developments of problems, from processes of education to current problems. Through empirical research, it can also question seemingly obvious trends, such as the history of childhood as a history of increasing liberalisation instead of an ambivalent relationship between increasing institutionalisation and nationalisation on the one hand and breaking away from formerly binding lifestyles on the other.[43] These are all achievements and insights which "empirico-analytical theory construction and methodology themselves cannot yield".[44] Pierre Bourdieu's statement in a 1985 interview may be read thus: "Totality, to me, is thus nothing that eludes definition; that can only be sought through the *theory* of society. To me, totality is something that has a social origin and may be explained scientifically. We are always situated in particularity, historicity. The problem of generality, universality, presents itself from here".[45] Thus, criticism of theories and science is one of the

[42]See Ulrich Herrmann, „Historische Sozialisationsforschung" in Neues Handbuch der Sozialisationsforschung ed. Klaus Hurrelmann & Dieter Ulich (Weinheim, Basel 4. völlig neubearb. Aufl.: Beltz, 1991), pp. 231-250, p. 237.

[43] See Tenorth, „Historische Bildungsforschung", op. cit., p. 136.

[44] Herrmann, „Historische Sozialisationsforschung", op. cit., p. 237. [translated by the author] „die empirisch-analytische Theoriebildung und Methodologie ja selbst nicht hergeben kann".

[45] Pierre Bourdieu, „Vernunft ist eine historische Errungenschaft, wie die Sozialversicherung. Bernd Schwibs im Gespräch mit Pierre Bourdieu" in Lebensstil und Lernform. Zur Kultursoziologie Pierre Bourdieus (= Neue Sammlung 3/85, Themenheft) ed. Eckart Liebau & Sebastian Müller-Rolli, pp. 376-394, p. 387. [translated by the author] „Daher [...] [ist] für mich [...] die Totalität kein der Definition sich Entziehendes, einholbar nur durch die Theorie der Gesellschaft; für mich ist Totalität etwas, das eine soziale Genese hat [...] und wissenschaftlich expliziert werden kann. [...] Jedenfalls befinden wir uns immer in der Partikularität, im Historischen. Und das Problem des Allgemeinen, Universellen, stellt sich von hier aus."

tasks of the history of education.

From this epistemological and discipline-historical position, we may make the transition to the relevance of the history of education to society. Identity can be described as a self-reflective conscience which requires not only the continuity of self-experience and a positive self-image but also the capacity for self-distance. This applies both to individual as well as collective identity formation processes. However, it takes historical analysis to interpret why societies differ in their collective identity and their action orientation and it is the history of education that, due to its special cognitive interest, explains the course of the individual and collective process of identity formation.

The history of education suggests no course of action but, through its particular educational scientific cognitive interest, it teaches a better understanding of oneself as an individual, a specific collective, a scientific discipline within the context of nation or society, thus teaching how to distance oneself from one's self. Apart from the arguments referenced above, I believe this to be a unique accomplishment of the history of education.

3.2 Discourse Theory and Science Policy

Due to reasons often discussed and analysed, the so-called life and natural sciences as well as engineering sciences currently are not only highly esteemed among the general public but also have a high standing with government research funding at universities and certain research centres. However, the distribution of student figures does not mirror this. Nevertheless, facilities and prestige differ greatly between the humanities and social science on the one side and life and natural sciences on the other. A more obvious scope of application, a perceived greater benefit to society and an assumed immediate utilty of research results from the latter, force the humanities and social sciences into a defensive position in the public and the scientific and academic communities.

According to Foucault,[46] discourse is not merely a debate on a specific subject, but a comprehensive set of rules concerning what can or cannot be spoken of, how and where we speak in certain areas of knowledge and action and the assignment of the privilege to speak. For the humanities and social sciences, as fully developed and theoretically and methodically substantiated disciplines, to be dismissed as redundant

[46] See Michel Foucault: Die Ordnung des Diskurses. Inauguralvorlesung am Collège de France 1970 (Frankfurt a.M., Berlin, Wien: Suhrkamp, 1977).

is thus impossible, both in educational policy and in the field of science. It is nevertheless possible to suggest the rules and goals of other sciences: an orientation towards application (research on learning and instruction) and the direct utility of research results (quantitative empirical educational research).

The rules of discourse are not 'made', they emerge through a process of development involving society as a whole. It is thus impossible to influence discourse at will and the idea that sound arguments alone could substantially change the standing of the history of education within the scientific system and the public sphere is an illusion. Historical knowledge is currently – as opposed to the nineteenth century – not an important reference in scientific or public debate. Whether it will ever be again remains to be seen. However, sound arguments for (educational) historical research are never idle. They enable (education) historians to stand up for themselves in the scientific and public discourse, thus not seeming powerless. While it will not put an end to ever-increasing challenges, it might reduce the risk of being 'overpowered' in discourse.

The above mentioned section of the *Journal of Pedagogic Historiography* proposes a solution to the concrete question of the discipline-historical positioning of the history of education: to avoid marginalisation of the history of education at least in educational science, the history of education should respond to the postmodern fragmentation of lifestyles and construction of meaning with corresponding research which does not strive to do justice to a 'big picture'.[47] Further, the formation of a stronger connection between the history of education and current socio- and cultural historic issues such as transculturality or multi-ethnicity is advocated.[48] The case for this could easily be argued against the backdrop of the science-historical observation that patterns of justification of the history of education remain almost the same throughout the 20th century: namely consisting in orientation. But what about the highlighting and distancing of oneself from current institutional structures (or de-institutionalisation) and conventional thought forms, even when they appear as scientific approaches? The history of education needs the whole plurality of its research to achieve this, thus fulfilling its task as a critical historical memory of the discipline and beyond, by not only consulting similarities and precursory developments in historic eras, but

---

[47] See Marcelo Caruso, „Abdankung der Geschichte: Chancen der Fragmente", op. cit., p. 69f.

[48] See Wolfgang Gippert, „Transkulturelle Perspektiven in der Historischen Bildungsforschung" in Zeitschrift für pädagogische Historiographie, op.cit., p. 73-74.

also emphasising the differences and 'the other' of these eras compared to the present. Plurality of research and the communication of variety do not lessen the need for legitimisation of the history of education – quite the contrary. However, they are necessary for the history of education to fulfil its responsibilities.

From descriptive to theory-oriented research: Norwegian historical-educational research in a historical perspective

Alfred Oftedal Telhaug

The focus of this article is exclusively on historical pedagogy as a subdiscipline in Norwegian pedagogy and in particular in Norwegian scientific pedagogy. With this as the point of departure, the author of this article focuses on the historical development of Norwegian historical pedagogy over the last hundred years, and the presentation is closely connected to the division into epochs that the Norwegian history research community has established over time. The main questions thus are: What position does historical pedagogy enjoy under the various state formations? What importance or purpose is it assigned in a social perspective? Which issues has it examined and does it continue to examine in our time? The article is critical to the overly pessimistic tone of the introduction to this anthology by Jesper Eckhardt Larsen, and tries optimistically to defend the new grounds that have been broken in through new historical educational research in Norway.

The liberal state epoch and the formative years of historical pedagogy – 1880-1935/40

The formative period of historical pedagogy in Norway can be linked without hesitation to the epoch that recent Norwegian history research has found it appropriate to call the liberal state epoch.[1] It begins with the breakthrough of parliamentarism in 1884, and it is replaced by the social democratic regime and this regime's "blissful" moment with the formation of a Labour Government in 1935. Next to the breakthrough of the parliamentary system, the dissolution of the Norwegian union with Sweden was the great political event of this period.

The social democratic regime found inspiration for its political views in the French and American revolutions and their ideas of liberty,

[1] Rune Slagstad: De nasjonale strateger (Pax: Oslo 1998), Chapter II "Venstrestaten". Alfred Oftedal Telhaug and Odd Asbjørn Mediås: Grunnskolen som nasjonsbygger. Fra statspietisme til nyliberalisme. (Oslo 2003), Chapter 3. See also Harald Thuen: "Skolen - et liberalistisk prosjekt? 1860-2010." Norsk Pedagogisk Tidsskrift (2010).

equality and brotherhood, and from the Norwegian Constitution of 1814 with its fundamental ideas of sovereignty of the people and division of power. The cultural community during this period drew from the philosophy of the Enlightenment, and perhaps more importantly, were inspired by Romantic idealism. This movement elicited a positive picture of the population from people from all walks of life. They felt that their most compelling duty was to identify the real Norway; that which was genuine and common to Norwegian features. In other words to identify Norway's special national characteristics. Each nation, including Norway, had to learn to know itself. The time was ripe to establish a national awareness. Based on this glorification of the Norwegian people and the spirit of the people, the great project of the liberal state was to reawaken the national spirit or the character of the Norwegian people. More than anything else, this required a historical perspective.

In this political-cultural context it became the task of the elementary school to contribute to an ethnic-historical nation building project, and history was seen as one of school's most important subjects, or perhaps even the most important one. It was to nourish the national self-esteem and love of the fatherland. In terms of methodology, this goal meant that pedagogy cultivated the charismatic presenter who would narrate, describe, explain, ask and converse. The textbook used during this period, P.A. Jensen's 1863, *Læsebog for Folkeskolen og Folkehjemmet* (Reader for Elementary School and Homes) which provided both brief and longer narratives that appealed to the children, taught them how to be "Norwegian citizens" and "carried them along to that great thing we call the 'fatherland'".

At the beginning of this epoch, pedagogical theory had already established itself as a subject to be studied in teacher training that was designed to qualify a teacher for work in the compulsory primary school sector, then called elementary school.[2] This did not mean, however, that the subject of pedagogy had a dominant position within this education, and until the Act that came into force in 1938, pedagogy did not belong more generally among the main subjects in the curriculum for general teacher training. With the Act relating to teaching seminars of 1890, as the teaching colleges were called at the time, the teaching hours in pedagogy were halved both absolutely and relatively compared to the scope allocated by the regulations governing the seminars from 1869.

[2] See Torstein Harbo: Teori og praksis i den pedagogiske utdannelse. Studier i norsk pedagogikk 1818-1922 (Oslo, Bergen, Tromsø 1969)

This was due to the fact that pedagogy was considered to be far inferior to such subjects as Christian religion and Norwegian. When it came to the priorities of disciplines within pedagogic studies, until the 1930s, school history had a dominant position compared for example, to educational psychology. This was probably due to some extent to the fact that the theorists of the time were not convinced that psychological, experimental research would produce reliable knowledge, nor were they willing to perceive the teacher as a practitioner who would be supplied by the researcher or theoretician with psycho-technical insight that would improve their practice in a linear way. The pedagogical theory was primarily intended to give general pedagogical education. It was to stimulate independent reflection, build up teachers as cultural personalities and show how schools had been throughout history. This was a duty that historical pedagogy was well suited to discharging. Hence, historical pedagogy was not only highly appreciated due to its validity function, but also because of the wish to promote national awareness among the population. The "soul" of school was the dedicated and riveting teacher with stories that would speak to the heart as well as the mind.

If we then turn to pedagogy as an academic discipline, taking its place as a subject in higher education and as a research field, we can again confirm that the period of the liberal state was this discipline's formative period. In 1907, a pedagogical seminar was established at the University of Oslo to train candidates who wanted to work as teachers in upper secondary education. In 1909, Otto Anderssen was granted a personal professorship in pedagogy, a position, which was later changed into a regular professorial chair.[3] At the Teaching College in Trondheim, an institution which gave teachers in primary and lower secondary education one year of supplementary education, Søren Nordeide was appointed as a professor when the institution was founded in 1922.[4] While Nordeide divided his attention between a number of academic disciplines, including historical pedagogy, Otto Anderssen devoted himself exclusively to this discipline, eventually leaving behind a large number of scientific works.

Historical pedagogy was therefore established in Norway as an academic and research discipline in the golden age of the liberal state, thus in a historical phase dominated by endeavours to promote a

---

[3] Ibid., p. 220-227

[4] Anders Kirkhusmo: "Akademi og seminar" Norges Lærerhøgskole 1922-1982 (Trondheim 1983) Nils Søvik: Pedagogisk institutt NTNU 1946-1996 (Trondheim 2008)

common national culture. What characterised this discipline during this phase?

The foremost representatives of the historical discipline during this period were Otto Anderssen, Søren Nordeide, Helga Eng and Torstein Høverstad. The most typical representatives were undoubtedly Otto Anderssen and Søren Nordeide, who both wrote overviews that dealt with the pedagogical history of ideas and the history of the Norwegian school. Otto Andersen dealt with the pedagogical history of ideas in connection with great thinkers ("prominent personalities") and main approaches in, for example, his four-volume *Billeder av dannelsearbeidets historie* [Pictures from the history of education] which was published between 1908 and 1914, and with the real history development of Norwegian schools in his book published in 1914 *Norges høiere skolevæsen 1814-1914* [Norway's upper secondary school system 1814-1914]. In 1916, Søren Nordeide published *Soga om oppseding og skule* [The history of upbringing and school], which dealt with pedagogical history of ideas, as well as the real historical development of Norwegian schools. The two authors gave descriptive/narrative and chronologically ordered presentations, in part with a clear personality orientation ("the great heroes") or a biographical element. One could also claim that Anderssen and Noreide significantly highlighted "the great personalities". As other school historians, they carefully stayed clear of contemporary history.

Helga Eng held a rather special position because she primarily undertook empirical psychological research, in part in combination with historical pedagogy studies. In 1918, she published the book *Kunstpedagogikk. Nutidspedagogikk* [Art pedagogy. Contemporary pedagogy], which dealt with the reform pedagogy movements in international art education.

The only clearly original but also controversial school historian from the period of the liberal state was Torstein Høverstad, Doctor of Philosophy.[5] For many years he undertook intense research activities aiming to qualify for a professorship in pedagogy. In 1918, he presented his dissertation for his doctoral degree with what would be his main work, *Norsk skulesoga 1. Det store interregnum 1739- 1827* [Norwegian school history 1. The great interregnum 1739-1827], and he followed this with *Norsk skulesoga. 2. Frå einevelde til folkestyre 1814-1842*

[5] "Torstein Høverstad: Den norske skolehistorie og pedagogikk for nasjonal folkeoppdragelse." In Erling Lars Dale: De strategiske pedagoger. Pedagogikkens vitenskapshistorie i Norge (Oslo, 1999), p. 288- 345.

[Norwegian school history 2. From absolute monarchy to popular rule 1814-1842], which was published in Oslo in 1930. Høverstad's doctoral degree work has been characterised as a "ground-breaking work on the history of the Norwegian elementary school", and he is considered to be the founder of education policy and the historical-sociological perspective in Norwegian pedagogy.[6] He did not shy away from the conflicts and disputes that arose in the school debates that raged at the time. It has rightly been claimed about him that he "politicised pedagogy".[7] But in the political world, Høverstad was seen as a particularly authoritarian and contentious person, and after Stortinget (Parliament) both in 1931 and 1937 had rejected the Government's attempts to make him a professor, he was forced to content himself for the rest of his life with being a research fellow with a professor's salary. Høverstad was also controversial because he identified very strongly with the national unification idea of the liberal state ("One school, one class of teachers, for one class of teachers, for one fatherland"), and because he saw it as the foremost duty of school and the subject of pedagogy to present the development of *popular* cultural heritage through changing times. Part of the popular cultural heritage was in Høverstad's opinion a spiritual life that understood itself as a revelation of God.

If we then consider school history research in the time of the liberal state as a whole, asking why the school writers of this time chose a historical perspective in favour of other perspectives, the following explanations may be given:

First, we can state that the research was a consequence of tradition or *convention.* Pedagogy was a young, emerging science. The academics that devoted themselves to this discipline had been raised in a humanist tradition. The sciences which pedagogy drew its ideals from were generally historically oriented. The science of religion was primarily the history of religion, literary science was literary history, language science was language history and so on.

Second, the historical perspective was to serve what we may call an *identity-confirming* function. It was characteristic of this period that many of the historical dissertations dealt with upper secondary schools and in particular the cathedral schools, and they were written by the headmasters of this type of school. The researchers thus wrote about their own schools and to some extent also about themselves and

[6] Dale a.a., p. 288.
[7] Dale a.a., p. 328.

the tradition within which they belonged. With their presentations, they wanted to make their own school great and meaningful as an institution. Their intention was to create respect for the school and hence also promote a sense of pride in the teachers for belonging to this type of school.

Third, the recommendation from the Teacher Training Committee from 1914 stated that student teachers needed to be given "a vivid impression of *the man* who brought the generations on to new paths". In this was the idea that historical research would display the heroes of school development, and thus present good *role models* who would establish teachers as cultural personalities. The teacher training at the time thus did not see a teacher as a process technician, but rather as a cultural personality who would present and impart knowledge.

Fourth, the historical orientation may be explained by the fact that the Norwegian society at the time of the liberal state was still a religious and Christian society that believed in school as an important tool for the optimism about the future that dominated the times. Bearing this in mind, historical pedagogy's task was to explore and describe a God-willed development where man gradually managed to elevate himself from a primitive to a civilised state. In a more secular version, the evolutionary idea meant that historical pedagogy should show how over the centuries an increasingly deeper understanding of upbringing had been attained. And not least, the historical perspective was to display school as part of a broad cultural development so that it could serve this. In pointing out the limitations of psychological science as a supporting discipline for pedagogy, Otto Anderssen wrote the following in 1914:

> "We must also be aware that psychology can only to a limited extent exercise influence on the goals set for school. These must be determined by the human culture and the human society and the requirements these set. What young people must learn, that which belongs in the knowledge and culture of youths, that which forms its spirit and behaviour, cannot be decided by its nature or by scientifically based assessments of the nutritional value of psychology or pedagogy..."[8]

If we then summarise these explanations, it could perhaps be claimed that historical pedagogy assumed a strong position under the liberal state because school was looked upon as a culture-building institution

[8] Otto Anderssen: Billeder av dannelsesarbeidets historie. IV. Det sidste hundreaar. (Kristiania 1914), p. 274-275.

and the teacher was then a cultural personality. If we were to ask what characterised good teachers in this era, the answer would be that they were enthusiasts who were also ardently interested in their teaching task. Through the historical perspective, pedagogy would ignite a spark or two strengthening the teacher's enthusiasm.

The blissful moment of the social democratic state 1935/40 – 1965/70

The fundamental underpinning of the formation of the Norwegian state during the golden age of social democracy in this country was the fact that the working class and the Norwegian Labour Party became the dominant political power in Norwegian society from the end of the 1930s and up to the 1970s.[9] With rather insignificant breaks, Labour was the governing party in Norway from 1935 to 1965, and by and large, the non-socialist coalition government continued Labour's school policy from 1965 to 1970.

The main political conflict during this period was between the political left (Labour, the Communist Party and the Socialist People's Party) and the right/centre or non-socialist wing (Liberals, Conservatives, the Agrarian Party and the Christian People's Party). Within the framework of a liberal and democratic state based on the rule of law, these two opponents were not that distant from each other politically, and the transition from the nationalist liberal state with its liberal conservative hegemony to the social democratic state was not too acrimonious. This was also related in part to the fact that political conflict was side-stepped to some degree in Norway as experts made their way into the social debate.

Bearing this in mind, the golden age of social democracy may be characterised as follows: The political hegemony in Norway favoured the compromise that Georg Simmel has called "one of the greatest inventions of mankind". This solution included the tension between capital and labour, market and central planning, and hence also the tension between the social classes. The leftists accepted a moderate (state) capitalism or market orientation, while the conservatives accepted the ambition of full employment and Keynesian economic policy with a strong welfare state

[9] Where not otherwise stated, the presentation of the social democratic state's golden age is based on Alfred Oftedal Telhaug: "Velferdsstat og utdanning i Norge – to sider av samme sak." Uddannelseshistorie 2006. 40. årbog fra Selskabet for Skole og Uddannelses-historie. (København 2006). See also Rune Slagstad et al. (1998) and Francis Sejersted: Sosialdemokratiets tidsalder. Norge og Sverige i det 20.århundre (Oslo 2005)

and workers' rights to organise. The parties played their roles and arrived at compromises they were all able to live with.

The overriding goal of the compromise was to integrate all members of society in a national community with a strong sense of a common bond between the people. While the liberal state or the liberal-conservative state emphasised individual responsibility for one's neighbour (mercy), the new compromise placed greater emphasis on solidarity and caring for each other as the responsibility of the political system and the collective. The interests of the different classes would be accommodated under the national common interests and the national joint responsibility, while this common good meant liberation for individual members of society and in particular for members of the working class. This major integration project had in turn the goal that politics should endeavour to create the egalitarian society, which first and foremost, was understood as a society whose members had equal opportunities.

When it comes to political measures or governing instruments, we shall first take note of the fact that the classical Norwegian social democracy transformed the relatively passive non-socialist liberal state into a strong planning and comprehensive public authority. The requirements placed on the state as problem solver and supervisor of social developments thus increased, and in contrast to developments in the rest of the world, where confidence in the private sector was high, the state assumed responsibility for many tasks which the market or civilian sector previously had dealt with. The state should promote collective values and common social interests.

We must note that during this period Norwegian politics placed great faith in science, particularly social science and the expertise these sciences with their *positivist* orientation laid claim to. The positivist priority meant that the first decades after World War II had little respect for the grand theories. Natural science research ideals came a long way to also conquering the social sciences with their emphasis on facts, data and disinterested explanations. Historians should dig deep into their sources and not subject themselves to the tyranny of models. Speculation and sentimentalism would be replaced by good language skills and questionnaires. Pedagogical research, as with other social sciences, was assessed on the basis of an *instrumental* perspective and understood as *steering science*. There was a master-slave relation between science/theory on one side and practice on the other. Research was trusted to have the ability to produce knowledge about relations or general laws for human behaviour. It was then believed that this ordered knowledge could be translated into *imperatives*, and in the school context this meant some school policy imperatives, but first and foremost didactical imperatives. It was believed that research would be able to predict how individuals would behave and would be able to predict human behaviour under given circumstances thus providing authorities and teachers with the opportunity to control or direct the behaviour of members of society especially students and pupils. It was believed that positivist and empirical research would be able to inform politicians about which school structure would give the best pupil results, and it was also believed that the same style of research would be able to tell teachers how to organise their teaching in the classroom.

In the early post-war decades, the result of placing this faith in science as a steering instrument led to academic discussions dominated by faith in knowledge, truth, objectivity, rationality, neutrality and logic. This faith in empirical science was expressed in the establishment in 1954 of the National Council for Innovation in Education, a body which Parliament instructed to carry out pilot projects with new school reforms based on research.[10] When Parliament debated this case, the standing Committee for Church and Education Affairs released the following statement: "By employing empirical science in its service to test new school forms and educational methods, reform activities will have led the important social sector of schooling into modern forms."[11] Specifically, this instrumentalism also meant that teachers were to be understood less as enthusiastic presenters, as during the previous period, and more as planners, facilitators and guides who based their approach more on psychological and pedagogic knowledge grounds.

If we now look to this period's social theoretical debate within the field of pedagogy, there can be no doubt that natural science oriented research with its study of relation between cause and effect and with understanding of pedagogy as a social engineering art was in the ascendant. Already in Norway between the two world wars, the subject of pedagogy focused more on child psychology studies, ability and knowledge testing than on ideas and issues relating to aims and objectives. The emphasis was upon empirical measurements with quantification rather than interpretation of the ideas about school in the past and the present. There was more on the pupil than the teacher, more on

---

[10] Alfred Oftedal Telhaug: Forsøksrådet for skoleverket 1954-1984. En studie i norsk skoleutvikling (Oslo, 1990)

[11] Ibid. p. 27.

psychology than history. The school committee of the Norwegian teacher organisations stated the following in 1933:

> "It is actually just as impossible to speculate and point to the best teaching methods and teaching material, the most appropriate textbooks, the most favourable school organisation and so on, as it is to arrive at the best operational methods and operating equipment in, for example, agriculture and industry. *Truly real advances can only be effected by empirical means, also in school, first and foremost through various pilot projects".*

This statement, comparing school to the physical world (agriculture and industry), was often quoted by the dominant post-war figure in Norwegian education science, Professor Johs. Sandven, at the Institute for Educational Research, University of Oslo.[12] In 1966, he wrote about historical pedagogy:

> "Increasingly it has become clear, however, in upbringing as well as in mankind's other activities, that speculation and theory built on individual perceptions or experiences given by history do not give sufficient guidance in our endeavours to contribute to man's unfolding in the modern society".[13]

This new orientation over time led to pedagogy as a *taught subject* in teacher training and as a *study subject* on the level of higher education being divided into three main disciplines. First, there was *pedagogical psychology,* which included *learning psychology* and developmental psychology. Second, *didactics*, both general and pedagogical content knowledge for each school subject. Third, *historical* pedagogy, which comprised the history of educational ideas, the real historical development of school, and often also comparative pedagogy. In relation to the volumes of the various curricula and textbooks, pedagogical psychology probably had the most prominent position, closely followed by didactics. When it came to the position of the main disciplines in the teaching, some of the subject teachers were undoubtedly willing to place historical pedagogy into the background.[14] There was, however, no doubt that the national

---

[12] ohs. Sandven: Pedagogisk forskning i Norge. Stensil (Oslo, 1955), p. 5. See also Johs. Sandven: "Pedagogisk målsetting og psykisk funksjonssammenheng". In Johs. Sandven: Oppdragelse og vekst (Oslo, 1966), p. 13.

[13] Johs. Sandven et al. (1966), p. 5.

[14] This statement to some extent is based on observations and experiences I have made as a college and university teacher since 1962.

school policy leadership wanted a teacher training which continued to have room for historical pedagogy. In the "*Undervisningsplan for den 2-årige og 4-årige lærarskolen*" [Curriculum for the two-year and four-year teacher college] which the Ministry of Education and Church Affairs published in 1965, it was stated in the introduction and about teacher training in its entirety that: "The historical point of view must be heard in all the subjects, so that the pupils can see the growth of cultural life and see the relation between the past and the present".[15] When dealing with the pedagogical subjects, it established that the goal for the teaching in pedagogy was to be reached through five main tasks, and that one of the five was "to let the pupils see school and upbringing issues in a historical perspective".[16] The curriculum also to some extent, specified the content of the educational history of ideas in the history of the Norwegian school and the relevant school programme in Norway. In the "Guidelines" the curriculum provided for the teaching, emphasis was placed on imbuing the teacher training students with a "deeper understanding" of what is meant by the term "bringing up children" in our cultural context. To some extent, the curriculum specified the content of the pedagogical history of ideas and Norwegian school history within the contemporary school programme.

Pedagogical-psychological and didactic research together had a far greater volume than historical research. However, there is every reason to point out that the discipline of history still constituted a significant part of the total research effort. In 1975, Professor Helge Dahl at the Institute for Educational Research at the University of Oslo stated that up to the summer of 1974, the institute had approved a total of 456 Master's degree papers in pedagogy, and that 133 or 29 per cent of these could be characterised as historical papers. Twenty papers, or 15 per cent, could be called comparative studies. Dahl also stated that of the 31 doctoral degree dissertations dealing with a pedagogy topic that had been approved, 16, or more than half, were in historical pedagogy.

[15] The Ministry of Education and Church Affairs: Undervisningsplan for den 2-årige og 4-årige lærarskolen (Oslo, 1965), p. 7.
[16] Ibid., p. 70.

Helge Dahl concluded thus: "This says much about the strong position-school history research has in pedagogy".[17]

If we look in more detail at the topic areas the Norwegian historical pedagogy focused upon as a research discipline, we find that it worked with a wide range of topics. Many studies appeared to be chronologically oriented overview works dealing with the development of the Norwegian school. This was the case, for example, with the "classic" Den norske skoles historie [The history of the Norwegian school] by Einar Høigård and Herman Ruge (1947), Helge Dahl's Norsk lærerutdanning fra 1814 og til i dag [Norwegian teacher training from 1814 up to today] (1959) and Alfred Oftedal Telhaug's Den 9-årige skolen og differensieringsproblemet [The nine year compulsory school and the differentiation problem] (1969). A number of studies dealt with school development and school philosophy in other countries, more or less using a comparative perspective. Examples include Johs. Sandven's Pedagogisk idebrytning i USA [Pedagogical idea conflicts in the USA] (1949), Sigurd Nørstebø's John Deweys oppsedingsteori, opphav og utvikling [John Dewey's theory of upbringing, origin and development] (1953) and Bjarne Bjørndal's En studie i nyere amerikansk læreplantenkning [A study of recent American curriculum philosophy] (1969). The examples also show that historically focused studies during this period ensured that impulses were brought to Norway from the USA, and they also tell us that historical pedagogy dealt with the world of educational ideas then as now. Other more or less comparative studies comprised the Scandinavian countries and to some extent aspects of school development in Europe. Thus in general: Research looked at our geographical and cultural neighbours. With further delimitations but still mostly inclined towards the overview, research examined different types of school, as was the case with Hans-Jørgen Dokka's dissertation Fra allmueskole til folkeskole [From school for the general population to elementary school] (1967), and this was also the case with presentations of the history of individual schools. An example is the well-known study by Einar Høigård called Oslo katedralskoles his-

[17] Helge Dahl: "Historiske oppgaver ved Pedagogisk forskningsinstitutt, Universitetet i Oslo". In Torstein Harbo, Ole Korsen and Sverre Sletvold: Skolen og samfunnet. En pedagogisk essaysamling (Oslo, 1975), p. 76. Dahl's assessment is shared by Rolv Petter Amdam and Svein Lorentzen when in 1989 they write: "In spite of an increasingly strong emphasis on pedagogical psychology, the historical dimension retained a key place in pedagogical research until the end of the 1960s." See Rolv Petter Amdam and Svein Lorentzen: Skole og utdanning som etterkrigshistorisk forskningsfelt. (LOS-senter Notat 89/34). Harald Jarning: "Fri fra gullalderen". In Knut Tveit (ed.): Streiftog i historisk og komparativ pedagogikk. Compilation of articles published in connection with the celebration of Torstein Harbo's 70th birthday (University of Oslo, Institute for Educational Research, Report No. 2, 1997), p. 237.

torie [The history of Oslo Cathedral School] (1942). School history also examined the history of individual subjects, such as Sverre Sletvold's doctoral dissertation Norske lesebøker 1777-1969 [Norwegian textbooks 1777-1969] (1971).

These research works featuring overviews – often with much attention upon the system and organisation of school – were not only supplemented by studies of the history of ideas such as Bjarne Bjørndal's two dissertations: P. Voss og hans samtid. Pedagogiske idebrytninger 1869-1896 [P. Voss and his contemporary period. Pedagogical idea conflicts 1869-1896] (1959) and Frå formaldanning til allmenndanning [From formal education to general education] (1964), they were also supplemented by monographs/biographies, focusing on the actions and thoughts of individuals or their contributions to specific reforms. There were many dissertations in this latter category. Examples include Einar Boyesen's dissertation from 1947 on Hartvig Nissen, Reidar Myhre's dissertation from 1953 on Ludvig Holberg, Helge Dahl's dissertations Niels Treschow – en pedagogisk tenker [Niels Treschow - an educational thinker] (1965) and Knut Knudsen og latinskolen [Knut Knudsen and the Latin school] (1967), Olav Sunnanå's Georg Kerschensteiner og arbeidsskulen [Georg Kerschensteiner and the work school] (1960). The history of pedagogy as a subject also came under the microscope in one dissertation, Torstein Harbo's doctoral dissertation from 1969, Teori og praksis i den pedagogiske utdannelse [Theory and practice in pedagogical education].

To summarise, historical pedagogical research in the golden age of the social democratic state may be described as follows:

I. Compared to the previous period, the changes were minor. During the last epoch, some of the Norwegian school historians moved closer to the contemporary period than was the case in older times, but this was the exception rather than the rule. Hence, research was not only harmless, but it also cast little light on the school situation at the time. The discipline had no clear thematic focus beyond the public aspects of schools.[18] Otherwise, Norwegian school historians worked on a substantial number of themes and moved away from focussing on a grand narrative. The presentations were generally full of detail and descriptive, but also weak on theory. They cultivated factual aspects, eloquent prose and objectivity, in short the narrative tradition. For anyone interested in change and progress through school reform, historical pedagogy might easi-

[18] See R.P. Amdam and S.Lorentzen et al. (1989)

ly be found uninteresting and useless. The tension that existed at this time between an American-inspired positivism, primarily represented by Professor Johs. Sandven, and a conservative historical-hermeneutical pedagogy, represented by Reidar Myhre and Torstein Harbo, particularly appeared as a conflict between two quite different fundamental views on what pedagogical research is and should be. Many probably came to see historical pedagogy as lacking in challenges and usefulness. The following assessment from Swedish historian Gunnar Richardson had clear relevance also for what was happening in Norway:

> "The pedagogical ideals that previously could be found among the familiar characters of pedagogical history were found to be completely obsolete. Nor was it considered relevant to undertake in-depth studies in the discussions on the objectives of school that pedagogical history had offered earlier. The textbooks about the history of pedagogy that fledgling teachers were forced to read were also found to be hopelessly boring".[19]

II. When it comes to the role of historical pedagogy in what we have spoken of as a reform-oriented and practical pedagogical research or as school research, we can categorically admit that it was assigned little or no importance. This fact emerges clearly from the report *Utbyggingen av norsk skoleforskning* (The development of Norwegian school research) which was published in 1967-68.[20] Even if this report was written at the behest of Norway's General Scientific Research Council (NAVF), it was quite unilaterally concerned with promoting empirical research, quantification oriented and useful research which consisted of "follow-up" and a "cataloguing" of the effect of various reform measures. Where one previously had trusted philosophical speculation, the call was now for empirical research, this report stated. This not least meant that the pedagogical research now called for was to be focused on relations, and preferably relations between different measures in the teaching and the results of these same measures. To this end, NAVF placed great confidence in new and suitable measuring instruments, such as various forms of tests. It goes without saying that with such research ideals, historical

---

[19] Gunnar Richardson: "Utbildningshistorisk forskning i Sverige på 1980- och 1990-talen." Knut Tveit a.a. (1997), p. 308-309.

[20] NAVF: Utbyggingen av norsk skoleforskning (Recommendation published on 28 December 1967 by the Committee for School Research and adopted by the Council on 25 January 1968)

pedagogy would fare poorly, which needless to say, it did, when new school research funding of a substantial scope was granted to Norwegian pedagogical research starting in 1969.

This meant that when the new school research commenced in 1970,[21] historical pedagogy was not granted separate funding. On the other hand, funding was allocated to other scientific disciplines focusing on schools, and the Ministry of Education and Church Affairs as well as Parliament had greater influence on research because they could select the fields they wanted to illuminate. Thus developments, to some extent, headed in the direction of clearer political control of Norwegian pedagogical research.

The New Leftist radicalism of the 1970s

Towards the end of the 1960s, Norwegian school philosophy and Norwegian pedagogical research started to pick up signals from the international arena, possibly indicating that the golden days of the social democratic state were over.[22] The well publicised 1968 rebellion fiercely attacked the materialism, growth ideology and efficiency philosophy that was pervasive during the golden age of social democracy. The rebellion turned against efficiency philosophy in that it rejected the consumer society with its unilateral focus on economic growth and burgeoning affluence. The leftist radicalism, as this rebellion was often called, therefore was a new politicisation of the social and pedagogical debate. The generation of 1968 turned against positivism, which followed natural science paradigms and ideals, and introduced a constructivist view of knowledge in the sense that it was believed that knowledge must be discovered or construed.[23] According to Charles Taylor, this anti-positivism merged with a quest for authenticity, i.e. a genuine life where one is oneself and autonomous. Each individual would shape his or her own life, which meant rejecting all conditions that might impede the unfolding of life. In his major work from 2008 *(Sporten),* the historian of ideas Rune Slagstad, reproduced Taylor' interpretation of the 1968 rebellion thus:

---

[21] NAVF: Skoleforskning i Norge. Om videreføring av norsk skoleforskning og utviklingsarbeid. A report prepared by the Contact Committee for NAVF and the National Council for Innovation in Education (Oslo-Bergen-Tromsø, 1975) Particularly Chapter II.

[22] Francis Sejersted a.a.. Charles Taylor: A Secular Age. Cambridge, Massachusetts and London. Rune Slagstad. (Sporten). En idehistorisk studie (Oslo, 2008)

[23] Petter Aasen: "Læringsplakatens utdanningspolitiske kontekst". In Jorunn Møller and Liv Sundli (ed.): Læringsplakaten. Skolens samfunnskontrakt (Kristiansand, 2007)

> "The essential thing was not to be unified with God or the concept of the good, but rather becoming one with oneself – introversion as the basis for social actions in life. My life is mine – and not a copy. I will remain faithful to the original and the original is in me".[24]

Within the political debate, this new radicalism characterised post-war social democracy as an authoritarian society, and mercilessly attacked the dominant social democratic and American-inspired understanding of the legitimization of research. The word now was that scientific thinking that prevailed after the war stemmed from the interest in mastering reality technologically and that this pragmatic interest primarily was expressed through the so-called empirical-analytical sciences. Research in these sciences sought monologic knowledge, and it did this because it aimed to provide knowledge that would make it possible to master actions of a technical nature, which is to say actions that can exclusively be assessed based on their efficiency. As an alternative, the new radicalism turned to the historical-hermeneutic sciences, which did not aim to find predictive knowledge but rather wished to promote the understanding of meaning. Hermeneutics felt its task was to impart traditions, and the concrete activity of working with textual analyses gained in meaning and importance. To the same extent it promoted an unforced understanding of past and contemporary tradition. Its ultimate purpose was to make our own situation transparent. As a new and third science theory category, the radicalism of the 1960s and 1970s referred to the critical social sciences. They were also interested in ordered knowledge, but the decisive factor for them was that they aimed to unmask the ideological basis of dependency relationships that were only apparently immutable. The fundamental interest underlying critical science was to be found in the wish to liberate mankind by imparting information that would lead to a higher level of reflection. For educational thinking, the leftist radical understanding of society and mankind meant that pupils in schools no longer could be understood as things or objects that were shaped on the basis of psychological insights into causal relationships of the mind. School could no longer be considered a results-oriented enterprise, but rather needed to be understood as an arena for pupils' self-realisation. One aspect of this ideological shift was a desire to loosen the reins of central control over Norwegian schools and give more power to local authorities and generally encourage more local autonomy. The detailed

---

[24] R. Slagstad et al. (2008), p.438.

Acts, regulations and curricula should be replaced by framework laws and plans stimulating school development from below. It was also part of the new thinking about school history that it should not only focus on purely descriptive statements dealing with individual school history events (legislation, curricula, pilot projects). School history could no longer content itself with real history descriptions in a narrative form in chronological order. Narratives about the past and analysis of the past should take as their point of departure problems, issues, hypotheses and theories. If it became a '*Problemgeschichte*' (a history of problems), to borrow the words of German professor Rudi Maskus, it would also be relevant, not because it dealt with current issues, but because it dealt with relations and constants that will always exist.[25] Thus, the primary goal of research or theory should not be to instruct the teacher about what was good teaching, but rather to furnish him or her with perspectives, categories and concepts. One example was that the following question could be asked: Why has Karl Marx become the most influential social science researcher of our time? Simply because he wanted to furnish us with the class perspective or the class construct, i.e. with a perspective or construct that continues to be extremely useful when analysing our surroundings. Thus, rather than training teachers with the aim of making them more efective process technicians, educational research should teach them to become independent and reflexive practitioners.

What happened to historical pedagogy and school history *research* in Norway through the 1970s and '80s? Was its position further eroded? Did it retain its position? Was it perhaps strengthened? During this epoch, developments at the Institute for Educational Research at the Norwegian Teacher College in Trondheim (later the University of Trondheim and the Norwegian University of Science and Technology (NTNU)) proceeded in a more "history-friendly" direction than it did at the Institute for Educational Research at the University of Oslo. Professor Johs. Sandven, the dominant personality in the established university community in Oslo, continued to focus on psychometric research, showing little understanding of the new radical thinking.[26] The social pedagogy alternative at Blindern (where a section of the University of Oslo is located) that emerged in opposition to Sandven's psycho-technical line admittedly identified itself fully with Marxist and radical school

[25] R. Maskus: "Pädagogik als Problemgeschichte." in Zeitschrift für Pädagogik (1971), 17, p. 351-385. For a Norwegian presentation of this history, see NAVF et al. (1975), Chapter IV.
[26] Lise Vislie: "Den Sandvenske "gullalder" på 50- og 60-tallet". Norsk Pedagogisk Tidsskrift, hefte 6, (2009), p. 445-459.

thinking, but research activities fostered by this alternative did not lead to a new flourishing of a historical perspective.[27] The optimistic progressive view of practically oriented change, which characterised this alternative made the new generation of researchers and students virtually immune to the historical perspective. In Trondheim, Torstein Harbo and Reidar Myhre, both professors standing firmly on German scientific ground, made their mark through substantial effort in the service of historical pedagogy. They carried out research and produced textbooks on the history of pedagogical ideas and the Norwegian school. At the same time, younger researchers such as Alfred Oftedal Telhaug and Petter Aasen were to some extent inspired by new radical thinking. Alone or in close cooperation, they published through the 1970s, 1980s and 1990s a number of research works and textbooks where a central theme was the relation between society/politics and pedagogy, often with a historical perspective.[28]

The development described here, with clear differences between Oslo and Trondheim, can be documented by quantitative information. The available data show that while as much as 41% of Master's Degree dissertations in Trondheim from 1970 to 1988 had a historical character, there was a dramatic reduction in the number of Master's Degree dissertations with similar content in Oslo.[29] In Oslo, 31% of the dissertations had a historical character from 1960 to 1969, but the proportion declined to 19% from 1970 to 1979 and to 9% from 1980 to 1989. If we look exclusively at Oslo, we can also see that relatively speaking, the number of university posts dedicated to historical pedagogy diminished, and that the number of pedagogical-historical doctoral degree dissertations showed a steady decline.

Even if historical pedagogy lost ground as a research discipline in Oslo during the new radical epoch, we can still state that it in part retained its position as a *study subject* in what we may call the academic study of pedagogy. The discipline was part of the three main disciplines of the study of pedagogy as a university course and as part of the teach

---

[27] Birgit Brock-Utne: "Det sosialpedagogiske studiealternativ sett innenfra". Norsk Pedagogisk Tidsskrift, hefte 6, (2009), s. 460-471. Erling Lars Dale: "Kritisk pedagogikk ved PFI". Norsk Pedagogisk Tidsskrift, hefte 6, (2009), p. 472- 487. Lars Løvlie: "Kritisk pedagogikk – 1970-årene". Norsk Pedagogisk Tidsskrift, hefte 6, (2009), p. 488- 495.

[28] See for example Alfred Oftedal Telhaug: Den 9-årige skolen og differensieringsproblemet. Oslo 1969 and Norsk skoleutvikling etter 1945 (Oslo, 1982).

[29]See Alfred Oftedal Telhaug: "Norsk skolehistorisk forskning på defensiven? Beskrivelse og analyse". In Knut Tveit (ed.) et al. (1997), p. 212- 232.

er training. And when it came to the content of the discipline, tradition retained its strong footing.

If the picture of this radical epoch is to be correct, it is also necessary to refer to new measures initiated to promote the publication of historical-pedagogical research. Practitioners of the discipline also delved into organisational aspects to reach a greater and wider audience. This was realised when in 1977 Norwegian school historians founded the "Selskapet for norsk skolehistorie" [the Society of Norwegian School History], an association that since 1982 has managed to publish a yearbook on Norwegian education history. In 2009, the yearbook had had 26 volumes published, all under the editorship of Knut Jordheim and this yearbook shows every sign of continuing.[30]

When it comes to the content of Norwegian education history, the discipline to some extent expanded its field of research and widened its scope due to the new radical thinking.[31] Where it had previously focused completely on the institution of the *school* as a research object, it now increasingly turned to the *socialisation* of children and young people in a historical perspective. The focus was particularly strong on *the child* and on *childhood*. In 1985, a Nordic network was established for research on *the history of the child*, and in Norway Tora Korsvold, Liv Kari Tønnessen and Harald Thuen would make major contributions to this discipline.[32] School history research now rejected the biographical genre in favour of overviews and more delimited studies that considered school thinking and school developments in political, ideological and social contexts. This was important because far more consistently than previously, presentations and analyses would be brought much closer to the contemporary time. Vegard Kvam has stated the following about this development trend:

---

[30] See Årbok for norsk utdanningshistorie 2009. 26th vol. Published by "Stiftelsen SKOLEN-Årbok for norsk utdanningshistorie".

[31] Alfred Oftedal Telhaug: "Forty Years of Norwegian Research in the History of Education". Scandinavian Journal of Educational Research, Vol. 41, Nos. 3-4, (1997), p. 347. H. Jarning a.a. p. 235. Per Rand: "Pedagogisk Forskningsinstitutt, Universitetet i Oslo. In Einar Ness (ed.): Skolens Årbok 1980 (Oslo, 1980), p. 6987. "Vi trenger et historisk perspektiv på pedagogikken." Norsk Skoleblad, nr. 7, (1989), p. 14. R.P. Amdam and S. Lorentzen et al. (1989), p. 7-10.

[32] Tora Korsvold: Profesjonalisert barndom. Statlige intensjoner og kvinnelig praksis på barnehagens arena 1945-1990. No. 20 in Skriftserie fra Historisk institutt (NTNU: Trondheim 1997). Liv Kari Tønnessen: Slik levde småbarna før. Trekk fra barndommens historie i vårt land – med særlig vekt på de minste barnas liv og lek (Oslo, 1982). Harald Thuen: "Introduksjon". In Hugh Cunningham (ed.): Barn og barndom fra middelalder til moderne tid (Oslo, 1996).

> "From the end of the 1970s and to the present time we can trace a change in education history research in the sense that the narratives more than before are brought closer to the current time, and in the sense that the researchers are more critical and point out doubtful aspects of the contemporary education society in view of the historical material.... One characteristic of the research is that the researchers are not afraid of losing distance to the events and becoming part of the education policy conflict. The point of departure is current education reforms, which are then analysed in a historical perspective".[33]

In this way, school historical research became more a part of the political life and the political contemporary conflicts than it had been before.

The post-national phase 1985/90-2010: Globalisation, liberalism, postmodernism and knowledge competitions

The leftist radical or social critical pedagogy thinking that we connect with "May 1968" had a relatively short lifespan as a hegemonic regime of power and knowledge. Margaret Thatcher took over as the Prime Minister of Britain in 1979, Ronald Reagan became the President of the United States in 1981 and Kåre Willoch became the Prime Minister of Norway in the same year, representing the Conservatives. This was the result of a more or less clear opposition against the political left with its thinking in terms of class, its scorn of utilitarian considerations and its faith in social levelling. Moreover, in a relatively short period of time, great changes occurred in social conditions which pedagogical ideology had to deal with. When the twentieth century was drawing to a close, descriptions and analyses of international social developments were dominated more and more by the concept of *globalisation.* This term means that something becomes global in scope so that national borders and national political boundaries lose some of their importance. Economies, cultures and types of society are torn out of their territorial frames and transcend national and state borders. The world is woven together in a network of new types of contact, new groups of actors, relations of interdepend-

[33]Vegard Kvam: "Nyttige historier. Hvordan kan utdanningspolitikken ha nytte av utdanningshistorisk forskning?" In Årbok for norsk utdanningshistorie (2009), p. 117- 118. See also Alfred Oftedal Telhaug, Per Eivind Kjøl, Alf Inge Wallum, Rolf Th. Tønnessen, Nina Volckmar: Norsk utdanningspolitisk retorikk. En studie av utdanningstenkningen i norske partiprogrammer. Oslo 1999.

ency and self-interpretations. The exposure to a diversity of cultures is enlarged. Ideas, knowledge, goods and services are more easily distributed. In short, the world is becoming smaller, and two consequences of this development are of vital importance for pedagogical ideology and thinking.

First, the *economic competition* among countries is intensified. Danish professor Ove Korsgaard has stated as follows in his book *Kundskabs-kapløbet* [The Knowledge Race] from 1999:

> "The combination of sophisticated information technology, low transportation costs, new technology and the breaking down of political and structural barriers against free trade and capital movement is now melting the entire world into one market, dominated by cut-throat global competition".[34]

Economic rationality with its focus on competition and individualisation has given the market more clout than it previously had. Moving into 2011, this situation has not been changed. The term "the knowledge economy" with its requirement that schools maintain the basic and innovative skills has continued to exert a strong influence.[35] Competition between countries has also intensified at the level of *education and knowledge*. This is a result of the understanding that knowledge is now the basis for economic growth and economic competitiveness. Now, the living standard in a country and its level of welfare are far more clearly seen as hinging on the population's opportunity to sell brain power on the global market. Gudmund Hernes, Norwegian Minister of Education from 1990 to 1995, stated in an article in *Dagbladet* (a major Norwegian daily newspaper) in 1986:

> "We must increasingly live by our wits, the ability to develop new ideas, to work with advanced technology, to create products and to find imaginative ways of resolving problems. Of all our national resources, the trained intelligence and innovative ability will be most decisive."[36]

---

[34] Ove Korsgaard: Kundskabs-kapløbet. Uddannelse i Videnssamfundet (København, 1999), p. 225.

[35] See for example Gustav E. Karlsen: "Et snevert kunnskapssyn". Adresseavisen (18-09-2009).

[36] Gudmund Hernes: "Kan man ha ambisjoner i Norge?" Dagbladet 31 (December 1986).

This thinking has resulted in concrete actions, for example measuring international knowledge levels attracted much attention, in part posing new premises for the school debate in Europe and in Norway. The reason was that the results of these tests showed that Norway fared less well in these than anyone had imagined.

Second, many researchers (for example Marcuse and Ziehe) now became interested in describing changes of mentalities in children and young people, not least emphasising changes that did not favour the knowledge school. To some it appeared as though older values such as the struggle and efficiency of the frugal society had been replaced by the search for consumer gratification of modern society? Had the older social view, which included an authoritarian upbringing that believed in values such as obedience, orderliness and stamina, been replaced by the ideas of social autonomy, of self-realisation, pleasure-seeking and spontaneity? In *(Sporten),* Rune Slagstad claimed that in this country we had moved into a post-modern era that cultivated the moment instead of the future and aestheticism instead of ethics, a time of seeking pleasures that could be bought, the hunt for adventure and enjoyment instead of achievement, which cultivated a life of entertainment such that as expressed in the sports fanaticism which even King Harald of Norway confessed to, and which helped to break down divisions between "high" and "low" culture. Slagstad stated: "We are now seeing formidable movements in and between various art and cultural expressions. Cartoons and pop music have changed status from rubbish to culture in the space of two years. Hermann Hesse and Donald Duck are quite naturally literary night-table fellows".[37]

What, then, did this new climate for political and scientific theory and the new socialisation mean for school policy and general thinking about pedagogy in Norway? The answer may be given thus:

Norwegian as well as Nordic school philosophy lost some but not all of what made it special. This means that Norway now became "a part of the world" and that pedagogical thinking became more *post-national* or *international*. We might perhaps say that the Norwegian sense of self-satisfaction was dented. The reforms that appeared were now often in response to recommendations made by the UN. In debates concerning direction for schools, there was more reference to studies undertaken by the EU, WTO, World Bank and OECD, and thus to recommendations given by organisations that were primarily interested in the financial

[37] R. Slagstad et al. (2008), p. 765.

development of their member states.[38] The great school debate of the last decade in Norway, often only called the PISA debate, has as its point of departure the OECD's international knowledge and skill measuring scheme. Measurable results have come into focus for school policy and debates on education.

Norwegian school thinking has now come to use *socio-economic* considerations as the basis for reform measures. Over the last 20 years, school authorities have given greater priority to content and ways of working that have promoted Norway's economic competitiveness. The demand for greater efforts by pupils has become a recurring thread in the political and academic debate on education. Gudmund Hernes stated the following in a newspaper article in 1987:

> "The Norwegian knowledge industry will not acquire sufficient knowledge. Our competitiveness will depend on graduating students who have not been given an adequate ability to compete. The silver-spoon generation will have under-invested in themselves. Their easy start will give them a heavy burden. What was beneficial for enterprises in the 1990s will also result in a backlash from 2000. If this is to be avoided, today's practice must be changed. The strategic measure is education".[39]

With business and industry as the ideal, education has been understood on the basis of instrumental logic; a calculating enterprise where utility dominates with scant space for exploration and aesthetics. This idea prevails to this day. In 2009, the Research Council of Norway stated in the introduction to a report on a programme plan for Norwegian education research toward 2020: "What we learn in day-care centres, school, training and education institutions helps shape us as individuals, and creates an important foundation for the working life and business and industry of the future."[40]

So what has happened with Norwegian education history during this last phase? Is the pessimistic description correct when Jesper Eckhardt Larsen in the preface to this anthology writes: "What has been coined a new paradigm for research policy has functioned since at least the 1960s and 1970s, but increasingly so after year 2000. Positions in

---

[38] See Nytt Norsk Tidsskrift, no. 3-4 (2009)
[39] Gudmund Hernes: "Dessert med bakrus-fare". Aftenposten 14 November (1987).
[40] Norwegian Research Council: Programplan for utdanning 2020. Norsk utdanningsforskning fram mot 2020. (Oslo, 2009). See the preface.

basic research in the humanities are either cut, or never opened".[41] Is this description valid also for the current situation in Norway? Has historical pedagogy come under serious pressure due to the new knowledge economy?

If we first attempt to understand the perceptions or interpretations of situations that exist, we can state that they diverge substantially. As the editor of a major anthology featuring 18 Norwegian educational profiles (published in 2004), Harald Thuen asserted that, "This book reflects a sign of the times: A growing interest in insight into Norwegian pedagogical history and educational philosophy".[42] In his trial lecture for the doctoral degree in 2009, Vegard Kvam sounded moderately optimistic on behalf of the discipline when he stated the following based on studies carried out by Jostein Sæther: "From around the 1970s and toward the 1990s there was a significant decline in the interest in historical pedagogy in Norway, but starting around 1990 and up to the present, some research works of a historical nature are again being published".[43]

However, the assessments diverge, as mentioned above. In an article published in 2002, Kaare Skagen claims that, "Today the historical perspective has been virtually forced out of teacher training".[44] In his trial lecture in 2009, Vegard Kvam also referred to how the Research Council of Norway asserted in 2004 that education research and particularly education history research had little priority among researchers in Norway. The discipline had recruitment problems and the nation was lacking stable academic environments where research could be seen on context. In this same connection, Kvam also stated that the historical perspectives today are not given any emphasis in research policy.[45]

Looking at the more exact data that have been published lately, the following picture of the situation emerges. If we first examine the studies subject of pedagogy, as it has developed over many decades at the Institute for Educational Research at the University of Oslo, it might appear that the subject's volume on the basic course level has been relatively stable over a long period of time. A study from 2000, where

---

[41] Quote from the introduction to this anthology

[42] Harald Thuen and Sveinung Vaage (ed.): Pedagogiske profiler. Norsk utdanningstenkning fra Holberg til Hernes (Oslo, 2004), p. 11.

[43] Vegard Kvam et al. p. 123.

[44] Kaare Skagen: "Utdannelseshistorie og –politikk i norsk lærerutdannelse". UNIPED no. 3, (2002), p. 49.

[45] Vegard Kvam et al. p.124. See also Norwegian Research Council: Norsk pedagogisk forskning. En evaluering av forskningen ved utvalgte universiteter og høgskoler (Oslo, 2004), p. 109-110.

Knut Tveit examined the relative volume of the pedagogy subject at the Institute for Educational Research at the University of Oslo, shows the following percentages for the years from 1939 to 1996: 1939: 19%, 1958: 21% , 1975: 21%, 1985: 23% and 1996: 16%.[46]

In Kaare Skagen's study published in 2002 entitled "Utdannelseshistorie og – politikk i norsk lærerutdannelse" [Education history and policy in Norwegian teacher training], he restricted himself to a description and analysis of the pedagogy education given as part of the course offered by universities and colleges to fledgling teachers in lower secondary school and upper secondary school.[47] He found that the historical dimension was not counted separately and independently among the curriculum's five main topics but was rather considered to be a sub-topic under the main area of "Samfunnsoppgaver og verdigrunnlag" [Social duties and value basis]. How wide the topic was to be was left to each institution to decide. Skagen then found that education history and education policy on average were given no more than ten teaching hours a year. The position of the topic within the teacher training education programme was clearly marginal and would from time to time be completely dropped. Skagen also found that education history and school policy were rarely set as examination assignments. He summarised this as follows: "On average, the student teachers thus use approximately 2.5 per cent of the time they are taught to learn education history if the institutions at all offer teaching in this subject. ... Historically, there is no doubt that the history subject has been forced to the sidelines by other disciplines and topics in the teacher training".[48]

At the time of writing, general teacher training in Norway is again being reformulated, and the central political authorities have made it clear that the historical perspective must be maintained.[49] In 2009, teacher training and the subject of pedagogy were discussed by the

[46] Knut Tveit: "Utviklinga av Pedagogisk forskningsinstitutt". In E. Buk-Berge, T. Harbo and F. Hjartemaal: Pionerer i norsk fagpedagogikk. Helga Eng og Einar Høigård på nært hold (Oslo, 2000), p.208.

[47] K. Skagen et al. (2002)

[48] Ibid, p. 49.

[49] Ministry of Education and Church Affairs: St.meld. nr. 11 (2008-2009) Læreren. Rollen og utdanningen. Innst. S. nr. 185 (2008-2009) Innstilling til Stortinget fra kirke-, utdannings- og forskningskomiteen. St.meld. nr. 11 (2008-2009) Innstilling fra kirke-, utdannings- og forskningskomiteen om Læreren - rollen og utdanningen.

Government and Parliament, but this often lacked a historical perspective and the historical perspective in teacher training was not debated.[50]

If we are to understand this development, it is necessary to introduce two perspectives. Firstly, as Kaare Skagen so clearly has pointed out, thinking about school policy in Norway in our time has emphasised that teacher training should focus on what is practical and useful. Skagen wrote in 2002:

> "In Norwegian practical pedagogy, we may trace a strong yearning towards practice and action. This has caused concepts such as experience learning and action learning to become popular for action-oriented teachers and school managers who see themselves as leading the development of school. The new interest in action orientation may be deduced from the much used term 'experience learning' or its synonym 'action learning'. The concept is designed as a counterpart and alternative to knowledge-based learning. Experience learning is presented as meaning-creating, here-and-now-oriented, important and useful, and a life form that activates the emotions. Knowledge-based learning is, on the other hand, connected to facts, oriented toward the past, teacher dominated and primarily intellectual (...). Where experience learning is the primary teacher competence, historical knowledge is not in demand in the teacher training".[51]

Secondly, this way of thinking about education has overlooked the fact that education policy now as before, is controlled more by policy-cultural matters than by theories about development and learning. Vegard Kvam writes the following on this:

> "School is a cultural product. This means that if we are to understand school and its present development, and if educators are to deliver research that is useful for education policy, it is not sufficient to use psychology or the practical oriented learning theory, as traditionally was done in our country during the

[50] See Alfred Oftedal Telhaug: "Historieløst om helten". Kronikk, Aftenposten 13 February 2009.

[51] K. Skagen et al. p. 46.

> periods where political power has turned to pedagogical research. It is probably more interesting to analyse the forces that control social development, and to see school in a cultural connection. Then educators with an interest in history should be put to work".[52]

In saying this, Kvam suggests both implicitly and explicitly that the school history perspective has been eliminated in today's teacher training because "the powers that be" do not want to recognise that the development of school is controlled more by cultural forces than by learning theories and process technical competence. He also states in other contexts that the historical perspective should be strengthened because it enables the expertise and those charged with directing the system to reflect with more certainty upon the design of today's school.

In terms of volume, historical research appears to have a much weaker position in Norway over the last decades. If we focus on the doctoral degree level and on the Institute for Educational Research at the University of Oslo, we can state that from 1999 to 2009, a total of 122 dissertations were submitted, and that only nine of these may be characterised as historical pedagogical according to their thematic focus.[53] This means that only eight per cent of the submitted dissertations were based on historical pedagogy.

Even if the picture of the status of historical pedagogy in recent years that has been outlined above tells of a discipline on the defensive and a discipline that relatively speaking is being reduced in scope, the picture changes with a content analysis. This is because the negative trend is connected to the research volume and the demand for historical pedagogy at the political and bureaucratic level. We see a different picture if we examine the content of historical pedagogy as a research discipline, revealing more diverse activity than in previous times. It is now dominated by a new and young generation of researchers. Let us therefore examine the content of the research and publication in recent years:

Towards 2009, *overview works* maintain their strong position as part of Norwegian historical pedagogy. In the history of ideas, older works are appearing in new editions,[54] but new comprehensive works also appear which follow the development of thinking up to the most

---

[52] V. Kvam et al. p. 123-124.
[53] http://ask.bibys.no/ask/action/result? Fid=serieobjektid §term = 00089419.
[54] Reidar Myhre: Grunnlinjer i pedagogikkens historie (Oslo, 1996)

recent of times.[55] In Norwegian school history, older works are also being published in new editions, but this also applies to new presentations dealing with parts of the school system or the entire system.[56] While the voluminous overview works retain their position, the discipline is being renewed and expanded to some extent due to the more popular trend to study the relevant reforms in a historical perspective and because the research is now more interested than before in the conflicts in question or the political discussion about the school reforms. In this way, the historical research helps to illuminate the contemporary thinking about schools.[57] One might also speak of an expansion of the perspectives because the comparative contribution is reinforced. We also find works where the Norwegian school is compared to the Danish and the Nordic school, but this is also the case with the European and the entire international school development.[58] Again we may also state that the child and Norwegian childhood are in focus through a long series of histori-

[55] Kjetil Steinsholt and Lars Løvlie (ed.): Pedagogikkens mange ansikter. Pedagogikkens idéhistorie fra antikken til det postmoderne (Oslo, 2004)

[56] Odd Asbjørn Mediås: Skoledirektørembetet i Norge 1860-1992. Oslo 1996. Rolf Grankvist: Utsyn over norsk skole. Norsk utdanning gjennom 1000 år (Trondheim, 2000). Liv Kari B. Tønnessen: Den nye småskolen – bakgrunn og utforming (Kristiansand, 2002). Alfred Oftedal Telhaug and Odd Asbjørn Mediås: Grunnskolen som nasjonsbygger. Fra statspietisme til nyliberalisme (Oslo, 2003). Ivar Bjørndal: Videregående opplæring i 800 år – med hovedvekt på tiden etter 1950 (Halden, 2005).

[57] See for example Erik Sølvberg: Frå Hernes til Clemet – frå plan til marknad? Kvar går den vidaregåande skolen? (Bergen, 2004). Alfred Oftedal Telhaug: Kunnskapsløftet – ny eller gammel skole? (Oslo, 2005). Per Bjørn Foros: Skolen i klemme (Oslo, 2006).

[58] Alfred Oftedal Telhaug: Den nye utdanningspolitiske retorikken. Bilder av internasjonal skoleutvikling (Oslo, 1990). Anne Trine Kjørholt, Tora Korsvold and Alfred Oftedal Telhaug: Pedagogisk tilbud til 4-7-åringer i internasjonalt perspektiv. En studie av England, Frankrike, Japan og USA. Norsk senter for barneforskning (Trondheim, 1990). Alfred O. Telhaug and Rolf Th. Tønnessen: Dansk utdanningspolitikk under Bertel Haarder 1892-1992 (Oslo, 1992). Alfred Oftedal Telhaug: Norsk og internasjonal skoleutvikling. Studier i 1980-årenes restaurative bevegelse (Oslo, 1992). Rolf Th. Tønnessen: Demokratisk dannelse i tysk perspektiv (Oslo, 1992). Torstein Harbo and Thyge Winther-Jensen (ed.): Vi og de andre. Komparative- internasjonale- flerkulturelle pedagogiske studier i Norden (Oslo, 1993). Alfred Oftedal Telhaug: Politikk og profesjon. Engelsk skoleutvikling 1988- 1997 (Oslo, 1997). Torstein Harbo: Norsk skole i europeisk perspektiv. Takt eller utakt 1945-1997 (Oslo, 1997). Petter Aasen: "Det sosialdemokratiske prosjekt. Utdanningsreformer i Sverige og Norge i etterkrigstiden", in A. O. Telhaug and P. Aasen (ed.): Både-og. 90-tallets utdanningsreformer i historisk perspektiv (Oslo, 1999). H. Thuen and S. Vaage (ed.): Pedagogiske profiler. Norsk utdanningstenkning fra Holberg til Hernes (Oslo, 2004). Odd Asbjørn Mediås: Enhetsskolens utvikling i Danmark og Norge. (Aalborg, 2004). A. O. Telhaug, O. A. Mediås and P. Aasen: "The Nordic Model in Education. Education as part of the political system the last 50 years." Scandinavian Journal of Educational Research. Vol.50, no 3, (2006).

cal dissertations.[59] It must also be pointed out that the autobiographical genre is now making its way into school history,[60] and that pedagogy as a discipline is being given greater attention.[61]

The decisive element when it comes to the quality of the historical-pedagogical discipline may, however, be the following: During the last period, the discipline has moved in a quite different direction towards social science theory. This means that narrative and descriptive historical pedagogy has been significantly changed into *theory-based research*. As examples we can mention Rune Slagstad's great work inspired by political science *De nasjonale strateger* [The national strategists], Per Bjørn Foros' Baumann-inspired study *Tid for besinnelse* [Time for composure], Nina Volckmar's study *Fra solidarisk samværskultur til kunnskapssolidaritet* [From solidarity socialisation culture to knowledge solidarity] inspired by Habermas, Durkheim and Foucault, and Maria Øksnes' study of children's recreational time inspired by Foucault and Bakhtin.[62] It is definitely also of great importance for school history research that several younger researchers hailing from other disciplines such as sociology and political science (Tuastad, Skarpenes, Trippestad) have focused on school history and examined it according to theoretical perspectives.[63] Bearing this in mind, Norwegian historical pedagogy now positions itself as a critical discipline and has ceased to base research around separated national perspectives in favour of an international and social science perspective. The questions thus raised by historical-pedagogical researchers will be of a more general interest than has previously been the case with the specifically descriptive and narrative versions. One may ask whether there is reason to believe that research will gain in quality and thus attract more attention when it takes as its point of departure, the

---

[59] Petter Aasen and Ove Kristian Haugaløkken (ed.) Bærekraftig pedagogikk. Identitet og kompetanse i det moderne samfunnet. (Oslo, 1994). Tora Korsvold: For alle barn! Barnehagens framvekst i velferdsstaten. (Oslo, 1998). Kari Blom: Norsk barndom gjennom 150 år. En innføring. (Bergen, 2004). Tora Korsvold: Barns verdi: en barndom som evneveik på 1950-tallet (Oslo, 2006). Harald Thuen: Om barnet. Oppdragelse, opplæring og omsorg gjennom historien. (Oslo, 2008).

[60] Hans Østvold: Skolemann og skolepolitiker (Notodden, 1996). Per Kvist: En vandring gjennom norsk skolehistorie (Bergen, 1999). Alfred Oftedal Telhaug: Ensomhet og fellesskap. Erindringer om forskning og formidling (Oslo, 2009).

[61] Elisabeth Buk-Berge, Torstein Harbo, Finn Hjardemaal et al. (2000).

[62] Rune Slagstad et al. (1998). Per Bjørn Foros: Tid for besinnelse (Oslo, 2002). Nina Volckmar: Fra solidarisk samværskultur til kunnskapssolidaritet (Trondheim, 2004). Maria Øksnes: "Hvis det er noe vi ikke får lov til, så sniker vi oss til det!" (Trondheim, 2008).

[63] As examples, refer to the following doctoral dissertations: Svein Tuastad: Skulen og statsmaktsspørsmålet (Bergen, 2006), Ove Skarpenes: Kunnskapens legitimering (Oslo, 2007) and Tom Are Trippestad: Kommandohumanismen (Bergen, 2009).

insights and claims of the great theorists? Is there a possibility that this critical turn will create a stronger focus upon contemporary times?[64] This may mean that the prospect for historical-pedagogical research is brighter than it appears to be in the view of Jesper Eckhardt Larsen?

Conclusion

My conclusion is therefore that even if the field of historical-pedagogy in Norway has lost ground in terms of its presence in recent decades, as a research discipline it has developed considerably. The choice of themes and research questions is now broader. The presentations examine more boldly the contemporary situation. The Norwegian narrative tradition is increasingly being replaced by an internationally inspired re-theorization of the field.

[64] Vegard Kvam: Livsnær skole. En historie om Erling Kristvik og den fådelte skolen. (Oslo, 2009), p. 33.

Between "Freight-shippers" and Nordists – The political implications of educational historiography in Denmark.

Christian Larsen & Jesper Eckhardt Larsen

Introduction

In this article we attempt to propose a political analysis of the field of the history of education in Denmark from the late 19th century into the 21st century. A recently published bibliography of historical works in Danish educational scholarship encompasses over 10.000 posts – and barely spans the latter half of the 20th century.[1] This leaves us a wide and open field to analyze. The most we can do is to provide the reader with a very limited outline of some positions taken in this historiography – and try to frame these in the political context. This attempt builds upon the understanding of the development in scholarly fields as an expression of external forces just as well as internal dynamics. Here we will look at educational historiography as such a battlefield. We claim that the political economy of the educational field has been supported by historians of education trying to deliver and reflect on common premises for specific groups of both politicians and educationalists.

Secondly we try to frame the Danish historiography of education in the nexus of either reference to a continental continuity, first and foremost the tradition of Germano-phone *Bildung*, or reference to a Pan-Scandinavian area of common egalitarian and naturalistic educational traditions. This Scandinavianism (only Denmark, Norway and Sweden), is somewhat mixed with a wider Nordic reference (including Iceland and Finland and more recently the Baltic countries). We choose to call this an educational *Nordism*. The references to the Anglo-Saxon world are less overt, albeit important for the two most recent trends to be dealt with in this article. We pinpoint five distinct and broad trends in this historiography – somewhat in chronological order –represented by recent works in the history of education. Within this framework we have tried to analyze some "grand narratives" from the late nineteenth century

[1] Christian Larsen, Dansk Uddannelseshistorisk Bibliografi 1948-2004 (Odense: Syddansk Universitetsforlag, 2005).

into the twenty-first century. Our overview of central works within the Danish history of education supports distinct existing cultural-political viewpoints. The existing literature on this subject is surprisingly limited in the Danish case. There are only four articles on Danish educational historiography we found available, and they deal with history writing at Denmark's only institute for school history. *"Forty Years of Research into the History of Education in Denmark,"* published by the second professor at this institute Vagn Skovgaard-Petersen in the *Scandinavian Journal of Educational Research*, is the most comprehensive article until now. Other contributions in this issue deal with other Nordic countries and must therefore be recommended to the reader.[2] The other historiographical overviews will be commented on below.[3]

As a simplification of the overall development we will group the literature into five segments. These five segments fit more or less with similar groupings in the international literature on educational historiography. This literature tends to group educational historiography into four groups: 1) Conservative; 2) Whig; 3) Revisionist; and 4) Post-revisionist.[4] We will be adding a fifth group to this list separating two categories of the Whig tendency. The arguments for specific Danish variants to this overall succession will be presented below. We do however not intend to present our five groups in any linear chronological order, because we find new contributions to Danish historiography of education in all these groups.

Firstly, the neohumanist tendencies of much education in the whole of Europe have played a major role in defining the educated elites of Denmark since the breakthrough of these ideas in Northern Europe in

[2] Vagn Skovgaard-Petersen, „Forty Years of Research into the History of Education in Denmark," Scandinavian Journal of Educational Research 41, no. 3-4 (1997).
[3] Ingrid Markussen, "Uddannelseshistorisk forskning – nogle udviklingslinier," in Forskning for folkeskolen - undervisning og videre uddannelse, ed. Torben Broström, Ingrid Markussen, and Kaj Spelling (København: Danmarks Lærerhøjskole, 1981); Ingrid Markussen, "Forskningstendenser ved Institut for Dansk Skolehistorie," in Institut – Selskab – Museum : en skolehistorisk hilsen til Vagn Skovgaard-Petersen, ed. Inger Schultz Hansen and Erik Nørr (København: Selskabet for Dansk Skolehistorie & Dansk Skolemuseum, 2001); Lejf Degnbol, "Vagn Skovgaard-Petersen og Institut for Dansk Skolehistorie," in Institut – Selskab – Museum : en skolehistorisk hilsen til Vagn Skovgaard-Petersen, ed. Inger Schultz Hansen and Erik Nørr (København: Selskabet for Dansk Skolehistorie & Dansk Skolemuseum 2001).
[4] Jurgen Herbst, „Beyond the Debate over Revisionism : Three Educational Pasts Writ Large," History of Education Quarterly 20, no. 2 (1980); Jurgen Herbst, "The History of Education : State of the Art at the Turn of the Century in Europe and North America," Paedagogica Historica 35, no. 3 (1999); Andy Green, "Education and State Formation Revisited," History of Education Review 23, no. 3 (1994); Marc Depaepe, "Demythologizing the Educational Past : An Endless Task in History of Education," Historical Studies in Education/Revue d'histoire de l'éducation 9, no. 2 (1997).

the 18th century. The keyword in this tradition has been the term *dannelse* (Bildung or liberal education), along with differing definitions of *almendannelse* (allgemeine Bildung or general education). We choose to call this group both *borgerlig* (bourgeois) and *dannelsesbaseret*, i.e. building on the positive connotations of humanistic scholarship and Bildung, but with a somewhat conservative outlook. The continuing importance of specific German pedagogy and educational thinking in the first half of the nineteenth century brought an observer Jørgen Jørgensen to express the calamities of Danish educational thinking in 1848: "Just as much as we lack independent educational writers, the numerous are the pedagogical freight-shippers that make German works on the field accessible to readers not acquainted with this language."[5]

Early reactions to this trend were the realistic and/or national romantic movements that gained more and more political force during the late nineteenth century. We choose to call this assertive group both liberal and Grundtvigian – referring to their central ideology – somewhat framed – as it is – by the educationalist and protestant priest Nicolai Frederik Severin Grundtvig (1783-1872). Just as the references of the first group were chiefly continental, so were many members of this group nordist – ranging far into the twentieth century. The late romantic period where these ideas were born was the period of a conscious severing of any decisive connections to Germany. Instead, it was a reference to a common Nordic past. This was something new, and although politically insignificant it was culturally decisive. The native languages being a central part of the national romantic turn in education and culture formed a natural departure for the growing Scandinavistic and Nordist movements. Of the two national wars during the latter half of the nineteenth century one was won and one lost to the emerging German superpower. Seen from a Danish perspective the last one lost in 1864 had quite a long *Wirkungsgeschichte* in disconnecting Danish cultural connections to our southern neighbour. Tendencies in this historiography will be seen to be somewhat Whiggish. In other words, they will tend to be seen as the advent of egalitarian democracy realized through the educational counterforce of the Grundtvigian and liberal movements in the second half of the nineteenth century.

Moving into the first parts of the twentieth century we encounter in Denmark, as elsewhere in Europe and globally, more radical groups

---

[5] Jørgensen 1848, p.189 cited in Sven Erik Nordenbo, Bidrag til den danske pædagogiks historie (København: Museum Tusculanums Forlag, 1984). p.87.

within the progressive movement of educational reform. These tendencies have had differing proponents, but a positive evaluation of more child-centred pedagogies (along with the democratic urge to include all social groups in this educational form) serves as the common denominator of these scholars. We choose to call this group both cultural radical (*kulturradikal*) and progressive. This group shares characteristics of a Whig interpretation of history as the historiography narrates of more and more child-centred pedagogy and democratization through more and better schools. Research on the internationalization of educational thinking seen in a global perspective shows this period to be astonishingly international, not to be surpassed until the latter quarter of the century, in what many see as the true age of globalization of educational practices and reflection.[6]

Both before and after the ruptures of academia in 1968, a fourth group emerged with a very strong expansion into the present field of the history of education in Denmark. We choose to call these scholars *socialistic* and/or *emancipatory* in their view of the history of education. This group of Danish scholars fits quite well into the international revisionist movement in educational history. We see the development of the Danish revisionists from an initial socialistic or Marxist view on history in general, to a more post-modern critical and emancipatory line that expresses the aspirations of the underprivileged groups or subgroups in what could be considered as an advocative voicing. Workers and peasants were the "folk" to be initially emancipated in Marxism – women, children, the handicapped, ethnic minorities etc. were later identified as groups who were also in need of emancipation from a more or less well defined power-holding subject. The initial nexus of reference of this group was clearly a child of Cold War Europe. The heroes and heroines of a western Marxist turn (very often German!) could be observed in connection with an anti-capitalist reverence for the Eastern Block. Educational historiography was by no means actively trying to drive Denmark into the communist camp – but the tensions of the Cold War could trigger a deep critique of the perpetual structural inequalities of education in the capitalist block - including little social democratic Denmark.

We are not keen on defining all subsequent literature under the well-known heading of post-revisionism; however, we do find a new

[6] Jürgen Schriewer et al., „Konstruktion von Internationalität : Referenzhorisonte pädagogishen Wissens im Wandel gesellschaftlicher Systeme (Spanien, Sowjetunion/Russland, China)," in Gesellschaften im Vergleich, ed. Hartmut Kaelble and Jürgen Schriewer (Frankfurt a.M.: Peter Lang, 1998).

pragmatic and more optimistic view of certain school developments. Our version of a post-revisionist approach could be called an all-inclusive, *laissez-faire* view of educational history writing. Some choose the view of everyday life, with a turn to materiality or affects while some focus on a strong state as a positive and progressive actor. Others find some inspiration for didactics in heroes of the past. One could agree with Gary McCulloch in a recent debate with Marc Depaepe that a new testament is needed in light of the historical Puritanism of the revisionists. We too do not find that Marc Depeape is all the way right in his purist ten commandments.[7] The two contributions from McCulloch and Depeape in this volume can also make this controversy apparent.

Before we enter into a characterization of the views on educational history of these five groups of scholarship in the history of education in Denmark, we will take a brief review of institutional developments within the field of the history of education, where it has been shown that the Nordic references are dominant in the Danish educational self-perception. Secondly a short prehistory of what has been called the *Danish schism* will provide a key to understand the Danish situation in its comparative differences and oddities as opposed to both German and Scandinavian developments at our point of departure: late nineteenth century Denmark. This provides at the same time an outline of the first opposition mentioned above: neo-humanistic elites with continental references challenged by assertive national romantic and realistic movements with nordist references. These two positions are also described in an influential external view on Denmark. Margaret Archer suggests that at its inception the Danish history of education was heavily influenced by the elites and these assertive groups.[8]

Institutional developments for the history of education

In Denmark educational research was recognized as a specific academic field relatively late. A brief attempt at the University of Copenhagen in early nineteenth century was soon abandoned. It was only after World War II that a professor of education was appointed at the University of Copenhagen. But as an early example of the Danish schism another institution *Danmarks Lærerhøjskole* (the Royal Teachers' Training

[7] Marc Depaepe, "The Ten Commandments of Good Practices in History of Education Research," Zeitschrift für pädagogische Historiographie 1(2010); Gary McCulloch, "The Gospel according to St Marc," Zeitschrift für pädagogische Historiographie 1(2010).

[8] Margaret S. Archer, Social Origins of Educational Systems (London and Beverly Hills: Sage Publications Ltd., 1979).

College), was intended to serve as a continuing educational institution for the teachers.

This institution was founded in 1867 but was not granted the status of an institution of higher education before 1963. In 1965 an institute for the history of education was established with the Scandinavian-based Roar Skovmand (1908-1987) as the first full professor. The institutionalisation at the college meant that there was now an academic impetus and focus on writing a general national history of education, as opposed to the histories of individual institutions. This change came about exactly at a time where history as a social science of broad historical trends was gaining strength as opposed to the history of actors and ideas. The institute was seen from the start as a Nordic project, and the first three researchers to be appointed positions at this institute covered all of the Scandinavian countries. A Dane, Vagn Skovgaard-Petersen (1932-2006) was supplemented by a Swede, Ingrid Markussen (b. 1938), and then by a Norwegian, Ellen Nørgaard (b. 1933). The work of Professor Skovmand and these other writers made reference to the whole of the Nordic area. They will be commented on below.

The sphere of activity for the institute was closely connected to the aim of the Royal Teachers' Training College: to serve the interests of the primary school (*at tjene folkeskolens tarv*), which, however, did not prevent the institute from looking into other areas of the educational system, especially through the yearbook of *Selskabet for Dansk Skolehistorie* (the Society for the History of the Danish School). The society was founded in 1966 with the aim "to disseminate knowledge to and interest in the history of the Danish school", and in cooperation with the institute to ensure research into this field. They also set out to collect and preserve historical source material from schools. The new society began publishing a yearbook in 1967.

The focus on the primary school underlined the gap between two cultural segments, i.e. between the primary schools/teachers' training colleges and the universities/gymnasiums. Vagn Skovgaard-Petersen tried to compensate for this in his thesis *Dannelse og demokrati* (Bildung and Democracy), which dealt with the connection between the said institutions. Despite this a lasting schism in the self-understandings continued to exist. This is a theme that is emphasized in *Institut – Selskab – Museum. En skolehistorisk hilsen til Vagn Skovgaard-Petersen* (2001). This work underlines the desire that the history of schools should interact with the practitioners of the primary school segment, and raises the concern of this being lost with the new much larger institution *Dan-*

marks Pædagogiske Universitet (the Danish University of Education), established in 2000. The old schism between *folkeligt* and elitism is still alive in Danish culture. It had its symptomatic expression in the Danish history of education which neglected the universities, and that only to a limited extent (beside Vagn Skovgaard-Petersen) dealt with the transformation of the gymnasium into an institution of the people. The history of education at this institution largely became the history of the primary school. The history of the university was not seen as a part of the history of education until the foundation of *Danmarks Pædagogiske Universitet*. With some exceptions, the existing history of the university was written by representatives of the university subjects. This was the case with the great jubilee publication of the University of Copenhagen in 15 volumes.[9]

The institute was closed in 1992 due to financial cut-backs and the staff became a part of the new Institute for Pedagogy and Educational Research. Another, more institutional, turn in the story of the history of education in Denmark was the merger between a number of institutions including the Royal Teachers' Training College with *Danmarks Pædagogiske Institut* (the Institute for Educational Studies) and other smaller institutions in 2000. Hereby *Danmarks Pædagogiske Universitet* was founded. The first rector of this institution, the historian of ideas Lars-Henrik Schmidt (b. 1953), began his work with a disregard for any historical studies in the vein of individual school histories; he considered this to be an out-dated discipline. The new institutes were not clearly performative in outlook, but definitely focussed on the present not the past. In a framework of sociology, anthropology, philosophy and psychology the historically interested researcher had to find a way to legitimize herself/himself. This was – and we speak from the heart – an uphill battle. It was mostly in the framework of comparative education that work was done, and now combining a comparative- with a historical- viewpoint.

The Danish university reform of 2003 has lead to what, in polemic terms, could be called an "informed absolutism" taking over from "constitutional democracy" of the faculty laws of the 1970 and 1973. Inspired by the OECD a top-down management of the universities and the research policies has had the consequence of strongly personalized management. After the merger of *Danmarks Pædagogiske Universitet* in 2007 into *Aarhus University,* it was firstly a separate faculty called

[9] Svend Ellehøj and Leif Grane, eds., Københavns Universitet 1479-1979, 14 vols., vol. 3, Københavns Universitet 1479-1979 (København: GEC Gads forlag, 1979-2005).

the *Danish School of Education* and the history of education had again become a legitimate endeavour, at least when funding was found outside the institution itself. Now, in 2011, the faculty is merged as an *Institute of Education* together with the Aarhus Faculty of Theology and the Aarhus Faculty of the Humanities into the large (and unmanageable) *Aarhus Faculty of Arts* and became a department within the enlarged faculty. This raises a very important question: What does this mean for the field of educational research and the field of the history of education? Until now the new institute leader Hanne Løngreen has terminated the previous leaders efforts to establish a new chair in the history of education, without any other reason, than this is not a relevant topic.

Explaining the metamorphoses of Danish institutions of research in education, and as a part of the new age of cognitive capitalism, must be the endeavour of future historians. Here we will suffice with mapping the long twentieth century of grand narratives of education. Before each of the five mentioned viewpoints are analyzed a view of the situation in late nineteenth century Denmark could be helpful in understanding the oddities of Danish educational historiography. This will enable us to view ourselves from outside, as it were.

The Danish Schism – the situation in late 19th century

To begin with a somewhat strange statement about Danish educational history: the *light* turned *upside down* already entering the 20th century. This statement from the educational historian Ove Korsgaard refers to the large political and "bottom up" influence of liberal, peasant movements in the late nineteenth Denmark and the metaphor will be elaborated on later in the article.[10] The landowning peasants formed an alliance with the Grundtvigian movement in both church and politics. Grundtvig was a theologian and priest, as well as being the most productive poet in the Danish standard book of psalms for church life. In an educational context his quite aggressive attack on the established institutions of learning was to be decisive in the Danish educational self-understanding. His attacks were inspired by Johann Gottfried Herder's view of the people's organic growth into a cultural unity. This view brought him to the conviction that the very heavy Latin and Greek impetus in the gymnasiums (secondary education) should be supplanted by a national educational curriculum, putting new stress on the Danish language and history. His

[10] Ove Korsgaard, Kampen om lyset: Dansk voksenoplysning gennem 500 år (Århus: Gyldendal, 1997).

own idiosyncratic hatred of Latin and German was an extra impetus to work for new institutions of education. A trip to Great Britain in the eighteen-thirties inspired him to form a programme of folk high schools (*folkehøjskoler*). His idea gained royal attention, and he managed to persuade King Christian VIII (1786-1848, King 1839) to establish a royal folk high school in Sorø, south west of Roskilde on the Island of Zealand. As an irony of fate democracy ran faster than this grand plan. In 1848 the new King, Fredrik VII, after political pressures, accepted a democratic reform establishing a two-chamber parliament. The second-first government had a national liberal politician and famous Latin scholar as the minister of educational and ecclesiastical affairs (*Kultusminister*), Johan Nicolai Madvig (1804-1886). With the words: "There shall be no educational institutions in Denmark that form a monopoly on Danishness" [11] he discontinued the plans for the royal high school. Grundtvig was disappointed with the rush of democratic reforms; somewhat ironic as history grants him a reputation as one of the most important democratic thinkers in the Danish tradition.

Despite these moves, the folk high school movement continued with financial support from the state (awarded in later legislation not least supported by Madvig), but freely and without much central state guidance, or royal influence. The proliferation of folk high schools in the late nineteenth century was to change the scene of Danish education with a strong *Wirkungsgeschichte* into present day Danish politics of knowledge. The romantic notion combined with the British college model formed a new cultural movement, where young peasants found a year or more to spend in these boarding schools, best-described as being half church, and half institution of Danish song-culture, historical culture and mythology.[12] This was present to an extent where a Danish writer wrote to the also famous cultural radical Georg Brandes (1842-1927) in the eighteen-eighties that the "Danish schism lies between the wet, thoughtless Grundtvigianism and the dry, non-intuitive Madvigianism." The first had its own institutions in the folk high schools, independent (free) schools (*friskoler*) and to some extent private teachers training colleges. The latter had its institutions of learned (secondary) schools,

---

[11] Jesper Eckhardt Larsen, J.N. Madvigs dannelsestanker, vol. 111, Studier fra Sprog- og Oldtidsforskning nr.337 (København: Det filologisk-historiske samfund Museum Tusculanums Forlag, 2002). p.97ff.

[12] Uffe Østergaard calles this movement the Danish variant of a civil religion in: Uffe Østergård, "Nation-Building Danish Style," in Nordic Paths to National Identity in the Nineteenth Century, ed. Øystein Sørensen (Oslo: The Research Council of Norway, 1993).

later to be renamed into "gymnasium" and the stronghold of the then only Danish university, University of Copenhagen, where Madvig was *rector magnificus* for some time and professor of Latin for a lifetime.

This brief history is to frame the most insisting grand narrative of the Danish educational history writing: a liberal peasant cultural story of the "light from below." A song written by Grundtvig expresses that, in his view, "The sun rises with the peasant – not at all with the learned." Until nineteen-sixties both the liberal party (*Venstre*) as well as the Social Liberal Party (*Det Radikale Venstre*) emphasised that seven years primary schooling was enough to make every boy and girl able to adapt to adult life. There was almost a fear of educating too many high school and university graduates because they would not want to work at the farms or in industries. During the debates concerning the 1958 School Act the minister of education Jørgen Jørgensen from the Social Liberal Party said that he saw no reason for expanding the mandatory seven years schooling. He pointed to his own story as evidence. With only seven years of schooling in a small village school he became a government minister, as he proclaimed. At the teachers' training colleges, politicians were reluctant to have high school exams as admission on the grounds that it would exclude "the man from the plow" (*Manden fra ploven*): a central phrase in Danish educational politics until fifty years ago.

This "Herder-narrative" has been the guiding narrative of Danish education, with the other classicist strand somewhat into the shadows in discussions of defining the nation. One must add that being a very well educated person, Grundtvig was himself a humanist, and on top of that a nordist. His plans included the establishment of institutions of higher learning on a more international – for the time being inter-nordic – level. He foresaw a true university institution in the Swedish town of Gothenburg, where learned scholars could develop his programme of a science/scholarship (*Videnskab*) "for life" as he expressed it in opposition to dead culture. This was a university in the old fashion, but it should also, Grundtvigs's words, move beyond what he called *Drenge-Videnskab* (Boy-Science). Instead this should be *Vidskab*: a broad, education for life. An institution was founded in 1947 as a result of the later pan-Scandinavian reception of the folk high school movement and a new scandinavianism after World War II, but never as a full university. The University of Gothenburg today does not stand in this tradition.

This strife between Madvig and Grundtvig was, as already indicated, also a battle of defining a Danish *dannelse* (Bildung) as either classical and continental (with Germany as closest present affinity), or as scandinavistic or nordist with a pan-scandinavian view of a common culture (having no hesitation in stretching its narratives of continuity back to the Vikings). When Madvig in 1844 declared that we are "human beings before we are Scandinavian," and therefore our Bildung should follow the long cultural developments from ancient Greece, he was referring to a high culture doctrine of continental universalism from antiquity that stretched to the present day and privileged European culture nations.[13] Grundtvig, on the other hand, consciously wished to free Danes from our "inner Germans" and argued to exchange dead languages of the "black school," such as Greek and Latin, with living languages from "the school for life." The curious conclusion he drew was to propose present-day Greek for the secondary school curriculum, along with the ancient pan-Nordic language. The only common trait was to keep Danish Bildung strongly humanistic and language-based, as opposed to the strong line of realistic reformers on the Danish scene at that time.

The folk highs schools were not only a Grundtvigian movement, but divided into Grundtvigian folk high schools (1844ff), Inner Mission high folk schools (1889ff), Social Democratic folk high schools (1910ff), and Socialist folk high schools (1970ff). Amongst the independent schools and local teachers' training colleges we also find Grundtvigian schools, Christian schools, and socialist schools. This means that there are many versions of the folk high schools and free schools movement: a Grundtvigian version, a Socialist version, a Christian version etc. and this has an influence on how the history of the folk high schools and the independent schools is being told. The local teachers' training colleges founded on Grundtvigian, Christian or other specific values have lost those values within the last 5-10 years as they have been merged into larger university colleges (*professionshøjskoler*) with a NPM person/technocrat in charge.

The establishment side of the Danish schism - neohumanism

The Danish historiography of education that has held a more top-down, positive notion of higher learning and *dannelse* has of course also had its development through the twentieth century. Here we will examine the influences of central proponents that illustrate our view that the mentioned opposition is still active in present day historiography.

In the time between the two world wars the archivist and historian Dr. Bjørn Kornerup (1896-1957) published histories of individual

[13] Larsen, J.N. Madvigs dannelsestanker, 111: p.75ff.

institutions in the learned neohumanistic vein. His two most ambitious works were histories of the two institutions: Ribe Cathedral School (in Jutland) and Frederiksborg State School (on Zealand north of Copenhagen).[14] These are both examples of a celebration of the learned tradition of neohumanist *dannelse*. The line of teachers is mentioned to praise the high academic standards and traditions of scholarship. The "spirit" (*Geist*) of the individual institution is narrated in a long historical perspective with a focus on great personalities of learned culture at the gymnasium and the University of Copenhagen. The ethos of learning and upbringing are connected in the definition of a high-brow local tradition. Learning and *dannelse* are both seen as valuable in themselves. Certainly this fits the model of history discussed above. The functions of this type of educational history can be seen to create or stifle the elite identities of students and teachers from these unique institutions and the University. Dr. Kornerup actually copied large passages on the history of Danish learning between the two books and his contribution to the 5 volumes history of the Danish church.

Kornerup shares elements of the Whig interpretation that the number of students and schools lead to a larger inclusion and higher levels of quality. Being conservative, however, separates him largely from the Whig side of history writing. Indeed the learned schools have had a growth, like the one seen internationally. Until the end of the nineteen-fifties only 5 % of a cohort graduated from a gymnasium, and a large percentage of them had parents with an academic degree or parents working as civil servants etc. Only 10 % came from the working class. The enormous growth in this level of education came after Kornerup's ouvre.

The neohumanistic tradition of the celebration of knowledge in the *kulturnation* (Kulturnation), as a value of high culture in itself, actually survived well into the post World War II period. The politicians and new national research councils continued to argue for the relevance of humanistic scholarship seen as high culture. The *high culture-argument* must be understood as a reminiscence of the neo-humanism that dominated university life through most of the nineteenth century. Humanistic scholarship was considered to promote the moral culture of nations. An elitist view of a moral *avant-garde* was connected with vague ideas of

---

[14] Bjørn Kornerup, Frederiksborg Statsskoles historie 1630-1930 (Hillerød: Frederiksborg Amts Historiske Samfund, 1933); Bjørn Kornerup, Ribe Katedralskoles Historie (København: Gyldendal, 1947-1952).

national dissemination of high culture, but these views were strongly contested after the student revolts in the late nineteen-sixties. By then *Dannelse* was seen as a carrier of bourgeois ideology and the ideas of *kulturnationer* were exchanged with concepts of research for "society" (*samfund*). However the long tradition of neohumanist *dannelse* and *almendannelse* in the Danish context actually survived more strongly in Denmark than in Norway or Sweden. Because of the drive for upper secondary gymnasium education to become more and more inclusive, about 50% of a cohort now, this development did not lead to a total break with the neohumanistic curriculum; something that was, of course, in a modernised version by now.

As a reaction to the leftist vogue of the seventies and eighties a new, somewhat postmodern, notion of *dannelse* could again raise interest in historical re-evaluations of the learned traditions. In his book on the concept of *dannelse* with regard to the fore mentioned Madvig , Jesper Eckhardt Larsen (b. 1967) consciously picked the opposition to Grundtvigian educational history: this position is a red thread through his book.[15] At the turn of the 20th century a strong argument for the continuing importance of *almendannelse* was proposed by the educational historian and former gymnasium teacher Harry Haue (b. 1941) for his thesis *Almendannelse som ledestjerne* (Allgemeinbildung as leading star). In a span of over two-hundred years he believes that the neohumanistic concept of *almendannelse* has had central importance in defining the special role of the Danish gymnasiums. In his last book on the subject, published in German, he surprisingly states that *almendannelse* should still, in spite of more than two-hundred years usage in Danish, be called a "German" concept.[16] This is, we believe, an attempt to give a more highbrow importance to a concept that certainly has had its own life in the Danish context. The publication of another recent volume on the concept of *dannelse* in Denmark shows, however, a clear (and not very German) line of Danish thinkers' views on *dannelse*. A more existential and less curricular sense of the word has flourished among Danish educators and philosophers from Søren Kierkegaard (1813-1855) to Knud E. Løgstrup (1905-1981).[17]

---

[15] Larsen, J.N. Madvigs dannelsestanker, 111.

[16] Harry Haue, Allgemeinbildung : ein deutscher Begriff im dänischen Gymnasium 1750-2007 (Odense: Syddansk Universitetsforlag, 2008).

[17] Joakim Garff, ed. At komme til sig selv : 15 portrætter af danske dannelsestænkere (København: Gads Forlag, 2008).

To sum up: the neohumanist and thus high brow history of education as the history of *dannelse* still has some importance in supplying a strong educational ethos to educators of all kinds, but maybe it is especially strong in secondary education. In a time where PISA surveys and an ideological war against supposed leftwing teachers from the side of the liberal-conservative government threatens to kill all self-esteem among teachers and educators in Denmark, this is a stronghold not yet abandoned. As mentioned this tradition is clearly stronger in Denmark than in our Nordic neighbours that have all had stronger social democratic and modernist reforms of secondary education severing the bonds to traditions of *almendannelse*.

The Grundtvigian and liberal stream in Danish educational historiography

Grundtvig has, as already indicated, a central role in defining the specific national narrative of Danishness through most of the twentieth century. Originally being connected to what Margareth Archer calls the "assertive" groups of liberal peasants Grundtvigian notions of nationhood have influenced both left and right wing movements in Denmark through to the present day. A social democratic historian, Henrik Nissen (1933-2005), could still in 1983 write, that "Grundtvig is the sea the little Danish pixie chooses sometimes to mirror himself in, whenever he feels the urge to see himself as something special."[18]

The comparative educationalist Thyge Winther-Jensen can be seen in this tradition, putting a large emphasis on Grundtvig and showing his strong and prolonged impact on Danish educational politics. He states that the grundtvigian triad of: 1) folkelighed (Herderian populousness); 2) life enlightenment; and 3) free school choice; is actually carried further by the social democratic educational politicies as the triad of: 1) equality; 2) social solidarity; and 3) local influence on school politics. So there is, states Winther-Jensen, a strong connection between the nineteenth century mastodon Grundtvig and the present politics of schooling in Denmark.[19]

A quite critical article on the more direct political impact of Grundtvigian notions of education contrarily suggests that his role is often overestimated. Under the heading "Making Danish School History

[18] Henrik S. Nissen, "Samfundsudviklingen og det grundtvigske," in Efter Grundtvig. Hans betydning i dag, ed. Henrik S. Nissen (København: Gyldendal, 1983).
[19] Thyge Winther-Jensen, Komparativ pædagogik - faglig tradition og global udfordring (København K: Akademisk Forlag, 2004).

into Myth", Susanne Wiborg (b. 1969) and Ove Korsgaard (b. 1942) balance between references to historiography that truthfully argue for the Grundtvigian impact, and other historical works that seem to attribute all of the Danish liberal, egalitarian educational *Sonderweg* to one person and his followers.[20]

As a reference of historiography that is positive towards Grundtvigs' indisputable centrality, these two authors mention the first professor in the history of education in Denmark: Roar Skovmand (1908-1987). His works had the fate of landing in the middle of fierce fights about the definition of Danish national identity. His first works were published before WWII but his first major significant work on the Danish democratic tradition of Folk High Schools in the Grundtvigian tradition was published in 1944 during the German occupation of Denmark. Another major work on the Nordic democratic traditions of Folk High Schools in the same tradition was published in 1983.[21] During the war a new democratic consensus found support in the "bottom up" view of educational reform that was connected to Grundtvigian movements in all the Nordic countries. The overt anti-German cultural self-definition of cause gained new "relevance" in the time of war. Another important figure in this definition of democratic resistance on a cultural level was the historian of religion Hal Koch (1904-1963), who left his desk in the University to travel all over Denmark. He presented talks about the democratic national identity that he saw was the result of long and strong development both in the biography of Grundtvigs own views, and so of Denmark itself. Political historians like Henrik S. Nissen have often made the point that Grundtvigian influence made the Danish peasantry more resistant to National Socialistic tendencies in a time of severe crisis during the nineteen-thirties and during the German occupation of Denmark 1940-45. In a micro study of North Zealand the historian of education Søren Ehlers presented another quite critical view on the social and cultural developments of Grundtvigianism.[22]

In spite of the more critical reappraisal of Grundtvigian influence Ove Korsgaard cites his own works from 1997 and 2004 as works that

---

[20] Ove Korsgaard and Susanne Wiborg, "Grundtvig – the Key to Danish Education?," Scandinavian Journal of Educational Research 50, no. 3 (2006).

[21] Roar Skovmand, Folkehøjskolen i Danmark 1841-1892 (København: Gyldendal, 1944); Roar Skovmand, Samspillet mellem Nordens Folkehøjskoler indtil Anden Verdenskrig (Århus: Universitetsforlaget i Aarhus, 1983).

[22] Søren Ehlers, En lokal grundtvigsk bevægelse : etableringen af grundtvigske institutioner i Nordvestsjælland 1864-94 (Odense: Landbohistorisk Selskab, 1983); Søren Ehlers, Ungdomsliv : studier i den folkeoplysende virksomhed for unge i Danmark 1900-1925 (København: Alinea, 2000).

support a view of the central importance of Grundtvig himself and Grundtvigian movements in the special narrative of Danish national identity. He emphasizes the Danish *Sonderweg* of democratic and inclusive educational institutions that somehow managed to create an assertive takeover of the Danish educational identity, as well as its democratic definitions of the term *folkelighed,* and how this was in contrast to the special German National Socialist definitions of the term *völkisch*. In what we see as an extremely self-satisfied view of this Scandinavian *Sonderweg*, the Norwegian historian, Rune Slagstad (b. 1945), who also includes the history of education in his very well-known works on the "national strategists," writes: "the democratic folkishness (folkelighed) is the Scandinavian gift to the modern world".[23] It is very clear that this line of historiography in education has certainly played a central role in both Danish, Norwegian and (to some extent) Swedish nation building processes. Historians like Eric Hobsbawm have illustrated how the national romantic turn in education served democratization purposes in many western countries. This has shaped an assertive line of educational historiography dealing with the heroes and heroines of equality, national reforms in content, and a democratic view on the dissemination of knowledge to the *folk* (the People). Or, to summarize, this is why peasants are not considered to be unlearned and barbaric in the Scandinavian countries. On the contrary, they are the heroes of national educational reforms. This tendency in the historiography we interpret to be somewhat Whiggish – tending to celebrate the advent of egalitarian democracy realized through the educational counterforce of the Grundtvigian and liberal movements in the second half of the nineteenth century. The analysis of the Whiggish historiography by Andy Green includes these traits. The protestant affinities, and the celebration of democracy antedated to times where this word was hardly as celebrated, marks a clear affinity to a Whig interpretation of history.[24]

We choose to include Joakim Larsen's three volumes of school history in this category of works.[25] Larsen (1846-1920), a pioneer in the Danish historiography on education, was the head of schools in the large

---

[23] Rune Slagstad, De nasjonale strateger (Oslo: Pax Forlag, 1998); Rune Slagstad, "Folkedannelsens forvandlinger," in Dannelsens forvandlinger, ed. Rune Slagstad, Ove Korsgaard, and Lars Løvlie (Oslo: Pax Forlag A/S, 2003).
[24] Green, "Education and State Formation Revisited."
[25] Joakim Larsen, Bidrag til den danske skoles historie (1784-1818), vol. 2 (Viborg: Unge Pædagogers Serie, 1893/1984); Joakim Larsen, Bidrag til den danske skoles historie (1818-1898). , vol. 3 (Viborg: Unge Pædagogers Serie, 1893/1984); Joakim Larsen, Bidrag til den danske skoles historie (1536-1784). , vol. 1 (Viborg: Unge Pædagogers Serie, 1916/1984).

Copenhagen suburb Frederiksberg. In his work he is not overtly dealing with Grundtvig's importance as Skovmand did, but is rather acting as the Whiggish liberal historian who narrates the history of primary schooling in Denmark around 1900 as a steady victory of more and more inclusive, modern and democratic schools. The sheer volume and lightness of the new schools – buildings and curriculum – were, for Larsen, signs of this steady victory of liberal school politics. As a sign of the absence of overviews in Danish school historiography his works were republished – photocopied – from the originals during the nineteen-eighties. They appeared in a period of another educational atmosphere, which is to be described below as an emancipatory line of educational historiography.

To sum up: the liberal peasant movements have played a very central role in Danish political life, and often in connection with Grundtvigian thoughts about Danish educational self-understanding. The hostilities between the liberals and the conservatives were once central in defining Danish politics, but somehow Grundtvigian views on education have had an appeal to all political groupings from the far left to the far right. In the politics of knowledge a hostility towards the learned university elites can – in our view – be traced directly back to Grundtvig's populist sarcasms vis a vis the "black schools" and highbrow neohumanist universities in the vein of Madvig. Danes tend to love everything that is not elitist – to view learning as dull and dead – but at the same time love a speech in an open and liberal spirit in a summer course in a Folk High School. The identical content in a humanities department of a highly-esteemed university is considered with utmost contempt by the very same people for using tax money to support the self-realization of – in their opinion - the self-indulgent learned elites.

The culture-radical and progressive line in educational historiography

Proceeding chronologically into the first parts of the twentieth century we encounter, here as elsewhere in Europe, more radical groups within the progressive movement of educational reform in Denmark. These tendencies have had differing proponents – but a positive evaluation of more child-centred pedagogies, along with the democratic urge to include all social groups in this educational form, serves as the common denominator of these scholars. The group is diverse but the connection between the modern breakthrough in literature and intellectual history, in Denmark called *kulturradikalisme* (culture-radical) and connected with the Danish intellectual Georg Brandes (1842-1927), and the progressive movement in education, is relatively stable throughout the twentieth century. The political party, *Det Radikale Venstre* (the Social Liberal Party), represented the small farmers and somewhat the city-educated left side of the *Bildungsbürgertum*. Through their close collaboration with *Socialdemokratiet* (the Social Democratic Party), they managed to influence Danish educational politics much more than their numbers would indicate. To speak generally, Danish politics through the short twentieth century was dominated by the combination of a Social Democratic prime minister and a Social Liberal minister of education. While social liberal historians have written a large part of general Danish political historiography through the twentieth century, more than a few of the social liberals were also loyal to Grundtvigian views of Danish culture and education. This helps to explain why we chose to define five groups in this paper, and not the four commonly in use in international literature. As mentioned above this group shares characteristics with a Whig interpretation of history now as the historiography that narrates of more and more child-centred pedagogy and of democratization through better schools.

The first obvious example in this group of scholars, Sofie Rifbjerg (1886-1981), was a practitioner who wrote her own educational history. Already the title itself *Træk af den moderne opdragelses historie* (Trends in the history of modern education) indicates that she saw herself as the Danish pioneer of the progressive movements of *reformpædagogik* (Reformpädagogik). Narrating from the international precursors Montessori and Freinet in Europe, via school experiments in the UK and USA, she tells the story of how she brought the ideas back to Denmark. From 1926-1931, the so-called *Vanløseforsøg* (the Vanløse experiments – Vanløse is a suburb to Copenhagen), based on progressive methods, stands as a central defining event for this group of scholars. Here as elsewhere in Europe the progressive educational movement was dedicated to opening new paths for the individual pupil in the light of child-centred methods and/or the more egalitarian and class-driven ways to present the child with art, music, movement and expression.

Later in the twentieth century the scholar Ellen Nørgaard (b. 1933) chose to write her doctoral thesis on exactly these developments in *reformpædagogik*. Her view was to combine the individual pedagogic self-understanding of the reformists with a critical view of their supposed "liberation" of the children from discipline and harsh schooling.[26]

[26] Ellen Nørgaard, Lille barn, hvis er du? : en skolehistorisk undersøgelse over reformbestræbelser inden for den danske folkeskole i mellemkrigstiden (København: Gyldendal, 1977).

The second professor of the history of education in Denmark, Vagn Skovgaard-Petersen (1931-2006), was more interested in the modern, broad and democratic dissemination of *dannelse* to all groups of society, but he too chose to combine a positive view on the individual reformist politician or school-holder with a critical re-evaluation of the true impact of the democratic reforms from the period around 1900.[27]

Seen in retrospect these scholars all have some degree of sympathy towards the reformist actors whom they chose to describe. Skovgaard-Petersen phrased this view as follows: "This book can be read as the story of how some people have tried to change both the school system and the teaching and thereby change society." This view also gives this group of scholars a certain Whiggish tendency: this is the loyal story of how better schools and more democracy came about though individual progressive agents in a political struggle against existing structures.

From socialist to emancipatory historiography – revisionism in Denmark

Scholars of both history and education from the other Nordic countries tend to see the left wing dominance of academic life following the student revolts as significantly stronger in Denmark than in that of Norway or Sweden. The cry was for emancipation and equality in education through the whole educational system, and scholars were urged to do research for "society." This was most often defined as *forskning for folket* (research for the people). Both before and after the ruptures within academia of 1968, a fourth group emerged. We choose to call label this group as socialistic and emancipatory in their view of the history of education. In international literature this group of scholars would be seen as radical revisionists.[28] We see the development of this group moving from an initial socialistic or Marxist view of history in general into a broader post-modern critical and emancipatory viewpoint. What characterizes all of these scholars as "emancipatory" rests on the views held that almost any group or subgroup of society was supposed to get its share of emancipation. Workers and peasants were the "classes" to be emancipated in Marxism – women, children, handicapped, ethnic minori-

[27] Vagn Skovgaard-Petersen, Dannelse og demokrati : fra latin- til almenskole : lov om højere almenskoler 24. april 1903 (København: Gyldendal, 1976).

[28] We are conscious of the broad usage of the term revisionism by Jurgen Herbst but we tend to agree to a development of the revisionism in Denmark as from a harder neomarxist revisionism into a softer broadly emancipatory revisionism. Herbst, "Beyond the Debate over Revisionism : Three Educational Pasts Writ Large."

ties etc. have later been groups who were in need of emancipation from a more or less well-defined power-holding subject. It is not our intention to scorn this endeavour, but rather to refer to the very broad reception in Danish academia of the German Frankfurter Schule of societal thinking. Jürgen Habermas was of central importance calling the knowledge interest of social sciences "emancipatory." Scholars like Michel Foucault and Pierre Bourdieu have had a very large impact on this stream of Danish educational scholarship, too. The idea of a history of education also moved significantly into a social science self-understanding as opposed to a humanistic one. The nineteen-seventies were the time where humanists tended to copy the methods and outlooks of the social sciences, be it Marxist, structuralist and/or quantitative in outlook.

Gunhild Nissen (b. 1936) forms with her thesis from 1973 an early example of a more materialist or Marxist view of Danish school-history.[29] She places her work *Bønder, skoler og demokrati* (Peasants, School and Democracy) in the context of a transition from works that deal with named, more-or-less influential historical actors into more anonymous, broadly defined social trends. She includes statistical work in her view on democratisation and social inequality. She writes: "In opposition to earlier research in the history of Danish schools that primarily viewed schools from above, the present problem (in her research, CL/JEL) indicates that the schools are viewed from below and from outside."[30] This tendency was mirrored by the sociologist Erik Jørgen Hansen (b. 1935), who created a quite influential piece of contemporary history by following a cohort from its youth into adulthood and tracking life-long economic and educational status development, thereby confirming the unequal distribution of educational opportunity. Denmark, he showed, was still a society constructed around the basis of class.[31]

The trends in recent historical work covered here include a reappraisal of traditional history writing by taking the viewpoint of underprivileged groups. For example, the history of women's education was central to the historian Birgitte Possing (b. 1952) who chose the form of a biography to show the fight of an individual against structural sexism. The story she told concerned the late nineteenth century female pioneer

---

[29] Gunhild Nissen, Bønder, skole og demokrati : en undersøgelse i fire provstier af forholdet mellem den offentlige skole og befolkningen på landet i tiden ca. 1880-1910 (København: Insitut for dansk skolehistorie, 1973).
[30] Ibid p.14.
[31] Erik Jørgen Hansen, En generation blev voksen : den første velfærdsgeneration (København: Socialforskningsinstituttet, 1995).

educator Nathalie Zahle (1827-1913).[32] The issues of another underprivileged group were studied by Birgit Kirkebæk (b. 1938) in her works on the educational treatment of mentally handicapped children and adults.

Finally, one could include Ning de Coninck-Smith's (b. 1953) work on child history. Her focus is also to examine history from below using methods of historical anthropology and micro-studies with international references to the French and the Anglo-Saxon scholarly communities. She is not interested in looking at school curriculum and its history. Her focus is, instead, on aspects of everyday life in school from the length of the school day to school buildings, school meals, youth centres, parents' evening etc. In her doctoral thesis from 2000, she shows how new definitions of childhood, disciplinary practices and urban physical surroundings fundamentally changed the lives of children around 1900. Her thesis is that the new state school came to play a central role in the democratization, i.e. universalization, of what has been described as middle-class childhood. Childhood became a phase of life in its own right and was invested with an independent significance for later adult life.[33]

In her latest book, de Coninck-Smith examines the history of school buildings in Denmark during the last 300 years. She is inspired by Philippe Ariès but where Ariès emphasizes the objects, de Coninck-Smith emphasizes the spatial aspects of childhood history and their meanings as a way to illustrate the changing conceptions of the good childhood as well as societal expectations, norms and values. She describes her book not as an architectural or pedagogial study but as socio-material. "I will think thoughts through space," she says, as a way to examine the threads between architecture, the view of children's upbringing and education, and social changes through time.[34]

A large work in progress is to rewrite the whole Danish history of primary education. Led by de Coninck-Smith, and including eleven historians, the collaborative project is to be a history written "bottom-up" in opposition to the histories of jurisdiction and politics viewing schools from above. Three issues will be investigated and pursued in all volumes: How have perceptions of schooling and the conditions for school attendance changed over time? Who struggled to influence the develop-

---

[32] Bigitte Possing, Viljens styrke : Natalie Zahle : en biografi om dannelse, køn og magtfuldkommenhed (København: Gyldendal, 1992

[33] Ning de Coninck-Smith, For barnets skyld : byen, skolen og barndommen 1880-1914 (København: Gyldendal, 2000).

[34] Ning de Coninck-Smith, Barndom og arkitektur : rum til danske børn igennem 300 år (Aarhus: Klim, 2011). p.13-15.

ment of schools, by which means, and with what results? Finally, what (and how diverse) are the specific ways in which every day school life has manifested itself at different times, and what has school meant to pupils, parents, and teachers? [35]

To sum up this historiography: there is a focus on groups in society who are looking for their own legitimacy, autonomy and voice. The emancipation is of gender, sexual orientations, life phases, handicaps etc. The function of this historiography is a political attempt for a critical analysis of modern society and power-holding elites. The continuity from the practice of ideology-critique of the nineteen-seventies is obvious. The demythologizing attempt mirrors international revisionist historiography. Marc Depaepe is the foremost active international proponent of this view of educational historiography: a conscious departure from hagiography and stories of progression, into a conscious demythologizing of the educational past.[36]

Post revisionism – anything goes?

With this fifth category we are, as noted above, not keen on defining all subsequent literature under the heading of post-revisionism; however, we do find a new pragmatic and more optimistic view of certain school developments. We agree with Gary McCulloch that a "new testament" is needed instead of the historical purism of the (self-declared) revisionist Marc Depeape's Ten Commandments that we here consider in the tradition of revisionist and emancipatory historiography.[37] This is a radical departure from defining post-revisionism as the project of the right wing. Our version of a post-revisionist attitude could be called an "anything goes" view of educational history writing, or to phrase it differently: it is acceptable to address both professionals, historians, the general public, social scientists etc. as interested constituencies with their legitimate but broadly differing claims to relevance. Some choose the view of everyday life, with a turn to materiality or affects, some focus on a strong state as a positive and progressive actor, and again some find inspiration for didactics in heroes of the past. The following examples from Danish his

---

[35] See: http://www.dpu.dk/fileadmin/www.dpu.dk/forskning/projekter/danskskolehistorie/20100512091403_schools-in-denmark---final-version.pdf.

[36] Marc Depaepe, "A Professionally Relevant History of Education for Teachers: Does it Exist? Reply to Jurgen Herbst's State of the Art Article," Paedagogica Historica 37, no. 3 (2001).

[37] See the highly relevant discussion on "good practice in educational history writing" between among others Marc Depaepe and Gary McCulloch: Depaepe, "The Ten Commandments of Good Practices in History of Education Research."; McCulloch, "The Gospel according to St Marc."

toriography may outline too broadly what we find to be post-revisionist; herefore, the addition of a question mark after asking "anything goes?"

The scholarly environment around the project rewriting the history of the Danish schools includes several *turns* in its approaches. Lisa Rosén Rasmussen in her PhD dissertation represents a turn to materiality by analysing everyday school ethnography. Helle Bjerg is a representative of the affective turn in a similar ethnography of everyday life in modern Danish schools. Ning de Coninck-Smith recapitulates this development as a succession of turns: from the linguistic and cultural turns into the material and visual turns.[38]

A more general societal focus that also had special attention in the nineteen-eighties was literacy studies, where there were a number of contributions about the levels of literacy in the general population from circa 1550-1900.[39] Charlotte Appel has continued this trans- disciplinary development in her work on literacy and book-markets in seventeenth century Denmark.[40]

Another tendency in the newer historiography is a turn to a more international outlook. In his PhD dissertation Christian Ydesen looks at international networks of educators and pedagogical theorists on *testing*. Susanne Wiborg analyses in a long tour de force the uneven development of comprehensive schooling in both the Nordic countries, UK and Germany.[41] Jesper Eckhardt Larsen's PhD dissertation looks comparatively and with a contemporary historical approach at the discussions on the humanities in higher education.[42] Yet another tendency among some historians is consciously seeking policy relevance. In his PhD dissertation, Christian Larsen looks into the Danish education system between 1814 and 1923. He traces the development with an increased recogni-

---

[38] Lisa Rosén Rasmussen, "Livet i skolen – skolen i livet: Eleverindringer om den materielle og sansede skolehverdag" (Aarhus Universitet, 2010); Helle Bjerg, "Skoling af lyst : fantasier og fornemmelser i tre elevgenerationers erindringer om livet i skolen – 1950-2000" (Aarhus Universitet, 2011); Ning de Coninck-Smith, "Skolens hverdag – en historisk udfordring," in Skolen lærerne, eleverne og forældrene : 10 kapitler af den danske folkeskoles historie i det 19. og 20. århundrede, ed. Ning de Coninck-Smith (Aarhus: Klim, 2002).

[39] Ingrid Markussen and Vagn Skovgaard-Petersen, "Læseindlæring og læsebehov i Danmark, ca. 1550-1850," in Ur Nordisk Kulturhistoria (Jyväskylä: XVIII Nordiska historikermötet, 1981).

[40] Charlotte Appel, Læsning og bogmarked i 1600-tallets Danmark (København: Museum Tusculanums Forlag, 2001).

[41] Christian Ydesen, "The Rise of High-Stakes Educational Testing in Denmark 1920-1970" (Aarhus Universitet, 2010); Susanne Wiborg, Education and Social Integration : Comprehensive Schooling in Europe (London: Palgrave Macmillan, 2009).

[42] Jesper Eckhardt Larsen, ""ikke af brød alene..." Argumenter for humaniora og universitetet i Norge, Danmark, Tyskland og USA 1945-2005" (Danmarks Pædagogiske Universitet, 2006).

tion that education was a public amenity and not a private business, and that either the borough or the state was ultimately responsible for its provision. Public schools were seen as the only natural place for youth to develop and be educated. Education was a task for the state and the local authority, available to all after their ability.[43] An example of the history of educational ideas that can be mentioned is the doctoral dissertation by Thyge Winther-Jensen on Plato, Comenius, Rousseau and Dewey. This book has been widely read in the Danish educational context and indeed shows that we, in post-modern times, still need heroes and inspiration from the past in some form or other. The view is here educational in a broad sense.[44]

An overview – thoughts on the long development

One can view the five positions we have examined here as part of a long societal development from classicism into romanticism, and from modern into post-modern societies. The first steps of the process of democratisation of reality suggested by the sociologist Alwin Gouldener were taken in the transition from classicism into romanticism: "The Classical view of the world had generated excluded enclaves of underprivileged reality, whose neglect it had no hesitation in justifying. The Romantic view believed that the insignificance of things was born of a failure of imagination: reality was now democratised."[45] One can criticize this view by the observation that romanticism (not least exemplified by Grundtvigian ideas), to the same extent as classicism, created new groups of underprivileged reality: the non-native and the Creole, for example, were not welcome in the romantic notion of social reality. Modernism was hoping for the equality of all in a uni-linear historiography of more and more, better and better schooling. In a radical sense Revisionism was modern society's critique of itself on its own terms of egalitarian and rational politics. It seems as if the last developments find a new plurality of voices with equal claims on legitimacy – and that actually takes us full circle to the place where old bourgeois values and dannelse (Bildung) can – in the name of post-modern pluralism – serve individual self-constructive

---

[43] Christian Larsen, "Fra skoleanordninger til Den Store Skolekommission : studier af forandringer i dansk uddannelsestænkning 1814-1923 med særligt henblik på decentral uddannelse, privat uddannelse og professionsuddannelse" (Aarhus Universitet, 2009).

[44] Thyge Winther-Jensen, Undervisning og menneskesyn belyst gennem studier af Platon, Comenius, Rousseau og Dewey - en antropologisk betragtningsmåde (Århus: Akademisk Forlag A/S, 1995 (1989)).

[45] Alwin W. Gouldner, For Sociology. Renewal and Critique in Sociology Today (London: Allen Lane, cop., 1973). p.331.

needs in the twenty-first century. Now – anything goes. The total democratization of reality is accomplished, at least in politically correct parts of academia.

To reiterate, we do not attempt a full prophecy of what will be the analysis of the present situation. A few projections will have to suffice. In the vogue of the globalisation discourse a new curiosity of many in the field may consciously let go of purely national narratives. Secondly, lessons for praxis tend to be gaining new legitimacy in the vein of either politically relevant or otherwise performative knowledge – or more simply put: *historia magistra vitæ.* To assume any linear relation between the "lessons" of historical works and praxis is not what is suggested, but rather, as in other educational research, "to inform social praxis, not to guide it."[46]

It is equally clear that our nexus of reference countries that we have indicated as creating our national educational self-understanding - German *Bildung* or Nordic democratic *folkelighed*, and concepts like *almendannelse* and *folkeoplysning* - is under severe pressure by a very strong both Anglo-Saxon and supranational globalization orientation. The language of power in the Danish educational field looks more to PISA and the London Institute of Education than to either continuities of the Humboldtian idea of Bildung durch Wissenschaft or to the happy experience of a summer spent at a non-exam Nordic folk-high-school.

[46] As the educational comparativist Jürgen Schriewer cites Meinolf Dierkes in Jürgen Schriewer, "Comparative Education Methodology in Transition: Towards a Science of Complexity?," in Discourse Formation in Comparative Education, ed. Jurgen Schriewer (Frankfurt a.M.: Peter Lang, 2003), p.52.

Contributors

List of contributors

Gary McCulloch

is the Brian Simon Professor of the History of Education at the Institute of Education, University of London. He is a former President of the History of Education Society (UK) and a previous Editor of the journal History of Education. His recent publications include Cyril Norwood and the Ideal of Secondary Education (Palgrave Macmillan 2007) and The Struggle for the History of Education (Routledge 2011).

Marc Depaepe

is full professor at the Katholieke Universiteit Leuven. Co-editor-in-chief of Paedagogica Historica, since 2005, and member of several editorial boards of national journals in the history of education. Former president of the International Standing Conference for the History of Education as well as of the Belgian Dutch Society for the History of Education; former vice-president of the Internationale Gesellschaft für Historische und Systematische Schulbuchforschung. Since 2010, "Fellow" of the International Academy of Education. Published a lot of articles and books on the history of educational sciences, the history of education in Belgium and in the former Belgian Congo, the historiography, theory and methodology of the history of education as a discipline.

Jukka Rantala

is Professor of History and Social Studies Education at the University of Helsinki. His research has focused on the historical construction of teacherhood in Finland, particularly the political ethos of Finnish teachers. He is the editor-in-chief of Kasvatus & Aika (Education & Time), a Finnish scientific quarterly in the field of history of education. He is also the chairman of The Finnish Society for the History of Education.

Pierre Caspard

attended the Ecole normale supérieure (Paris). His initial research and thesis focused on Swiss economic, social and demographic history. He directed the Service d'histoire de l'éducation within the Institut National Recherche Pédagogique from 1977 until 2010. During these years, this research and service laboratory produced over one hundred books as well as the journal, Histoire de l'éducation that P. Caspard founded in 1978. In addition to his scholarship on the social and cultural history of teaching in Switzerland and France in the 18th and 19th centuries, P. Caspard has published in many languages survey articles on French research in the history of education as well as analyses of its historiography.

Rebecca Rogers

is Professor in the history of education at Université Paris Descartes (Paris 5). Specialist in the history of girls' education in France, she has also published methodological and historiographical articles on the history of education. Two recent examples of this approach include: "The Politics of Writing the History of French Girls' Education", History of Education Researcher, 80 (2007): 136-144 and "Do we need commandments," response to Marc Depaepe's "The Ten Commandments of Good Practices in History of education Research", Zeitschrift für pädagogische Historiographie, 16/1 (2010): 35-38.

Barry M. Franklin

is Professor of Education and Assistant Dean for Global Teacher Education in the School of Teacher Education and Leadership in the College of Education and Human Services at Utah State University. His research is in the areas of curriculum reform, policy, and history with a focus on urban schools. His most recent books are Curriculum, Community and Urban School Reform (Palgrave Macmillan 2010) and The Death of the Comprehensive High School? Historical, Contemporary, and Comparative Perspectives (Palgrave Macmillan 2007), co-edited with Gary McCulloch.

Patricio R. Ortiz

has a PhD in Cultural Studies in Education/Anthropology from University of Texas at Austin (2007), and is Assistant Professor of ESL/Bilingual and Multicultural Education at Utah State University. His research and writing focuses on culturally and linguistically diverse student populations, indigenous education, migration and education and multilingualism in the

USA and Latin America. Using ethnographic methods, critical pedagogy and ethno-historical perspectives, his work has been published in both English and Spanish languages in the USA, Canada and Latin America.

Harry Haue

is Dr. Phil. and professor em. of history didactics and educational history at The Institute of Philosophy, Education and the Study of Religions at University of Southern Denmark in Odense. His main contribution to educational history is his doctoral thesis: Almendannelse som ledestjerne from 2003, a shorter version of which was translated into German in 2008: Allgemeinbildung. Ein deutscher Begriff im dänischen Gymnasium 1750-2007, both published by University press of Southern Denmark. He has written a number of articles on educational history, and some of them are translated into English in "Didactics of History and Educational Policy in Denmark. Five Lessons", in Yearbook for International Society for History Didactics 2006/07, and in E. Erdmann and W. Hasberg (eds.): Facing, Mapping, Bridging Diversity. Foundation of a European Discourse on History Education, Wochen Schau Wissenschaft 2011, vol 1, 173-209. He has been member of the committees preparing the latest reforms of history education in Denmark on all levels.

Esbjörn Larsson

has a PhD in History and is Senior Lecturer in History of Education at Uppsala University. Larsson defended his doctoral thesis From Upbringing to Education: The Swedish Royal War Academy, 1792 to 1866 in 2005. From then on he has continued his research on Education and Social structures during the 19th Century. At the moment he is working within the project "Between discipline and self-activity: Differences in the implementation of Monitorial Education for different social classes in Sweden, approx. 1820-1870" funded by Bank of Sweden Tercentary Foundation.

Else Hansen

is PhD and senior researcher in the Danish National Archives. Within the field of university's history, she has among other things, published "En koral i tidens strøm" (A coral in the flow of time - Roskilde University, 1972-1997) (1997) on the establishment and history of a Danish reform-university; and "Masseuniversiteter på tegnebrættet? 1950'ernes universitetsplanlægning i kommissioner og udvalg." (Mass Universities on the drawing board? University planning in the 1950s' commissions)

(2009). She is now working on a monograph on Danish university policy in the 1950s and 1960s.

Marcelo Caruso

is PhD (University of Munich, Germany) and B.A. in education (University of Buenos Aires, Argentina), is full professor of History of Education at Humboldt University, Berlin (Germany). His main research focuses are in the field of the history of educational technologies and in the global history of schooling. He is a member of the editorial board of Paedagogica Historica, the Zeitschrift für Pädagogik and current editor-in-chief of the German Yearbook for history of education.

Carola Groppe

is Prof. Dr. and Professor for History of Education at Helmut-Schmidt-Universität (Universität der Bundeswehr Hamburg, University of the Federal Armed Forces, Hamburg, Germany). Her main research topics are the history of the family, childhood and youth, the history of the educational system, and the history of the theory of education. Relevant publications: Die Macht der Bildung. Das deutsche Bürgertum und der George-Kreis 1890-1933. Böhlau-Verlag, Köln, Weimar, Wien 1997, and „Erziehung, Sozialisation und Selbstsozialisation als epochale Leitbegriffe und Deutungsmuster" In: Lothar Wigger, Winfried Marotzki (eds.): Erziehungsdiskurse, Verlag Julius Klinkhardt, Bad Heilbrunn/Obb. 2008, 75-93.

Alfred Oftedal Telhaug

has during 42 years (1962-2004) been a nationally distinguished researcher and teacher in education at the Teacher Training College and the University of Trondheim. As associate professor at the University of Trondheim he engaged strongly in the history of education focusing especially on the contemporary school development and on school politics. Together with the professors Reidar Myhre and Torstein Harbo he made Trondheim the Norwegian center of history of education and school politics as a research discipline. He has lectured at all levels in the Scandinavian countries, and he has also participated in the national school-reform work in Norway. From 1974 to 1982 he was editor of Norsk Pedagogisk Tidsskrift. Alfred Oftedal Telhaug has published around 40 books and many hundreds of reports and articles in national and international journals.

Christian Larsen

is Ph.D. and senior researcher at the Danish National Archives. His main fields are the Danish educational system from the end of the 18th century to the beginning of the 20th century. His dissertation was on the changes in Danish educational philosophy 1814-1923 with special reference to urban schools, private schools and teacher training. He has published articles and books on teachers' training, primary and secondary schools, bibliographies of Danish educational history, and was the editor of Realskolen gennem 200 år - kundskaber og erhvervsforberedelse (A History of Primary and Lower Secondary Schools in Denmark, 2010, 2 vols.). He is a member of the editorial board of the Danish Yearbook of the History of Education and secretary in the Danish Society of the History of Education.

Jesper Eckhardt Larsen

is assistant professor in the history of education at the Institute of Education at Aarhus University. He holds a Ph.D. in comparative education. This thesis dealt with the role of the humanities in contemporary societies, comparing Norway, Denmark, Germany and the USA since 1945. He is vice-president of the Danish Society for the History of Education. He has published internationally about the role of the humanities in the Bologna area and the USA. He has published books and articles about the concept of dannelse (Bildung) seen in a Danish historical perspective and on colonial Danish school history.